Knowledge
for
ACTION

Chris Argyris

Knowledge
for
ACTION

A Guide to Overcoming Barriers to Organizational Change

Jossey-Bass Publishers · San Francisco

Substantial discounts on bulk quantities of Jossey-Bass books are available to corporations, professional associations, and other organizations. For details and discount information, contact the special sales department at Jossey-Bass Inc., Publishers. (415) 433-1740; Fax (415) 433-0499.

For sales outside the United States, contact Maxwell Macmillan International Publishing Group, 866 Third Avenue, New York, New York 10022.

 The paper used in this book is acid-free and meets the State of California requirements for recycled paper (50 percent recycled waste, including 10 percent postconsumer waste), which are the strictest guidelines for recycled paper currently in use in the United States.

Library of Congress Cataloging-in-Publication Data

Argyris, Chris, date.
    Knowledge for action : a guide to overcoming barriers to organizational change / Chris Argyris. — 1st ed.
      p.   cm.—(A Joint publication in the Jossey-Bass management series and the Jossey-Bass social and behavioral science series)
    Includes bibliographical references and index.
    ISBN 978-155542-519-7
    1. Organizational change—Handbooks, manuals, etc. I. Title.
II. Title: Guide to overcoming barriers to organizational change.
III. Series: Jossey-Bass management series. IV. Series: Jossey-Bass social and behavioral science series.
HD58.8.A744   1993
658.4'06—dc20   92-42861
                                                  CIP

FIRST EDITION
HB Printing   10 9 8 7 6 5 4 3 2 1   *Code 9316*

A joint publication in
THE JOSSEY-BASS MANAGEMENT SERIES
and
THE JOSSEY-BASS
SOCIAL AND BEHAVIORAL SCIENCE SERIES

Contents

Preface

Knowledge for Action is about two of my lifelong goals. The first is to produce actionable knowledge that individuals can use to create organizations of any type, in which the search for valid knowledge, a commitment to personal responsibility and stewardship, and a dedication to effective action and learning are paramount. I believe that such a goal facilitates human competence, confidence, and efficacy and, at the same time, leads to innovative, flexible, and effective organizations.

My second lifelong goal is to design the research methods that will produce this valid actionable knowledge. I seek research methods that require high standards for testing the validity of researchers' propositions. I am especially concerned that we, as researcher-interveners, do our best to make sure that we are not kidding ourselves—and those who use our knowledge—about the validity and actionability of that knowledge. I especially seek research methods that empower participants to be genuine partners with researchers. A genuine partnership means that the researchers take on the primary responsibility for the technical features of the research; the participants and researchers jointly focus on the strategic goals of the researchers; and the participants are especially

responsible for implementing the research results in such a way that
their validity is always tested in everyday life.

Background of the Book

About five years ago, seven owner-directors of a consulting firm
dedicated to the highest quality of value-added management consulting asked me to help them in their quest to create a consulting
firm with qualities of learning and responsibility similar to those
I have been describing. I was, and still am, impressed with their
dedication, integrity, and brightness. I was especially impressed
with their commitment to learning. I agreed to work with them, and
the techniques and results of that project are used throughout the
book to illustrate how my two goals were achieved in that project
and might be achieved in many other projects.

There are at least two types of organizational learning. One
focuses on changing organizational routines. It is incremental and
adaptive. The second focuses on practices that lead to a new framework for learning and to new routines. The ideas in *Knowledge for
Action* apply to both types but, in keeping with my goals, especially
to the second. For example, I focus on changing organizational
politics that discourage organizational learning—especially around
problems that are embarrassing and threatening—and I make this
change occur first at the highest level of management.

Audience

Knowledge for Action is aimed at organizational researchers
who diagnose and help to change organizations. One primary
group of these researchers is composed of faculty and graduate students interested in field research that has organizational learning as
its main objective. The second primary group is composed of full-
time researchers in organizations, organizational development professionals, and planners and implementers of management
education.

The book is also aimed at line executives who wish to create
learning organizations. Line executives of consulting firms of all
types should find the studies in the book especially relevant.

Overview of the Contents

The book is divided into three parts and an appendix. Part One focuses on defensive routines at the organizational, intergroup, group, and individual levels. In Chapter One, I show that social scientists have conducted much research to conclude that defensive routines represent massive and pervasive causes of ineffective learning. I also show that most of the research gives little actionable advice about overcoming defensive routines. Indeed, where the research says something that is actionable, the advice may actually exacerbate the problem. In Chapter Two, I focus on the theory of action and its accompanying assumptions that I used to conduct the research project described in the book.

Part Two focuses on the case study of the consulting firm. I show how I diagnosed the defensive routines of the seven director-owners, and I describe the impact those routines had on learning throughout the organization (Chapters Three and Four). In Chapter Five, I describe the feedback session in which the directors commented on my findings, and in Chapter Six, I discuss the change seminar in which the directors participated.

Part Three illustrates what happened afterward for a period of five years. I have selected five exemplars of the kinds of changes that occurred during these years. I selected these examples because they illustrate problems that the directors had said at the outset were critical and were unlikely to be solved. The reason for their pessimistic prediction was that these issues, although well known in the organization, were undiscussable. Some directors reported that on the rare occasions when the issues were discussed the resulting group dynamics led to polarization and distancing among individuals, which in turn cast the problems outside the realm of influence. One of the criteria for assessing the effectiveness of interventions is, as we shall see, the degree to which issues that hitherto cannot be discussed or influenced become discussable and correctable.

Each example is described by means of conversation transcribed from a tape recording. Each is also accompanied by discussions of how and why I, as the intervener, acted as I did. Chapter Seven describes how the CEO (who was also a director-owner) and a director explored how they pushed each other's buttons instead of resolving their problems. Chapter Eight illustrates how two directors explored their degree of mutual mistrust in ways that built trust. Chapter Nine addresses an age-old problem in consulting firms that use a rigorous analytical procedure and theories: how do you recognize, evaluate, and teach rigorous analysis? Chapter Ten describes what I believe to be a very rare event. The CEO asked for a performance review from the other directors, his immediate reports. He asked that it be done in a group setting so that he could use the directors as resources and so that they too could perhaps begin to see each other as resources. In Chapter Eleven, I describe a situation in which two directors expressing their anger with each other "went ballistic," yet they were able to manage the episode so that their relationship became closer and more effective. A summary and the implications of the case study are presented in Chapter Twelve.

The Appendix deals with the implications for conducting research that produces actionable knowledge that can be used by practitioners, and whose use becomes a test of features of that knowledge. I focus on the nature of the theory and the empirical research required to produce actionable knowledge. I suggest that the present concepts of causality used in designing and executing research will have to be supplemented with an additional concept. Finally, I show why the traditional differentiations between basic and applied research, scholarship, and consulting are not only counterproductive but will eventually be outdated. The ways these distinctions are presently made may illustrate researchers' defensive routines more than valid rules about the conduct of research.

Knowledge for Action is a follow-up to *Action Science* (Argyris, Putnam, & Smith, 1985). In that book, my coauthors and I attempted to define the scholarly linkages of action science, to show how action science differs from traditional descriptive research, and to show how the education of researcher-interveners requires that they construct experiences similar to those they will have to create for individuals in organizations when they attempt interventions to change the status quo. Researcher-interveners will have to show that they are competent in the concepts and skills that they intend to teach others. Otherwise, it is unlikely that they can help to produce learning organizations or, indeed, learning societies.

The present book builds upon *Action Science* in three ways. It shows in detail how action science methods can be used in real life to produce actionable knowledge that causes lasting changes in the status quo. It also presents a more explicit concept of "design causality." If knowledge is to be actionable, I believe that design causality is a more relevant concept of causality than researchers' presently preferred concept.

Finally, *Knowledge for Action* illustrates how theory that is actionable can be tested by practitioners as they implement it in everyday practice. Continual testing by practitioners means that theory is no longer limited to testing by scholars.

I would like to thank Dianne Argyris, Richard Hackman, William Issacs, Donald Schön, and Richard Walton for their thoughtful comments.

Boston, Massachusetts   CHRIS ARGYRIS
February 1993

To Fellow Students and Colleagues

The Author

CHRIS ARGYRIS is James Bryant Conant Professor of Education and Organizational Behavior at Harvard University. He received his A.B. degree (1947) from Clark University in psychology, his M.A. degree (1949) from Kansas University in economics and psychology, and his Ph.D. degree (1951) from Cornell University in organizational behavior. Argyris has also earned honorary doctorate degrees from McGill University (1977), the University of Leuven, Belgium (1978), the Stockholm School of Economics (1979), DePaul University (1987), and IMCB of Buckingham, England (1987). From 1951 to 1971, he was a faculty member at Yale University, serving as Beach Professor of Administrative Sciences and as chair of the Administrative Sciences department during the latter part of this period.

Argyris's early research focused on the unintended consequences for individuals of formal organizational structures, executive leadership, control systems, and management information systems—and on how individuals adapted to change those consequences (*Personality and Organization*, 1957; *Integrating the Individual and the Organization*, 1964). He then turned his attention to ways of changing organizations, especially the behavior of executives at the upper levels of organization (*Interpersonal Competence and Organizational Effectiveness,* 1962; *Organization and Innovation,* 1965).

This line of inquiry led him to focus on the role of the social scientist as a researcher and interventionist (*Intervention Theory and Method,* 1970; *Inner Contradictions of Rigorous Research,* 1980). During the past decade he has also been developing, with Donald Schön, a theory of individual and organizational learning in which human reasoning—not just behavior—becomes the basis for diagnosis and action (*Theory in Practice,* 1974; *Organizational Learning,* 1978). Argyris's other books include *Strategy, Change and Defensive Routines* (1985), *Overcoming Organizational Defenses* (1990), and *On Organizational Learning* (1992).

Argyris is currently working on a project that will relate the perspective presented in *Knowledge for Action* to the ideas of other researchers and practitioners.

Knowledge
for
ACTION

Introduction:
Action and Learning

The study of learning that serves action reaches to the core of human social life. Action is how we give meaning to life. It is how we reveal ourselves to others and to ourselves. It is through action that we create social structures intended to create and preserve the social order necessary for managing our lives, our organizations, and our societies (Arendt, 1958, 1963).

Researchers have long been interested in producing knowledge that is applicable to our daily lives. Campbell and Stanley (1963) defined the interest in creating applicable knowledge as concern for external validity. I suggest that concern for external validity is necessary but is not a sufficient condition to produce knowledge that can be acted upon by practitioners in everyday life.

Actionable Knowledge

Actionable knowledge is not only relevant to the world of practice; it is the knowledge that people use to create that world. The word *action* conjures up images of individuals doing, executing, and implementing. In this book, I will focus specifically on these actions that are designed to produce intended consequences. I focus, therefore, on behavior imbued with meaning by individuals as they

1

interact with others in the world of practice. In this view, action is not simply the discovery of new ideas or the development of new policies; it is the implementation of these ideas or policies and the evaluation of the implementation's effectiveness.

I focus on two domains of action. One is the action around difficult problems, which are likely to be embarrassing or threatening. I claim that the skills most individuals, groups, intergroups, and organizations use to solve such problems are learned early in life. They are protected and rewarded by the culture. Yet they are counterproductive because they fail to produce effective actions— that is, actions that achieve the intended result of reducing problems. Therefore, if the ideas in this book are to lead to effective action, they must show us how to change the status quo, to change what has been taken for granted to be effective action. Any change that does not first change the meaning of effective action cannot persist because it continues to expose individuals to potential embarrassment or threat. This causes them to resort back to their old actions because their senses of competence and esteem are largely based on personal values and skills that are consistent with the old status quo. This individual embarrassment or threat is what has led to the organizational embarrassment and threat that has resulted in limiting genuine organizational learning.

The second domain of action concerns the way actionable knowledge is produced by researchers and then used by practitioners. It must be produced in such a way that its use represents a valid test of the theory of action that informed the production of the knowledge. In principle, the test can weigh the validity of "technical" theories of action, such as competitive analysis or activity-based cost accounting, as well as the validity of "human" theories of action, such as those that govern effective leadership, interpersonal relationships, group or intergroup dynamics, or organizational cultures. In actuality, this book is primarily about the latter category. A comprehensive actionable theory of management and organizational behavior will require the integration of both technical and human theories of action. I will indicate some possible steps to take for such an integration in the Appendix.

Knowledge that is actionable, regardless of its content, contains causal claims. It says, if you act in such and such a way, the following will likely occur. That means that actionable knowledge is produced in the form of if-then propositions that can be stored in and retrieved from the actor's mind under conditions of everyday life.

Action and Learning

Learning occurs when we detect and correct error. Error is any mismatch between what we intend an action to produce and what actually happens when we implement that action. It is a mismatch between intentions and results. Learning also occurs when we produce a match between intentions and results for the first time.

As it is used in this book, learning is also an action concept. Learning is not simply having a new insight or a new idea. Learning occurs when we take effective action, when we detect *and* correct error. How do you know when you know something? When you can produce what it is you claim you know.

Learning as just defined is intimately connected with action for three reasons. First, it is unlikely that any propositions of the if-then variety that we have stored in our heads can fully cover the richness and uniqueness of a concrete situation. There will always be a gap between our stored knowledge and the knowledge required to act effectively in a given situation. In order to fill the gap, learning about the new context in the new context is required.

Second, even after the knowledge gap has been relatively closed, it is unlikely that the action we design and implement will be adequate. Most contexts or situations that concern us are constantly changing. We cannot assume that other individuals or groups will react as we had thought they would when we designed our actions. There is a continual need for vigilant monitoring of our and others' actions. These processes too require learning, often performed iteratively.

Third, learning is not only required in order to act effectively; it is also necessary in order to codify effective action, so that it can be reliably repeated when it is appropriate. This means that effective actions are not only stored as rules in actors' heads; it means that their requirements are known publicly, usually in the form of formal and informal policies and routines that are rewarded by organizational cultures. Building policies, routines, and culture requires learning.

This book, therefore, focuses on both the actions and learning necessary to produce on-line effective actions that address problems that may be embarrassing or threatening because their solutions require changing the status quo. I demonstrate that in order for propositions to be actionable, they have to specify the action strategies that will achieve intended consequences, and they also have to specify the underlying values that must govern these actions. The action strategies have to be specified as rules that can be used both to design and produce (or craft) conversations and to construct criteria to assess the actions' effectiveness.

In the preface, I described the consulting organization that is the subject of the case study that provides the empirical part of this book. I and my research colleagues helped the seven owner-directors in this organization to see that they held personal theories of effective action. These theories had several similar governing values, including "always be in unilateral control" and "strive to minimize losing and maximize winning." We also helped the directors to see that they held action strategies such as "advocate a position in order to win" or "evaluate others in ways that do not encourage testing the validity of the evaluation." We then were able to help them see how such theories of action inhibited learning and overprotected them. Moreover, we also demonstrated how they produced organizational defensive routines (in the form of policies, practices, and norms) that reinforced the anti-learning and overprotective consequences that they condemned in the governing values they publicly espoused.

We also helped them to learn an additional theory of action to turn this defensive, anti-learning behavior around and reach their goal of creating a learning organization that would put them on the cutting edge of consulting practice. The new theory of action would facilitate learning at all levels and especially the learning that could address nonroutine problems that were embarrassing or threatening (precisely the conditions in which learning is especially needed). Our theory had to specify a new set of governing values and a new set of action strategies. It also had to inform the directors (and later others in the organization) how to get from here to there. Finally, it had to inform them how to drastically reduce their organizational defensive routines and how to build routines for effective organizational learning.

The research focused primarily on actionable knowledge within an organization for several reasons. First, the best way to monitor and manage our environment is to help develop organizations that are good at learning and quick at turning around. I acknowledged the importance of the environment by creating a learning competence within the participating organization that would pay careful attention to it at all times. Second, the environment itself is often composed of other organizations and networks. The skills, competencies, and theories of effective action that we help individuals to use within one organization can also be used in managing these other organizations and networks. This was especially important in the project described in this book, because the participants were members of a consulting organization whose very existence depended on dealing effectively with external clients. Moreover, the consulting firm used many concepts and analytical procedures to teach its clients to assess and deal effectively with their own environments.

The Importance of Specificity

In order to produce actionable propositions about human action that, once implemented, can be used as an acceptable field-test of the propositions, it is necessary to specify the actions that will produce the predicted consequences. Moreover, practitioners are not able to produce what they intend without knowing the appropriate behavioral specifications and having the skills to produce them. Applicable knowledge, unlike actionable knowledge, is not dependent upon these requirements.

The difference between applicable and actionable knowledge is illustrated by a recent thoughtful study. Nagel (1991) made an analysis of the 1985 MOVE disaster in Philadelphia, in which a fire that started when police firebombed the headquarters of the MOVE organization spread to other houses and eleven people died. He was able to explain Mayor W. Wilson Goode's actions by utilizing concepts developed by Janis (1989) and Janis and Mann (1977). For example, he explained Mayor Goode's delaying to act and then acting hastily as a textbook example of defensive avoidance followed by hypervigilance and defensive blindness as the mayor shielded himself from his responsibility for violating values crucial to him.

Defensive avoidance, hypervigilance, and defensive blindness to consequences seem both sensible and plausible as the key concepts that explain Goode's actions. But, as Nagel states, using the concepts to explain is one matter and using the same concepts to prescribe is quite another. Individuals who wished to derive actionable knowledge from identifying these concepts would have to describe the dynamics of defensive avoidance and hypervigilance to the people who wanted to avoid this behavior. They would have to teach these people how to protect themselves against rationalization, denial, selective perceptions, and wishful thinking in everyday life.

Nagel agrees with Janis's advice to individuals to institutionalize a set of anti–defensive-avoidance procedures, and he adds that Goode (and other decision makers) should learn to recognize the behavioral symptoms of defective decision making. Decision makers should also encourage trusted advisers to confront them when the advisers see them behaving defensively. Moreover, they should identify the central no-win dilemmas and grasp problems firmly.

As they are stated, these recommendations represent applicable knowledge but not actionable knowledge. In order for the knowledge to become actionable, so that practitioners could use it in everyday life, the authors would have to specify what skills are required to produce it and what contextual conditions are necessary to maintain it. I will attempt to meet these requirements in the study described in this book.

One of the basic tenets of my approach is that action is informed by theory. The importance of this tenet can be shown by looking at the opposite point of view. Lindon (1991), in a recent review of his thirty years of practice, questions whether action needs to be prompted by theory. He bases his doubt on the fact that he used four different theoretical perspectives to help patients who had the same disorder. He concludes that the key to a therapist's effectiveness is not acting on any one theory but acting in ways that make the patient feel genuinely understood.

However, one possible explanation for his experience is that the four theories may not be as different as he thinks. It may be that he was able to express genuine understanding of each patient's central affect because he could combine any of the four theories with his interpersonal therapeutic skills.

Lindon recommends that therapists make theory of as little import as humanly possible. Such advice is applicable but not actionable. In order for the advice to become actionable, Lindon would have to specify how therapists can produce the type of understanding that he defines and, at the same time, specify how they can make their respective theories about how to organize reality of as little import as possible. In order to produce such specifications, Lindon would have to hold a theory of suppressing theory in order to understand human beings. Moreover, he would need to operationalize these concepts so that a therapist could produce them during a therapeutic session in such a way that their consequences would provide a test of the theories.

Gabbard (1991), who comments on Lindon's paper, notes that it is rare to find an analyst who is sufficiently open-minded and flexible enough to "try on" different theoretical perspectives with different patients. Moreover, continues Gabbard, Lindon has the "courage and skill to apply psychoanalytic techniques to patients who are far more disturbed than the typical neurotic outpatient" (p. 23). If Gabbard is correct, then one way to acquire some insight into making Lindon's advice more actionable would be to study how therapists can become committed to theory and remain open-minded.

In his rebuttal to Gabbard, Lindon again acknowledges the relevance of theory but advises a "know-nothing" stance. He approves Bion's advice that "each session should be treated as if it were an initial consultation, [that is], with the analyst's being without preconception and having every sensitive antenna alerted for clues" (p. 31). Again the knowledge is applicable but, as described, is not actionable, because it does not include knowledge on how to produce such behavioral consequences.

Finally, Lindon quotes Freud as advising that it is not a good thing to work on a case scientifically while treatment is proceeding. Freud found that thinking scientifically was likely to interfere with thinking therapeutically. The argument of this book is that this is not necessarily the case. The right type of theory and the correct skills will lead to an interweaving of the two in such a way that science and practice will gain. Whyte (1991) makes this point eloquently in his new book on theory and participative action research.

The Example of Kurt Lewin

Kurt Lewin was a pioneer researcher in producing actionable knowledge, and his work (1948, 1951) is an exemplar of research activity that is both basic and actionable and that often has a consulting relationship. Lewin was one of "those few men whose work changed the course of social science" (Cartwright, 1951, p. viii) because he combined commitments to solving problems and to contributing to basic theory. Unfortunately, in my opinion, Lewin's and some of his colleagues' ideas about conducting action research were altered by later researchers, so that basic and action research were once again separated.

I believe that Lewin's works contain four core themes. First, for Lewin, sound theory was practical, and he integrated theory with practice in several ways. To begin with, he framed the social sciences as the study of problems. He also elected to study problems that were critical for society. For example, he was concerned about promoting leadership and democracy, educating informed and responsible citizens, and reducing prejudice of all kinds. He uncovered contributions to fundamental theory in solving such practical problems as selling war bonds during World War II or helping parents induce their children to drink orange juice and eat liver or spinach. In addition, Lewin began his studies by observations of real life. The original monographs of many of his early classical group experiments contain nontrivial amounts of ethnographic description. Finally, Lewin connected all problems, no matter how small or temporary, large or long lasting, to theory. No problem was studied that would not be a test of theory. Theory was not formulated that could not be tested through the study of problems.

Immediate problems were put in the service of testing timeless theory.

In short, Lewin integrated theory with practice in every study. He took actionability so seriously that he designed its requirements at the outset of each research project, demonstrating a concern that was not a norm among academic social scientists at that time.

Lewin described his research strategy as one that seeks truth by "successive approximations," and this reveals a second core theme in his work. He designed research by framing the whole and then differentiating the parts. Using this strategy, a researcher would be less likely to lose sight of the forest for the sake of the trees.

Instead of striving to produce generalizations of the type $X = f(Y)$, researchers who study wholeness should make more use of metaphors and representations. Examples of Lewin's metaphors are "space of free movement," "group atmosphere," and "gatekeeper." Lewin assigned rigorous meanings to these metaphors, so that the reader could clearly see what was included or excluded.

For example, the gatekeeper was in control of the gate that permitted players to fulfill their goals or inhibited them from fulfilling goals. Lewin showed how such a situation led players to become dependent upon and submissive toward the gatekeeper, how they became concerned about his or her needs and curried his or her favor, and how that could lead to competitive relationships among players. These predictions applied to any gatekeeper—a business leader, a camp counselor, a parent, a teacher, and so forth.

Lewin was a master at drawing representations that included what he hypothesized to be the relevant variables, no matter what discipline or level of analysis they represented, and he made explicit the logical and empirical interdependence of the factors. His representations showed how the factors formed self-maintaining patterns, and they provided insights into the sequence of actions that would be necessary to change the patterns.

Lewin had hoped that the mathematical discipline of topology could be used to produce these representations. I do not believe the use of topology was successful in this regard, but it was successful in a different way. His topological models were insightful diagrams, with a property which cognitive scientists now tell us is necessary for knowledge if it is to be usable in everyday life. The representations "chunked" the relevant variables into forms that could be stored and retrieved efficiently. These chunks contained micro-causal theories that explained how events came about and that could be used to design changes in the patterns.

A third important area in Lewin's work is that he produced constructs that could be used both to generalize and to understand the individual case. His work suggests that the dilemmas of statistical versus clinical or nomothetic versus ideographic methods and observations could begin to be resolved with the use of metaphors and diagrams such as those I have described here.

Lewin tested these assertions in many of his experiments by trying to bring about changes in individual, group, and organizational behavior. He was the pioneer researcher-intervener. He showed that the experimental mode could be placed in the service of change and that one of the most rigorous tests of understanding phenomena is to change the phenomena systematically. He saw experiments as a form of social management.

Lewin, like Dewey, was concerned about placing social science in the service of democracy. This is the fourth important value that I see in his work. Lewin was bewildered by how many Americans took democracy for granted. This concern for developing a better world was not something that he hid or played down. It was as if he felt that social scientists had a personal responsibility to be concerned about issues that deal with the quality of life. Responsibility to understand and initiative to act were core features of his sense of stewardship. In this regard, he predated Freire and other activists who sought to awaken the disempowered. Lewin, for example, advised minorities that, in addition to confronting the bigotry of the oppressors, they had to examine their own bigotry and their willingness to be disempowered.

In acting on these four values, Lewin changed the role of those being studied from subjects to clients. He made it explicit that he was there to be of help because the help, if effective, would both improve the clients' quality of life and produce more valid actionable knowledge. And he effected changes without submitting to pressures from clients who, thinking they were acting in the interest of solving practical problems, encouraged him not to meet the standards for making contributions to basic knowledge.

I seek to bring together researchers and practitioners in the service of both understanding and taking action. I share Lewin's belief that social science researchers should produce valid actionable knowledge from their research without compromising the requirement that the research be tested rigorously.

Part One

UNCOVERING ROADBLOCKS TO IMPROVEMENT

Part One defines and suggests some reasons for defensive routines that exist at organizational, intergroup, group, and individual levels.

In Chapter One, I review the existing literature to illustrate that much social science research reveals not only that these defensive routines are pervasive in human life but also that they are a massive cause of ineffective learning. I also show that, although most of this research may provide advice, it does not provide the actionable knowledge required to overcome and change defensive routines. Moreover, the information that is actionable may actually exacerbate the problem it claims to solve.

In Chapter Two, I discuss the theory of action that I used to conduct the research presented in parts One and Two, and I present the concept of design causality.

1

Ineffective Learning
in
Organizations

In this chapter, I review a selection of social science literature to assess the degree to which organizational defensive routines exist in business, governmental, and educational organizations. An *organizational defensive routine* is any policy or action that inhibits individuals, groups, intergroups, and organizations from experiencing embarrassment or threat and, at the same time, prevents the actors from identifying and reducing the causes of the embarrassment or threat. Organizational defensive routines are anti-learning and over-protective (Argyris, 1990c).

I also inquire whether the advice this literature offers to the practitioner to help him or her overcome defensive routines is in fact actionable. I conclude that we know quite a bit about the nature of these routines and their counterproductive effects on organizations, especially on organizational learning capacity. I also conclude that most of the advice provided to overcome organizational defensive routines is not helpful and, if implemented, in many cases would actually strengthen the routines.

Note: Portions of the material in this chapter are adapted from *Reasoning, Learning, and Action: Individual and Organizational,* by Chris Argyris (Jossey-Bass, 1982).

15

Business, educational, and governmental organizations—
and the people who work in them—exhibit similar defensive routines. I have chosen to look at each type of organization separately
in order to focus on different aspects of the routines in each case.

Defensive Routines in Government

There is an extensive literature that tries to explain how "informal"
or "political" behavior within public, or governmental, organizations may inhibit performance and organizational learning (Allison, 1971; Bardach & Kagan, 1982; Brown, 1978; Brunsson, 1989;
Halperin, 1974; Hawley & Nichols, 1982; Kaufman, 1977, 1981; Keggunder, Jorgensen, & Hafsi, 1983; Levine, Ruben, & Wolohagran,
1981; NAPA, 1983; Neustadt & Fineberg, 1978; Pressman & Wildavsky, 1973; Stockman, 1986). For example, Halperin (1974) writes
that pet projects and defensive games in governmental organizations are almost never made explicit but are nonetheless well understood by the participants, that personal challenges are often
wrapped in substantive guise, that people may take the opposite
stand to the one they prefer if their preferred stand is seen as deviant,
and that people accept such rules as necessary in order to survive.

Etheredge (1985) details blocks to learning that occurred during crucial decision-making governmental meetings. The blocks
included lying or deception within the executive branch; engaging
in politically sophisticated behavior that produced a system that
moved increasingly further from reality; ignoring orders and cutting corners, thereby keeping the president ignorant of reality; accepting neither bureaucratic nor personal responsibility; and
holding ritualized meetings that discouraged reexamination and
rethinking. Etheredge suggests that these games are consistent with
competitive, power-oriented individuals who enjoy playing hard-
ball politics (p. 161).

Brunsson (1989) studied Swedish local authorities. He reports that actors would agree that they had failed and that they
could not justify their behavior, but "although they knew they were
doing the wrong thing, they went on doing it" (p. 58). He describes
behavior patterns in which local authorities "administer" problems
in ways that inhibit the changes they admit are relevant (p. 68), yet

they see no way out. These patterns, they suggest, are in the nature of politics.

Kaufman (1981) describes how White House staff dealt with their fears of agencies becoming too independent by increasing controls. The agencies responded by complaining and by trying to bypass the controls. The White House then increased the controls again. This created self-reinforcing, self-sealing processes with a life of their own.

A similar process appears in the report of the Rogers Commission, which investigated the *Challenger* disaster. The commission determined that "safety was inexplicably poorly dealt with given the attention, personnel, and commitment the participants had to the subject. A disastrous situation was developing. While NASA and the others were capable of recognizing the problem and reporting it, the relevant players did not do so. The "can-do" attitude at all levels of the task at hand led everyone to focus on operational objectives. Once the focus was on getting the shuttle launched, the attention of the participants was diverted" (Presidential Commission, 1986, p. 56). The commission recommended strengthening the emphasis on safety by adding new roles with power to deal with safety and new rules to make sure safety was not ignored. The implication was that a czar for safety and new control procedures would solve the problems. What was not focused upon was why safety was handled in a poor way in an organization that understood the importance of safety.

David Stockman's White House education and disillusionment as director of the Office of Management and Budget began with the early meetings of the president and the cabinet (1986). Often, the president did not understand the essence of the argument. Even more often, Edwin Meese (counselor to the president) would manage the meetings so that no thorough airing of views was possible, and actions like these were not discussable.

Stockman and his associates decided on several bypass strategies. For example, Stockman reports, they learned to generate noncontroversial ideas for discussion during the meetings: "We had to scramble all week to find enough of these 'safe' items to fill Meese's Cabinet agenda while 'big ticket' spending-cuts and economic forecast items receded further and further" (p. 102). Stockman concluded that the tough decisions were not going to be made in the cabinet meetings "because Ed Meese was protecting the President from having to choose sides among his Cabinet members" (p. 109). Stockman had to devise a bypass strategy that would work over time but would not be viewed as a means to bypass Meese's and others' protection of the president's and cabinet members' intellectual and interpersonal limits. Stockman hit on a structural solution often used by individuals in this predicament.

Stockman proposed to Meese that he create a committee called the Budget Working Group, which would review all budget cuts with affected cabinet members before the cuts went to the president and the full cabinet. Even though Meese and Chief of Staff James Baker would be members of the group, Stockman knew that neither of them would attend the meetings unless the president did. Meese agreed, and Stockman selected his team. It was this group that made most of the difficult choices.

The Budget Working Group meetings also became the setting for Stockman and his associate Martin Anderson, a policy analyst, to educate new cabinet members and their staffs about the rigors of budget cutting. Anderson, says Stockman, knew how to cut the resisters down to size without humiliating them. Unfortunately, Stockman does not describe exactly how Anderson accomplished this feat. People can sense when they are being cut down to size and when the cutting down is being covered up. They play along by covering up their humiliation and anger. These bad feelings accumulate, however, and soon these people find appropriate ways to retaliate.

Stockman's descriptions suggest that humiliation and anger may have been present and that retaliation did occur. He notes that the cabinet members and their staffs began to resist. He also overheard cabinet members talking with each other about his heavy-handedness. Moreover, cabinet members and their staffs developed their own defensive actions. Secretary of Defense Caspar Weinberger and Secretary of the Treasury Donald Regan were especially skillful here.

On reflection Stockman admits it could appear that cabinet members acted irresponsibly, sweeping issues under the rug and basing short-run policy and political gains on weak facts

(*Frontline*, 1986, p. 14). But the actors, Stockman insists, were not clearly aware of their own actions: "I don't think anybody lied. . . . [There was] no deliberate deception . . . we were confused . . . but nobody said, 'we know we're lying, but we're going to go ahead and do it anyway.' . . . And we were all caught up in those daily tactical battles; . . . we never had time to raise . . . the big picture doubts" (pp. 15–16).

Actions That Inhibit Organizational Learning

What can we infer from these examples about the way governmental agencies are administered? The immediate impact of the policies, practices, and behavior described in the literature was to inhibit the detection and correction of error. The second-order consequence was to inhibit problem solving and decision making. This consequence led to a third-order consequence: less effective organizational performance.

In addition, all the actions occurred where a wide variety of issues were being dealt with. The issues were complex and nontrivial, and they contained a potential for, or an actual component of, embarrassment or threat. Moreover, the embarrassment or threat could be aimed at individuals, groups, intergroups, or whole organizations.

The actions violated formal managerial principles and managerial stewardship. In neither the official policies nor the administrators' espoused values was there encouragement to deceive, to manipulate, or to distort information. Nevertheless, the actions were robust; they appeared in spite of (and even because of) their deviancy from ideas in good currency on how to administer governmental agencies.

Let us now dig a bit deeper. Since these defensive actions inhibit problem solving and decision making, since they violate formal policies and managerial stewardship, and since they involve embarrassment or threat, it is unlikely that they are discussable while they are being executed. For example, it is not likely that someone would say that he or she was about to deceive, manipulate, or distort, because that would make the person vulnerable to the charge of acting unethically. Moreover, to admit and then to deceive is not to deceive; to admit and then to manipulate is to reduce the likely effectiveness of the manipulation; to admit and then distort is to tell the truth.

All these actions require that human beings communicate inconsistent messages but act as if they are not doing so. In order for these actions to be effective, they must be covered up while being enacted. In many cases, the cover-ups must also be covered up. To do this, individuals learn to communicate inconsistent messages, act as if the messages are not inconsistent, make the previous actions undiscussable, and make the undiscussability undiscussable. Individuals on the receiving end of these actions must collude. If they recognize the cover-up, they learn to act as if they do not recognize it. They also expect the deceiver, distorter, or manipulator to recognize the collusion.

These actions are organizational defensive routines. They overprotect individuals or groups and inhibit them from learning new actions. They are routines because they occur continually and are independent of individual actors' personalities.

Defensive actions are highly skilled. Skillful actions are executed immediately and automatically. Skillful actions "work." Most of the time they are executed without the actors' conscious attention. Indeed, paying attention may reduce the skillfulness. Thus, skillful actions are taken for granted (Argyris, 1985b).

Another feature of these skillful defensive actions is that they are learned early in life. To my knowledge, no formal organization theory requires organizational defensive routines. They exist in the first place because human beings learn early in life to deal with embarrassment or threat. Each individual has what I call a *theory-in-use,* which prescribes actions that will skillfully bypass the embarrassment or threat and cover up the bypass. The individual's espoused theory (in the form of values and attitudes for example) is typically quite different (Argyris & Schön, 1974). (I will discuss theories-in-use in depth in Chapter Two.)

The use of defensive routines learned early in life is reinforced by the organizational cultures created by individuals implementing strategies of bypass and cover-up. These strategies persist because organizational norms sanction and protect them. Once this occurs, individuals find it rational to hold the organization responsible for the defensive routines. Thus, there is a circular self-reinforcing process, from the individual to the larger unit and back to the individual.

Skillful behavior may be said to be guided by master programs in individuals' heads, programs that automatically produce the behavior in everyday life. Successful use of these master programs also increases an individual's confidence and self-esteem in managing himself or others. Therefore, changing the human predisposition to produce organizational defensive routines and the organizational norms that protect those routines requires altering both individuals' master programs and organizations' protective norms. It is unlikely that suggestions to deal with organizational defenses are going to work persistently if these alterations are bypassed.

The skillful and automatic use of defensive routines is illustrated by research that I conducted in a class I taught for several years with Lawrence Lynn at the Kennedy School (Argyris, 1982). About 100 students representing varied backgrounds and roles in government were asked to evaluate the behavior of the two competing groups that tried to define welfare policy during President Jimmy Carter's administration (Lynn & Whitman, 1981). During the first session, the students identified the following causes for the problems the two groups encountered (all classes were tape-recorded, and most of the students' remarks are verbatim):

- Working groups
    Had entrenched positions.
    Were unwilling to change.
    Had lots of disagreement.
    Were miscommunicating.
    Were not accustomed to working with each other.
    Had no one confronting the real issues.
    Had delegates from Moscow.
    Pushed their own agendas any time they could do so.
- Secretary of Health, Education, and Welfare Joseph Califano was "Washington-hip."
    He let things boil.
    He kept options open.

He was smart enough to know that if he accepted responsibility, he also would get all the trouble.

He appeared to have a secret agenda.

Vintage Califano behavior was that he had learned to humiliate his staff from Lyndon Johnson, he acted like a trial lawyer, he acted bored in order to collect his thoughts.

- The deadline placed people under pressure.
- No one was willing to make firm decisions. Each player thought, "It is not my decision to make."
- This is the dynamic of the first six months of any administration. The players are finding their way around, jockeying for position. Turf is being defined.
- Califano did not know his staff.

  They were afraid to level with him.

  They told him what they thought he wanted to hear.
- The groups had the typical Washington mentality—throw money at problems and take care of constituents.
- Everyone was acting rationally—each group felt it had the answer and acted as if it did. It is rational to resist (carefully and adroitly) giving up one's position. Hence, Carter might have been able to push a button and launch a missile, but he pushed Califano and nothing got done.
- There was an underlying tension between the Georgia hicks and the Washington sophisticates.

The members of the second session repeated the causes the first session had described and added some different ones:

- The task itself contained conflicting features: on the one hand, redesign welfare; on the other hand, add no more cost, in order to keep inflation down.
- The situation set up a *classic power struggle.* Why do we expect anything but what happened? Why are we surprised? The players were heads of agencies and were born winners, ambitious men who wanted to win. If they lost, they would lose the respect of their staffs.
- The players were *selfish and self-centered,* looking out for number one, obsessed with maintaining "my truth." People's

self-esteem is wrapped up in game-playing, and they are fearful to say they do not know what to do.

- None of the players had a great vision, an important organizing idea about welfare.

    No one really seemed to care about welfare reform.

    We lack mature leaders; there is no one with wisdom.

    We have dropped the "philosopher" from "philosopher-prince."

- Each institution was self-centered, with its own learning experiences and perspective; none wished to cooperate.

- The task was too large to do all at once. It might have worked out if done incrementally.

The participants in both sessions judged the actors in the case of welfare reform to be largely ineffective. What reasoning processes did the participants use to make their evaluations? Two features of the responses are relevant to our inquiry. First, the responses represent unillustrated, untested attributions or evaluations; advocacy of participants' views with little encouragement of inquiry by others; and attributions that place the responsibility "in" individuals or in forces in the culture. These are all defensive routines. Second, the diagnoses contain an implicit causal theory of effectiveness that may be stated as follows: If individuals or groups use untested attributions, advocacy that curtails inquiry, and attributions which assign responsibility to individuals or cultural forces, the individuals or groups will harden their positions, develop rivalries, become mistrustful, and distance themselves from taking the responsibility for confronting process issues. These outcomes, in turn, will lead to escalating error, undiscussability of the counterproductive features in the settings where they are occurring (but discussability among friends or cliques), and players who act as if there were nothing undiscussable (one cannot discuss the undiscussability of the undiscussable).

Moreover, if the actors in the Califano case had asked the class to evaluate their effectiveness, and if the class had stated these causal views directly, the class would have been using the same counterproductive behavior, the same kinds of attributing and advocating, that they condemned the actors in the case for using. In

other words, if the Califano players had listened to the class dialogue, they would probably have become defensive.

During the class discussion, a number of opportunities arose
to illustrate this hypothesis. Frequently, a faculty member would
ask the class how they would communicate to the actors in the case
what the students were saying about them in class. Almost always,
the students would try to ease-in to the criticism. In the few instances when students were forthright, many of the class members
laughed. When asked why, they answered that it was unrealistic to
think that one could be forthright with the president, Califano, and
the other major actors.

To summarize, the students diagnosed the players' actions in
the case as defensive, but the very way they framed their diagnoses
would also have created defensiveness if the players had heard them.
During the class, the students created defensiveness in each other
when they disagreed. The point is that the defensive behavior was
so skilled and automatic that the students behaved in the very ways
they condemned the players for behaving. In addition, the students
were unaware of their defensiveness, and most would never have
predicted that they would act as they did.

My associates and I have replicated these results, with both
similar and different cases as the students' topic, in over 150 classes
given during the past twenty years in schools of business, education,
and law, as well as in executive programs in private industry and
government.

Recommendations for Action

Although a number of governmental observers and participants
have suggested ways to overcome such symptoms of organizational
defensive routines as rivalries, increased errors, mistrust, and ineffectiveness, most of the recommendations fail to address the causes
of the routines. Halperin (1974), for example, recommends that the
president of the United States deal with people's games and defenses
by advantageous bargaining. According to Halperin, one of the
president's most powerful assets is his ability to persuade his principal associates that something he wishes to do is in the national
interest. People take him seriously when he delivers his ideas per-

sonally and evokes national interest. When this does not work, he negotiates. And if this is not adequate, he may bully and hector. Finally, he may simply take over as much of the execution as possible. The president may also fire certain players and bring in new ones.

It is not clear, however, how any of these tactics would engage, overcome, and reduce organizational defensive routines. Indeed, as I read Halperin's recommendations, it is almost as if the defenses did not exist in his situation—or, if they did, were not important. Clearly, Halperin's book documents that they did exist and that they were important.

Kaufman (1977) identifies three solutions to stronger control: reduce the size of government, strengthen controls, and provide incentives to private interests to do what the government is doing. After assessing the advantages and disadvantages of the solutions, Kaufman recommends that the government should treat symptoms, because they will relieve pain; have appeal processes that work; provide citizens with help, so that rules are not seen as barriers; and provide an ombudsman. But he does not say what specific actions are required to treat symptoms effectively, create appeal processes that work, or give help that actually overcomes the barriers. Again, the advice is abstract; it bypasses the very dysfunctional processes that Kaufman describes, and he himself finally concludes that we may have to live with a little red tape because that is the nature of the beast.

Wilson (1989) suggests that, in order for bureaucracies to become more effective, there should be more deregulation, executives who understand their organizational cultures, negotiations to identify essential and nonessential constraints, authority pushed down to the lowest possible levels, judgments based on results, and clear standard operating procedures (pp. 369-372). However, these recommendations also fail to deal with organizational defensive routines.

The same problem occurs with Janis's recommendations for overcoming "group think" (1972). For example, having someone play devil's advocate is unlikely to reduce defensive routines, as Secretary George Ball found out during the Vietnam era. Nor is

Bardach and Kagan's recommendation (1982) to impose budget constraints on regulatory unreasonableness likely to induce reason.

The literature on leadership in government is no more helpful (see Burns, 1978; Barber, 1977; Gardner, 1990; Paige, 1977; McFarland, 1969; and the scholars included in Kellerman, 1984). Burns speaks of transformational leadership at such an abstract level that it is difficult to see how that quality could be learned from his discussion, which omits important behavioral puzzles and dilemmas. For example, Bailey (1988) describes Roosevelt as designedly playing one subordinate against another. Edelman (1988) also describes Roosevelt as being skillful in acting deceptively and manipulating people. Yet Burns describes Roosevelt as a transformational leader. According to Edelman, John Kennedy, Lyndon Johnson, and Richard Nixon also acted inconsistently and deceptively. The actions mentioned are all consistent with the organizational defenses described earlier, and it may well be that transformational leaders succeed partially by being deceptive, but one would not know that from the research literature on leadership.

There are two recommendations that appear to have the potential to genuinely reduce the likelihood of embarrassment or threat. However, to my knowledge, neither strategy has been studied empirically to assess its practical strengths and weaknesses.

The first strategy—a strategy of group deliberation and decision making—is recommended by George (1972) as a way to develop more valid information and dialogue for the president regarding foreign policy. However, he supplies no discussion or research on how his strategy would work if the issues were threatening or embarrassing to the players. Perhaps the moment defensive routines become activated, the effectiveness of the structural arrangements suggested would be significantly limited.

The second strategy is recommended by Neustadt and May (1986), who suggest that actors examine their presumptions rigorously when reaching decisions about important issues. Neustadt and May illustrate that some important errors in Vietnam policy might have been averted if government officials had probed their own presumptions. Again, research is required to see how the reasonableness of this method might be sabotaged when individual, group, and organizational defenses are activated.

Defensive Routines in Education

As in the case of the literature on public administration, the literature on educational administration is full of examples of errors being introduced into the management of education in universities and schools.

For example, Hoyle (1988) describes micropolitics in educational settings. He includes such examples as materializing "professional" arguments against a proposed innovation that threatens the territorial interests of teachers, "losing" recommendations from working parties by referring the recommendations to other groups in the hope that they will disappear or be transformed, "rigging agendas," massaging the minutes of meetings, and "inventing" consensus where consensus has not been tested (p. 259). Blumberg (1989) cites examples of how teachers and principals have to deceive, go around regulations, play one group against another, and act as if they are not doing these things, in òrder to accomplish something that all agree would enhance teaching or learning in the classroom.

Sizer (1984) describes the lack of trust in teachers—how the constant control from "downtown" undermines even the ablest teachers and administrators, and how it leads teachers to withdraw or fight, which, in turn, leads "downtown" to increase the unilateral control. Broudy (1972) reports that the most common causes of school unresponsiveness include the rigidity of bureaucrats and the insensitivity of tenured civil servants whose major concern is maintaining the status quo.

Boyer (1985) agrees that good teachers and principals are caught in complicated bureaucratic webs and that "far too many schools are top-heavy with administration" (p. 224), which results in teachers performing menial tasks and busywork. Yet, despite all this administrative hierarchy and control, the public sees discipline as the schools' chief problem (Bunzel, 1985). Finally, Heath (1971) identifies mistrustful administrators who permit teachers little choice in everyday teaching matters. In the administrators' minds, the schedule is king and departmental barriers are necessary even though they inhibit cooperation.

Focusing on the classroom, Woods (1979) reports that teachers can be observed favoring boys, blaming students for some-

thing that has gone wrong (without examining their own responsibility), exercising unilateral control, and acting as if students are
not to be trusted. Students in turn produce their own defensive
routines, which look like aimless, pointless, and disorganized behavior—causing trouble for sheer delight, not paying attention, or
simply loafing. They also use laughter to deal with their sense of
futility and helplessness. A hidden pedagogy of survival results,
which the players act out skillfully and routinely. The acting out
is undiscussable, and undiscussability and uninfluenceability are
seen as "natural"; that's the way it is. Teachers' survival strategies
include dominating, fraternizing, and distancing. All these factors
make genuine change unlikely. Moreover, they provide teachers
with a "legitimate" excuse to explain away many of the difficulties
by blaming students. In other words, when student peer pressure,
immaturity, laziness, lack of ability, possession of deplorable attributes, and similar actions are seen as the causes of difficulties, these
"causes" then require and reinforce the teachers' dysfunctional behavior, including blaming the students.

Grant (1988) describes the counterproductive consequences
that developed in schools that attempted to experiment with new
practices. For example, at one school, letting students decide certain
issues led to leniency in discipline. This angered older teachers.
Teachers could no longer trust each other, and the administrators
gave confused signals but acted as if they were not doing so. For
example, teachers were "told" to be wary of setting high educational standards, but these messages were undiscussable. Teachers
who attempted to be tough could be indicted by the students for
abusing their authority. Indeed, the students could bring suits
against them. The resulting situation was anarchic. The faculty in
another school distanced themselves from each other. According to
Grant, the attitude was: You leave me alone and I will leave you
alone and maybe if I find out that you're dying of cancer I might
talk to you. As a result, many teachers did not feel they controlled
their fate. They had lost their sense of efficacy; yet the administrative superstructure continued to exist.

Jackson (1968) suggests that the types of dysfunctional behavior described here may have a profound effect on the typical
school culture as well as on the way teachers think about teaching
and schooling. The culture becomes one in which secrecy is a pre-

dominant way to survive and is used by some to manipulate institutional privileges. The teachers' view of teaching becomes one in which they shun elaborate ideas for dealing with complicated situations. They hold an uncomplicated view of causality, as if there were a one-to-one correspondence between cause and effect. They use intuition rather than a rational approach to explain classroom events. This reliance on intuition reinforces their simplified view of reality and makes them less open-minded when confronted with alternative teaching practices. Goodlad (1984) concludes that instructional practice is becoming more routinized. He predicts that this will conspire to limit the schools' role in the humanization of knowledge, the drive to make knowledge relevant to the lives of more people. Thus, the schools are producing the very consequences of ineffective schooling that they decry.

There is another theme in most of the research cited. Most of the writers report that none of what they have observed is new. As Adelson (1985) says, "The sorry state of American schools had been evident for years" (p. 18), or, as Blumberg (1989, p. 20) puts it, "So what else is new?" If there is a mystery, it is why it has taken so long to bring the problems out in the open.

Actions That Inhibit Organizational Learning

The underlying features of the defensive routines that inhibit organizational learning in schools are similar to those described for governmental organizations. The routines occurred when many different difficult problems were being dealt with; there were many different individuals and groups involved, and the defensive routines violated formal policies and practices; yet the routines appeared to survive, indeed to become more robust, even though countless studies had been conducted and literally millions of dollars spent in attempts to improve the schools' effectiveness.

Let us examine a representative sample of the advice given to overcome the schools' acknowledged problems, in order to develop hypotheses about why these defensive routines persist.

Recommendations for Action

Advice in the literature about how to correct educational ineffectiveness is abstract and distant. Almost no advice is given on how to engage the defensive activities and consequences just described. They are ignored, and the fact that they are ignored is also ignored (Scribner & Stevens, 1975; Hong, 1986; Fantini, 1986; National Board for Professional Teaching Standards, 1989). For example, it is suggested that teachers ought to be trusted and given greater autonomy (Grant, 1988), decision making should be delegated downward (Sizer, 1984; Boyer, 1985), and better financial support and laws more supportive of educational excellence should be provided (Chance, 1986). If schools are to be primarily instrumental, then more off moments and private areas should be given to teachers (Woods, 1979). Schools should clarify goals, train teachers to collaborate, require collective participation, and keep everyone on track (Frase & Hetzel, 1990). Accountability should be specified, but first goals must be clear, outcomes must be under the control of the school, standards of quality must be clear, and teachers must be recognized as experts (Broudy, 1972).

Lightfoot (1983) recommends that schools develop vision and boundaries that are permeable and that they provide teachers with autonomy and conditions where honest mistakes can be made and corrected. However, no insights are given that would specify the characteristics of effective vision, permeable boundaries, or adequate autonomy. Moreover, there is no information on how to achieve these goals. Heath (1971) advises concentrating on learning experiences that integrate intellectual consciousness with emotion and action, creating smaller educational units, and encouraging experiential education that confronts students with their own beliefs and values. Again. there is no insight provided as to how to recognize workable forms of these actions and how to implement them.

Scholars in the field suggest at least three reasons why defensive routines have been largely ignored. First, the administrative concepts used to understand schools do not focus on these issues (Reynolds, 1985; Westoby, 1988; Hoyle, 1988). Second, the measuring instruments used to diagnose schools do not include organizational defensive activities as variables to be studied (Abt, Magidson & Magidson, 1980). Third, teachers, like all of us, use a theory of action to guide their behavior that produces bypasses and cover-ups, especially when they are dealing with embarrassing or threatening issues. As Brodsky (1989) documents, teachers are often unaware of how skillfully they create defensive routines, how skillfully they compound them when they try to reduce them, how skillfully they blame others, and how skillfully they deny all of the above. Brodsky's study is rare because it provides relatively directly observable data, such as conversations, upon which she bases her conclusions.

Defensive Routines in Business

A review of the relevant literature suggests that business organizations have organizational defensive routines similar to those in government and education. And, once again, scholars' or practitioners' recommendations for overcoming the typical problems bypass the causes. Indeed, in the case of business, these recommendations actually reinforce the causes of the organizational defensive routines (Argyris, 1990c).

Rather than repeat concepts established earlier, I will review the literature about business organizations in a somewhat different way, in order to dig more deeply into the gap it displays between knowledge and action. To do so, I have selected some well-known studies where applicability of results, or actionable knowledge, was of concern to the researchers as they designed and conducted their research. After describing the gap between recommendations and their applicability, I turn to second-order consequences that are relevant if study results are to be used by practitioners.

The Gap Between Knowledge and Action

Lawrence and Lorsch (1967) show that the effective organizations in their research exhibited an appropriate balance between differentiation and integration, and that exact point of the balance was heavily influenced by environmental demands. A key to implementing the correct balance was the behavior of the managers. Their behavior was significantly influenced by their cognitive-emotional orientation, which was composed of each manager's functional orientation, his or her time orientation, his or her interpersonal orientation, and the quality and degree of the organizational structure's formality.

Lawrence and Lorsch focus on how managers might design their actions and the organizational and other structural features to develop more effective integration. For example, when focusing on designing actions to deal with conflict, they report that easing-in strategies were not as well correlated with organizational effectiveness as were confronting strategies. It is possible to "derive" from their findings the following action advice: In a conflict, constructively confront others *and* make sure that you are (and are seen as) competent and knowledgeable in the task, that you have organizational clout, and that the knowledge available and the knowledge required to make a decision coincide.

For the sake of illustration, let us assume that managers who want to apply this advice have the requisite competence, technical knowledge, and organizational power. This permits us to focus on the action steps the authors suggest to reduce easing-in and increase constructive confrontation. They recommend that the managers use organizational development (OD) consultants and such reeducative experiences as T-groups.

There are several problems with these recommendations. First, the authors' theory of differentiation and integration does not specify what behavioral skills the managers must learn to reduce easing-in and increase constructive confrontation. Second, if the managers go through a T-group experience and then fail *or* succeed to reduce easing-in and increase constructive confrontation, it would be difficult to use these results as a test of the theory. Third, the choice of action steps has been delegated to OD theory and practice, which, to my mind, does not deal with the challenges of helping managers act in ways that will integrate them with other managers and, hence, with the organization. Indeed, especially in the early days, T-group experiences aimed at reducing individuals' easing-in and thereby helping them confront the organization were often in the service of differentiating, not integrating.

Another example of the gap between action and knowledge in the research literature appears in Katz and Kahn (1966), who used the concept of role as the "major means for linking the individual and organizational levels of research and theory; [role] is at once the building block of social systems and the summation of the requirements with which such systems confront their members as individuals" (p. 197). Kahn and his associates (1964) conducted extensive research on role ambiguity and organizational stress that systematically explored the function of role.

In their research, the authors report that nearly half the individuals in a national sample described themselves as working under conditions of role conflict that had nontrivial consequences on individual and organizational stress. To understand the problem, the authors developed a model in which they were careful to point out the many variables and their relationships. For example, there was an apparent linear relationship between organizational size and the amount of reported role conflict and tension in the organization.

This research is clearly applicable to formulating organizational policy and to designing specifications for roles and role relationships. What would it take to make such knowledge usable by both managers in everyday life and those who wanted to test the model's features?

Prospective users would find a relatively complete list of prescriptions that are related to the design of organizational roles—for example, keep ambiguities in role definitions and between role expectations and role sets at a minimum. Let us assume that managers can translate these prescriptions into designs, have the skills to learn to produce these designs, and have the power to translate them into job definitions and policies about reporting relationships.

The next step would be for managers to implement the designs and monitor their effectiveness. At this point, personal and interpersonal factors would become activated. What if the managers found nontrivial instances of ambiguity still existing within many of the designed roles and found conflicts among roles? What behavioral skills would the managers require in order to correct these errors? The authors do not deal with these issues, yet if their research is correct, managers are likely to find that these issues exist.

Of all the empirical research that I have reviewed, Hackman (1987) represents the most thorough attempt to make explicit the challenges involved in moving toward actionable knowledge. He assesses the descriptive research on group behavior and shows why it is not possible to go from this research to prescriptions for the design and management of groups. It is a model presentation for researchers who may be concerned about going from descriptive research to advice.

Next, Hackman develops a normative model of what is likely to be required if groups are to be effective, and he defines effectiveness explicitly. It is possible to provide advice to managers (or interveners) from this normative model. For example, teams could be set up so that they ranked high on each variable in the model.

Hackman then turns to an action model that is concerned with ways to create the conditions that the normative theory suggests are necessary for a group to perform well. Hackman organizes his action model around four stages that are required if effective action is likely to occur, and he identifies critical questions to be addressed during each stage. For example, during the stages of prework and of creating performance conditions, the following key questions must be answered: What is the task? What are the critical task demands? How can the tasks be designed to be as clear and motivationally engaging as possible? What material resources (for example, tools, equipment, or money) will members need?

Again, let us assume that this knowledge is available because individuals can read and learn from the extensive literature on these topics. However, stage three (forming and building the team) and stage four (providing ongoing assistance) are more difficult to implement. For example, Hackman's discussion alerts us to the likelihood that forming group boundaries is often difficult because of internal group processes that lead to "process losses" and because defining group boundaries can activate problems such as organizational turf disputes. Defining and redefining tasks is also an action fraught with misunderstandings, tensions, and conflicts. Developing group norms and group members' roles is usually a natural process, but the norms and roles that develop may be heavily influenced by forces of which members are unaware. Moreover, the norms may conflict with core management values.

Once a group has begun to solve problems such as these, Hackman suggests, it will likely become a functioning system able to control its own destiny. Nevertheless, Hackman points out that attention must still be given to such crucial issues as renegotiating group design and context, promoting positive synergy, and learning from group experience.

The gap between knowledge and action is most apparent in the fact that no models are presented for taking the actions that are derivable from the theory. For example, the descriptive research documents "process losses." The normative model recommends reducing process losses through synergistic gains. The action model recommends creating positive group synergy. But there is no model for creating this synergy, only a reference to using "process consultation." But such advice may be problematic, because the practices of process consultation may vary significantly in some areas Hackman considers important. For example, in order to correct group process loss and to cultivate synergistic process gains, Hackman recommends determining whether groups are suffering from poor coordination, inappropriate weighing of members' talents, or flawed implementation. Most process consultation professionals will agree, I believe, on how to discover whether groups possess these traits. But process consultants differ significantly on how to cultivate the team spirit and encourage the group learning that will correct the traits. For example, Argyris (1990b) places constructive confrontation high on his list of types of interventions while Schein (1987b) places it last on his list. The interventions each would make to facilitate synergistic process gains would likely vary considerably.

Second-Order Consequences

The serious study of usable knowledge would benefit science by producing a more complete understanding of reality and practice and more effective ways to change practice than those I have just described. However, once change is activated, it may have counterproductive second-order consequences. Research to produce usable knowledge should pay explicit attention to such unintended consequences. I have found three categories of these second-order consequences that are dealt with incompletely in the current literature: errors are identified, but their persistence is not; undesirable, variable, and unethical results of implementing the research findings correctly are ignored; and inner contradictions are not identified, so that the paradoxical nature of organizations is not understood.

Failing to Deal with the Persistence of Error. There are several versions of this second-order consequence, which occurs when the causes of unintended errors are identified but the causes of the errors' persistence are not. For example, in discussing accidents, Perrow (1984) identifies three rationalities: absolute, bounded, and social. He believes that the first two have been overemphasized in understanding accidents while the third, social rationality, has been largely neglected. Social rationality, Perrow suggests, recognizes that individuals have different strengths that should be respected and that the process of integrating these differences can bring about social bonding. He says, "Bonding by diversity in skills . . . is more stable and perhaps more satisfying than bonding by addition of equal talents" (p. 322). Thus social rationality is recommended as a key resource in effectively handling or preventing major errors.

Hackman (1987), Janis (1989), and Argyris and Schön (1974, 1978), however, suggest that bonding is not a natural consequence of group processes. Thus, if one wishes to recommend social rationality, the next step in research is to learn how to create conditions that produce social rationality of the highest quality possible. Without such knowledge, Perrow is in the position of recommending a factor which, if the other research is correct, is unlikely to meet the claims he makes for it.

Hackman (1989) describes five design errors individuals make in bringing together and leading groups. They call the performing unit a team but manage members as individuals; fall off the authority balance beam; assemble a large group of people, tell them in general terms what needs to be accomplished, and let them work out the details; specify a challenging team objective, but skimp on organizational supports; and assume that members already have all the competence they need to work well as a team (pp. 493–501).

To the extent these errors exist because of ignorance, Hackman's research should reduce the ignorance and hence the design errors. However, if it is true that these errors persist over time, then the research question becomes, What prevents people from discovering and correcting the errors? Presumably, when individuals are given skimpy resources, they experience an inconsistency with the objective they have been given. If so, why do they not discuss what they know from this experience? If they do discuss what they know, what prevents them from correcting the error?

In my recent studies of similar errors, the primary reason the errors persisted is that they were covered up, and the cover-up was also covered up. The players reported that they acted in these ways because the organizational defensive routines required that they do so. To do otherwise, they reported, would likely open up a Pandora's box (Argyris, 1990c).

Another version of failing to deal with the persistence of error occurs when applicable research maintains the status quo in ways that are counterproductive to advice that can be derived from the research. In a review of advice given by well-known executives, I found two underlying difficulties (Argyris, 1990c). First, their advice may have been applicable, but, as stated, it was not actionable. Second, the advice often ignored the organizational defenses that created the errors in the first place, which meant that the advice could not alter the status quo. Moreover, the authors seemed unaware of the oversight. These difficulties were also found relevant for many studies in the social sciences (Argyris, 1980).

Researchers may unrealizingly add to the second-order consequence of maintaining the status quo and its errors by describing the universe (in this case, organizations) and then concluding directly or indirectly that it cannot be altered. It is one thing, for example, to conduct empirical research that documents (in my view accurately) the defensive routines of many organizations. It is quite another to state or imply that the defensive routines cannot be altered, without first conducting empirical research that substantiates this claim.

For example, Golding (1991) describes the "rituals" (routines) in an organization that restricted relevant financial information to the top level. Other managers who tried to get the information they needed concluded it was a waste of time to try. They also concluded that the meetings they attended were a waste of time, but they continued to attend them, covering up their true feelings. Golding also describes rituals to cover up secrecy. He concludes that many of this organization's rituals produced status degradation and intimidation to the point of becoming oppressive; but he also concludes, as I understand it, that these rituals will continue. He suggests that trying to stop these rituals would be as futile as trying to, as he puts it, stop the clock. Ironically, studies such as this make it less likely that social science research will be able to stop the clock by changing the status quo. Golding, in my opinion, describes the defensive reality of the organization accurately. But in stopping there and not conducting research on changing the rituals, he provides both the researchers who document and the executives who produce oppressive routines with an explanation that permits them to conclude that their defensive routines cannot be changed.

Brunsson (1989) produces insightful analyses of decisions to show that bounded rationality has its limits when organizations strive to mobilize support, deal with responsibility, and legitimate their actions and themselves. For example, he shows how the phenomena subsumed under the title of organizational "politics" can lead to conversations and decisions that may appear irrational but yet be quite rational, given the defensive routines within each organization and between each organization and its environment. Inconsistencies may indeed be useful. However, if I read Brunsson correctly, the inconsistencies were not discussable. Thus, it was difficult for the organizations to learn from their experiences. The inconsistencies' usefulness was in maintaining the status quo.

Yet another version of permitting errors to persist occurs when researchers take for granted what the actors take for granted. The result can be an unintended collusion, on the part of the researcher, with the status quo, including the defensive routines. As an example, I focus on the recent thoughtful and systematic research on group effectiveness by several cooperating scholars (Hackman, 1989). They studied mostly groups in everyday contexts. They used several different research methods. They relied heavily on interviews and observation. Yet, with all their intention not to be limited by the prevailing scientific methodology, they did take for granted features of the status quo that were critical, especially when it came to understanding organizational learning. I refer to what they called "self-fueling processes," which were largely counterproductive. For example, in the authors' studies of top management groups, the first prominent cause for the ineffective functioning of a top management group was that the internal processes of the team were such that, when things started to go wrong, fragmentation occurred—that is, the team tended to come apart. Because of this, top executives avoided using the team, which was the second prominent cause for ineffective functioning. Once a self-fueling cycle of fragmentation and avoidance was established, it was very hard to stop (pp. 82–83).

Some examples of the findings that show ineffective functioning occurring are the following:

"Yet FCG members typically did not acknowledge or address conflicts within the group. According to one member, 'There have been a few times when we have been on the verge of getting into it. But we never got over the hump'" (p. 230).

Over time, such behavior and norms produced "a unique history, [which led] the members of the FCG [to be] particularly wary of openly discussing their differences" (p. 230).

The behaviors just described made it difficult for members to deal with the aimless quality of their discussions. One of them said, "It's kind of like we have an FCG meeting because we have an FCG meeting. We don't have an agenda or anything" (p. 32).

It is possible to infer from these examples that the counterproductive group processes, such as avoiding conflict and not engaging the meetings' aimlessness, were bypassed during the meetings and that the bypass was covered up. Therefore, one explanation for the fragmentation and avoidance is that when things went wrong, the group members were faced with a problem that might have been embarrassing or threatening. This activated bypass and cover-up activities. These activities, in turn, activated the norms that made bypass and cover-up undiscussable. If they were undiscussable, bypass and cover-up were not likely to be correctable. Hence, the fragmentation and avoidance persisted.

Moreover, if the participants were acting as I suggest, they were doing so explicitly or tacitly. Bypass and cover-up were deliberate, intentional actions. So the participants not only knew that there were counterproductive group norms and that these norms and their impact were not discussable; they also knew that they colluded privately to reinforce the norms but acted publicly as if they were not doing so. This behavior would enhance the likelihood that the processes would be self-fueling once they were activated.

It is difficult to interrupt and correct processes of fragmentation and avoidance if they are not discussable; if group norms sanction their undiscussability; and if the participants privately know that they are acting in ways to encourage the persistence of group features that they criticize.

As researchers, I suggest, we have a responsibility to try to change defensive routines in order to develop empirical knowledge about their alterability. At the moment, because of the absence of such studies, coupled with the large number of studies describing organizational defensive routines, we may be encouraging scholars and practitioners to believe that the status quo, and its errors and defensive routines, is unalterable.

Failing to Uncover Variable, Undesirable, and Unethical Consequences. Yet other second-order consequences occur when recommended sequences of action lead to consequences that subvert the intended results or achieve the intended results through behavior that introduces a new set of errors. Users should at least be warned that these unwanted second-order consequences are possible. For example, Sayles has written a book (1989) full of interesting ideas and advice and carefully crafted statements about the degree of applicability of that advice. One example of his advice is that whenever superiors and subordinates disagree on an issue where concurrence is necessary, and the matter does not lend itself to simple directives, superiors should seek to establish a mutual give-and-take and reach an agreement that there is a problem; seek to understand the subordinates' natures, interests, anxieties, and desires through letting subordinates talk and explain in a way that communicates to them that the boss understands; and seek to get employees' interactions (big or small).

However, those who have observed leaders applying such advice or designed workshops to help them learn to apply it report enormous variances in the leaders' behavior. The actions one leader uses to produce a mutual give-and-take may be seen by another as unilateral and coercive or as abdicating leadership. Similar variances appear when leaders apply advice such as "letting subordinates talk" and "encouraging initiatives." Moreover, in the majority of the cases, the leaders are unaware of the gap between their designed interactions and the consequences they actually produce. They are also unaware that they have programs in their heads to keep them unaware (Argyris, 1978b, 1982, 1985b).

Sayles also advises using a "deceptively simple and direct" technique to deter backsliding on the part of others. Project managers, for example, should confront and challenge, raising questions such as "What makes you think that those hearings are comparable to the ones we discussed last week?" or "What is your evidence that the redesign is likely to solve the problem? Prove it to me" (p. 243).

The strategies used by senior NASA officials to deter what they believed was backsliding on the part of engineers who did not want *Challenger* to fly show a high degree of similarity to what Sayles recommends. As I interpret the Rogers Commission findings, the subordinates understood and accepted these strategies when they were used by superiors. The subordinates saw nothing illegitimate about the *way* they were being confronted; although they did experience frustration and bewilderment, they did not discuss such feelings. Therefore, one can hypothesize that these strategies can work in the sense that they deter backsliding, but they may also encourage a potentially disastrous distancing from feeling and acting responsible. The subordinates eventually gave up and took the attitude "Okay, wise guys—fly it!" (Argyris, 1990c).

Sayles reports that successful purchasing agents learn to deal with difficult requisitions or those that involve a conflict by using such strategies as these: appeal to superiors through the use of existing rules; evade rules by using personal-political tactics, such as going through the motions of complying but with no expectation of getting delivery on time; or exceed formal authority and ignore the requisition altogether. Sayles also suggests the following strategies for agents who must deal with an autocratic boss: prepare the ground carefully, instead of just springing the idea on the boss; do not present the problem and the proposed solution at the same time; present the problems in stages and in such a way that no solution will be immediately apparent to the boss, who should be kept uninformed (pp. 142–144).

The difficulty is that neither Sayles's studies nor his advice describe how the purchasing agents must actually behave when they carry out these actions. For example, going through the motions of complying by agreeing to a deadline they know they will not keep requires that the agents deliberately cover up that they have no

intention of meeting the delivery time or that they will exceed formal authority. However unethical the resulting behavior, the advice
is likely to "work," because it "tells" an actor to legitimize using
bypass and cover-up and to avoid embarrassment or threat by invoking two features of organizational defensive routines: overprotect
yourself and others and act in ways that inhibit learning and that
reduce the requirement to overprotect.

Another difficulty with this advice is that it is inconsistent
with other advice given by Sayles. For example, Sayles reports
strategies that purchasing agents use in order to reduce the conflicts
and mistrust described above (234–246). These strategies are, in effect, anti-overprotective and pro-learning. What are the consequences of advising managers to behave in opposite ways when they
are dealing with difficult issues? How credible will the learning-
oriented actions be if the same individuals use actions that bypass
the cover-up?

Additional Causal Factors for Defensive Routines

Hackman (1989, pp. 47–52) supplies an example that illustrates
more of the factors that surround defensive routines and that researchers should investigate. When the task of a corporate restructuring team changed from being conceptual and integrative to
assessing personalities and making highly politicized decisions,
counterproductive processes began to appear. As team members began to discuss potentially embarrassing and threatening issues—
such as assigning functional responsibilities, determining who
would work with whom, and asking whether the role of president
should be filled—the performance of the group deteriorated. The
top executive, who initially had given the team much autonomy,
reversed his actions and intervened more frequently and, at times,
counterproductively. For the first time, alliances were formed and
jockeying for position occurred behind the scenes. Members perceived and resented that others seemed to be positioning themselves
to become the next president.

In addition, members developed secrets that influenced their
behavior in team meetings and undermined the process of the
group. Meetings deteriorated in quality. Members often were absent

or late, and nothing was accomplished even when everyone was present. The group produced a report (through individual or dyadic efforts) that was well received, but once it was submitted, group members stopped working together. As the senior executive put it, the implementation of the report fell flat on its face.

It is possible to infer from these events that, first, the changes in performance conditions required tasks that were not only difficult but could lead to embarrassing or threatening interactions among the members and between members and outsiders. Second, members chose to deal with these features by bypassing them and covering up the bypass. For example, members reported to the researchers that they had feelings of resentment and that they knew about the existence of "secrets" around the issues. But they did not discuss these feelings of resentment or the existence of the secrets with the other members during their meetings.

Third, members knew that they and others were bypassing and covering up and that they were making these issues undiscussable during the meetings. They also knew that they acted as if nothing like this was going on, and they described these factors to the researchers. Fourth, the researchers reported that processes that were counterproductive, such as fragmentation and avoidance, and that were not discussable or correctable became self-fueling.

Finally, if participants in a group or organization know privately that they have acted in ways that reinforce fragmentation and avoidance, while they behave as if they did not know, and if they believe others are doing the same, then it seem predictable that they will feel a lack of confidence in the group's performance. Coming late to meetings or missing meetings, as members of this team did, is one natural consequence. These actions are empirical examples of distancing.

An additional cause of such distancing activities might have been the team members' fear that if they attended the meetings they might become so frustrated that they would make public the negative feelings and thoughts they had been keeping private. In groups with the processes just described, revealing these feelings would be seen as counterproductive. Hence, out of a sense of caring, of being realistic, and of getting on with work life, they adapt by withdrawal.

A Model of Self-Fueling Processes

It is possible to develop a model of defensive routines at the group and organizational levels to explain the counterproductive group processes and performance consequences described by Hackman (1989) and his fellow scholars for the corporate restructuring team we have been discussing (Figure 1.1)

The model begins with the existence of features in the group's "life space" that group members considered potentially or actually embarrassing or threatening. Examples of these features are dissatisfaction with group performance, attribution of politics, attribution that the causes of low performance were not discussable, and recognition of norms against dealing openly with conflicts or views.

Whenever these or other embarrassments or threats were perceived or experienced, the members' predisposition was to bypass

Figure 1.1. Self-Fueling, Uncorrected Group Processes.

Features that are embarrassing or threatening:	Bypass and cover-up	Actions that excuse and maintain bypass and cover-up:	Consequences of actions:
Dissatisfaction with group performance		Blame others—internal or external	Arrive late, leave early
			Miss meetings
Attribution of "politics"		Privately express dissatisfaction about group performance	Remain active while experiencing burnout—discuss only "boring" items
Attribution that causes of low performance are not discussable		Privately hold doubts about group's ability to change	
			Effectively disband group
Recognition of norms against dealing with conflicts or views openly		Experience helplessness	
		Distance oneself from one's own causal responsibilities	

the problems associated with these feelings. The bypass was then covered up; otherwise, it could have become public and the reasons for it made discussable. These consequences would violate the group norms that sanctioned the bypass in the first place.

Bypassing and covering up had two consequences. First, feedback to the original features maintained, protected, and reinforced those features. Second, actions were taken that made it possible for the participants to explain away bypassing and covering up. The actions protected the members and inhibited learning that could lead to self-corrective actions. They included blaming others—who might have been external or internal—while avoiding a public test of the validity of the blame, expressing private dissatisfaction with the way the group dealt with difficult issues by bypassing them, expressing private doubt about the group's capacity for change, experiencing helplessness about taking initiatives to change the group, and distancing oneself from one's own causal responsibility for any counterproductive consequences.

These protective actions that inhibited learning also fed back to reinforce the bypass, the cover-up, and the initial embarrassments or threats. In addition, they led to overt but "acceptable" signs of withdrawal such as coming late to meetings or leaving them early, not attending meetings because of conflicts, remaining active but experiencing burnout about group membership and therefore concentrating on "boring" issues, and disbanding the group as soon as it was organizationally permissible, while acting as if the group was still relevant (groups never die; they just fade away).

From my perspective, these self-fueling, counterproductive processes exist in all groups. (I address the reason for this in Chapter Two.) They lie dormant until embarrassment or threat activates them. Thus, risks can be transformed into opportunities only if the risks or the opportunities are not associated with embarrassment or threat. If they are, then these dysfunctional consequences will be activated. To put this in the language of the authors who performed the research discussed here, it appears that many of the groups studied had the same risk (of activating the defensive processes) and all had the same opportunities (to learn how to minimize their existence).

This model suggests that some of the causal explanations

described in Hackman's book require modification. For example, the researchers suggest that the changes in performance conditions were the primary causes of the group's ineffectiveness and that the counterproductive processes were second-order consequences (p. 52). The model indicates that the changes in performance conditions by themselves could not have been the causes; it was the way the group dealt with the embarrassment and threat embedded in the changed conditions that was the driving force behind what was observed.

This explanation emphasizes the causal responsibility group members have for dealing with any exogenous factors that suddenly impact group activities. For example, if performance conditions change, it is the responsibility of the members to make this change a central part of their agenda. The result could be that they decide they are not capable of dealing with the change. They could then identify the gaps in their competence. On the other hand, they could decide they are fully or partially capable of dealing with the change if certain other changes are implemented internally and externally. If I read the cases correctly, the latter opportunity was not explored when the performance conditions changed.

Ignoring Inner Contradictions

Inner contradictions occur when counterproductive consequences are produced by causes that also, in the eyes of the researcher, produce productive consequences. A good example of being blind to inner contradictions is found in my early writing. In one line of inquiry, I suggested that the way organizational controls and rewards were designed and implemented led to placing adult employees in contexts more appropriate to children. Adult employees who disliked such contexts adapted by actions such as being absent, changing jobs, supporting trade unions, becoming market-oriented, and psychologically withdrawing. Those who liked the conditions reported high job satisfaction yet were observed to be distant from feeling internal commitment to the organization (Argyris, 1957, 1964).

It took me a long time to see that the "inhumane" characteristics of organizations were probably created by humans paying strict attention to such human characteristics as finite information-processing skills, specific cognitive requirements for internalizing skills, and defensive actions learned through acculturation. Thus, organizations may have inhumane features because they are paying attention to what it means to be human.

Once I unfroze from the assumption that undesirable results could not flow from actions that seemed so clearly beneficial, it was possible to discover additional inner contradictions. For example, when organizational processes are rationalized, the rational knowledge used to improve performance may also differentiate between local and distant knowledge and managers who must use both kinds of knowledge can experience tension and frustration. Furthermore, given the ways most individuals have learned to deal with potential embarrassment and threat and given the organizational defenses that protect counterproductive consequences, escalating self-sealing processes will be created when organizations are burdened with these inner contradictions (Argyris & Schön, 1978).

The reason I finally had to deal with inner contradictions was not the descriptive research I was conducting or my concern for normative models. The reason was that, in trying to intervene in organizations to make them more humane *and* effective and to enhance their capacity for organizational learning, I came face to face with many of the tough questions that plague managers everyday about integrating the individual and the organization. I needed to close the gap between knowledge and action and to identify and avoid counterproductive second-order consequences.

Researchers Producing Actionable Knowledge

A few other scholars who study organizations are producing theory and empirical research intended to be actionable in organizational settings (see Alderfer, 1977; Alderfer et al., 1988; Alderfer & Brown, 1975; Bandura, 1989; Wood & Bandura, 1989; Blake & Mouton, 1961; de Charms, 1973; Golembiewski & Corrigan, 1970; Golembiewski, Hilles, & Daly, 1987; Hirschhorn & Young, 1991; Hirschhorn, 1991; Jaques, 1951, 1976; Likert, 1961; Luthans & Krectner, 1975; Luthans, Paul, & Baker, 1981; Luthans & Martinko, 1987; Manz & Sims, 1986, 1989; Torbert, 1976, 1983; Vroom & Yetton, 1973; Vroom & Jago, 1988). Mangham (1987) and Jones (1987) deal with the research and practice issues related to actionability in a manner that, although quite different, is compatible with the perspective described in this book. (For an example in another domain of research that leads to actionable knowledge and testing basic theory through the medium of intervention to change the status quo, see Kelman and Hamilton, 1989.)

There are several interesting patterns in this group's work. It has the explicit objective of helping users become more effective, and all of the writers conduct intervention-oriented efforts at the individual, intergroup, and organizational levels. The level at which each effort is primarily focused is determined by the theory that informs the effort.

These scholars focus on helping individuals (often acting as agents for organizations) become more aware of alternative ways of behaving or organizing and of the likely consequences of each alternative. The dominant theme is helping individuals become aware of their habituated behaviors in order to change them.

The assumption is that if new behaviors are learned, if the individuals wish to implement them, and if the individuals are permitted to do so by the context, then they will do so. Sometimes this assumption is realistic. For example, advice to be early or on time for the sale, to present positive features first, to hold group meetings, or to solve the problem or make the decision yourself describes behavior most individuals know how to implement without major changes or additions to their skills repertoire. However, advice to be supportive, to show concern, to exhibit trust and integrity while sharing ideas, to engage in a dialogue, or to develop a consensus is more difficult for most individuals to carry out with their ordinary levels of knowledge and skills. I explore this in more detail in the next chapter.

A review of the research on organizational behavior indicates that there is a wide recognition of organizational defensive routines and their consequences. There is also a gap between knowledge and action in this literature. Moreover, well-intended advice can have unintended negative consequences. Most of the scholars appear largely unaware of these unintended consequences.

2

Defensive Routines
That
Limit Learning

The first step to reduce organizational defensive routines is to explain how they develop in the first place. After all, they are not part of formal management theory or practice, nor are they taught in university courses or executive programs. Yet they are omnipresent. Why?

An even more perplexing question is illustrated by the organization studied in this book. We have a group of seven owner-directors who left other organizations because of the defensive organizational routines and who wanted to create a consulting organization that had minimal defensive routines but who found themselves creating an organization that had the very features they deplored. How do we explain the creation of defensive routines in a *new* organization by the very people who deplored them?

A Learning Framework

The framework I will use to answer these questions encompasses learning at the individual, group, intergroup, and organizational levels. Learning occurs whenever errors are detected and corrected. An error is any mismatch between intentions and actual consequences, such as the mismatch the directors detected between their

49

intention (an organization with few defenses) and the actuality (an organization with many defenses that seemed to be self-reinforcing and spreading).

In my view, discovery of a mismatch is only a first step in learning. Additional steps occur when the error is corrected in such a way that the correction perseveres. Furthermore, there are at least two ways to correct errors (Figure 2.1). One is to change the behavior (for example, reduce back-biting and bad-mouthing among individuals). This kind of correction requires only single-loop learning. The second way to correct errors is to change the underlying program, or master program, that leads individuals to bad-mouth others even when they say they do not intend to do so. This is double-loop learning (Argyris & Schön, 1974). If actions are changed without changing the master programs individuals use to produce the actions, then the correction will either fail immediately or will not persevere.

Theories of Action

Master programs can also be viewed as theories of action that inform actors of the strategies they should use to achieve their intended consequences. Theories of action are governed by a set of values that provide the framework for the action strategies chosen. Thus, human beings are designing beings. They create, store, and retrieve designs that advise them how to act if they are to achieve their intentions and act consistently with their governing values.

Figure 2.1. Single-Loop and Double-Loop Learning.

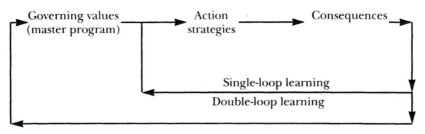

These designs, or theories of action, are the key to understanding human action.

Early in our research, my colleagues and I learned that there were two types of theories of action. One was the theory that individuals espoused and that comprised their beliefs, attitudes, and values. The second was their *theory-in-use*—the theory that they actually employed. We did not expect that individuals would customarily design and implement a theory-in-use that was significantly different from their espoused theory, nor did we expect them to be unaware of the inconsistency when the theories they espoused and used were different. Therefore, it was a major surprise—given our view of human beings as designing organisms—to find out that there are often fundamental, systematic mismatches between individuals' espoused and in-use designs. It was also a bit baffling to find that individuals develop designs to keep them unaware of the mismatch. And they do all this when the issues are embarrassing or threatening, the precise time when effective learning is crucial (Argyris & Schön, 1974; Argyris, 1982).

The second major surprise was that, although espoused theories varied widely, there was almost no variance in theories-in-use. We found the same theory-in-use, for example, in North America, Europe, South America, Africa, and the Far East. We also found it to be the same whether individuals were young (twelve years old) or old; poor or wealthy, well or poorly educated, male or female, and of any skin color.

I should like to be clear about the claim I am making. The behavior of individuals varied widely, but the theory they used to design and implement the behavior did not vary. For example, the actual behavior called "face saving" varies widely. But the proposition or the rule that is followed to produce face saving remains the same: when encountering embarrassment or threat, bypass it and cover up the bypass.

One important implication of these findings is that if theories-in-use are few in number throughout the industrialized world, then understanding and facilitating learning should be more doable than many have supposed.

A second important implication is related to producing actionable knowledge. In the introduction, actionable knowledge was defined as information that actors could use, for example, to craft conversations that communicate the meanings they intend. Actionable knowledge has to specify how to produce meanings but leave actors free to select the specific words. Thus, the theory-in-use defined for face saving is an example of actionable knowledge. It defines the action strategies (bypass and cover-up), leaving it up to the actor to craft the actual words to be used.

Model I Theory-in-Use

Model I theory-in-use is the design we found throughout the world. It has four governing values:

1. Achieve your intended purpose.
2. Maximize winning and minimize losing.
3. Suppress negative feelings.
4. Behave according to what you consider rational.

The most prevalent action strategies that arise from Model I are the following:

1. Advocate your position.
2. Evaluate the thoughts and actions of others (and your own thoughts and actions).
3. Attribute causes for whatever you are trying to understand.

These actions must be performed in such a way that you satisfice your governing values—that is, you achieve at least your minimum acceptable level of being in control, winning, or bringing about any other result. In other words, Model I tells individuals to craft their positions, evaluations, and attributions in ways that inhibit inquiries into them and tests of them with others' logic. The consequences of these Model I strategies are likely to be defensiveness, misunderstanding, and self-fulfilling and self-sealing processes (Argyris, 1982, 1985b).

Organizational Limited-Learning Systems

Organizations come alive through the thoughts and actions of individuals acting as organizational agents and creating the organizational behavioral world in which work gets done. If it is true that most individuals use Model I, then the consequence of this use will be the creation of organizational behavioral worlds that are consistent with and protect the use of Model I. I call these worlds, or organizational limited-learning systems, Model OI. This claim assumes that individuals are unlikely to act in ways for which they have no theory-in-use. If it can be shown that individuals can design and implement actions that are beyond and different from their respective theories-in-use, then this claim would be disconfirmed.

The directors in the organization that became the case study for this book espoused and sought an organization that rewarded double-loop learning and changes in governing values, because they believed this learning was necessary to remain at the cutting edge of new knowledge and practice. However, as we shall see, their theories-in-use were consistent with Model I. Therefore, it was not surprising that they were unable to create organizational behavioral worlds that encouraged double-loop learning. Instead, their Model I theories led them to create Model OI behavioral worlds that rewarded limited learning. These limited-learning systems are types of organizational defensive routines.

As we have seen, an organizational defensive routine is any action, policy, or practice that prevents organizational participants from experiencing embarrassment or threat and, at the same time, prevents them from discovering the causes of the embarrassment or threat. Organizational defensive routines, like Model I theories-in-use, inhibit double-loop learning and overprotect the individuals and the organization.

We are now ready to answer the question with which we began the chapter. Organizational defensive routines are caused by a circular, self-reinforcing process in which individuals' Model I theories-in-use produce individual strategies of bypass and cover-up, which result in organizational bypass and cover-up, which reinforce the individuals' theories-in-use. The explanation of organizational defensive routines is therefore individual *and* organizational. This means that it should not be possible to change organizational routines without changing individual routines, and vice versa. Any attempts at doing so should lead to failure or, at best, temporary success.

If this self-reinforcing process is valid, then researcher-interveners face at least two challenges when trying to help both individuals and their organizations become double-loop learners. The first challenge is that individuals' senses of competence, self-confidence, and self-esteem are highly dependent upon their Model I theories-in-use and organizational defensive routines. This dependence practically guarantees that when individuals are acting to produce double-loop learning, the consequences will be skillfully counterproductive because the Model I theories-in-use will not allow Model I governing values to be changed. In short, human beings are skillfully incompetent (Argyris, 1986). This message is not likely to be met with joy. Indeed, it is likely to create additional conditions of embarrassment and threat. Thus, one of the first messages required for reeducation will likely trigger the very organizational defensive routines the intervener is asking participants to change. The researcher-intervener must not ignore this dilemma but must see it as an opportunity for learning based on here-and-now data. So far, most of the individuals with whom my colleagues and I have worked have indeed become defensive upon hearing this message, but most of them have learned from their defensiveness (Argyris, 1982).

The second challenge is that individuals' theories-in-use are so internalized that they are taken for granted. They exist tacitly because they are used skillfully. We call behavior skillful when it works, appears effortless, and is produced automatically, without much conscious attention to the process.

Moreover, people customarily define social virtues such as caring, support, and integrity as consistent with Model I. This means that they are not likely to recognize the counterproductive consequences of Model I theories-in-use. To help them recognize their skillful Model I blindness, the intervener must introduce Model II theories-in-use. Model II theories are, at the outset, espoused theories. The challenge is to help individuals transform their espoused theories into theories-in-use by learning a "new" set of skills and a "new" set of governing values. Because many individuals espouse Model II values and skills, these traits are not totally new to them. However, the empirical fact to date is that very few individuals can routinely act on their espoused values and skills; yet they are often unaware of this limitation.

Model II Theory-in-Use

The governing values of Model II are valid information, informed choice, and vigilant monitoring of the implementation of the choice in order to detect and correct error. As in the case of Model I, the three most prominent behaviors are advocate, evaluate, and attribute. However, unlike Model I behaviors, Model II behaviors are crafted into action strategies that openly illustrate how the actors reached their evaluations or attributions and how they crafted them to encourage inquiry and testing by others. As a consequence, defensive routines that are anti-learning are minimized and double-loop learning is facilitated. Embarrassment and threat are not bypassed and covered up; they are engaged (Argyris & Schön, 1974; Argyris, 1982, 1985b).

To the extent that individuals use Model II theory instead of merely espousing it, they will begin to interrupt organizational defensive routines and begin to create organizational learning processes and systems that encourage double-loop learning in ways that persist. These are called Model OII learning systems (Argyris & Schön, 1978).

Defensive and Productive Reasoning

To understand more about the ways defensive routines are maintained, we must examine the ways humans reason. The function of reasoning in everyday life is to provide a basis for opinion, belief, attitude, feeling, and action. Reasoning explains or accounts for facts. It is through the act of reasoning that individuals can go from the beliefs and actions they know to new beliefs and actions.

In my research, I have found that individuals use two types of reasoning in everyday life: defensive reasoning and productive reasoning.

When individuals design and implement their actions through defensive reasoning, the premises they develop to support their causal explanations are tacit. The inference processes by which they go from their premises to their conclusions are also tacit. And the data they use to generate their premises and conclusions are soft. Soft data are relatively directly observable data such as conversations whose meanings are difficult to understand, especially by individuals with contrary views. Hard data are relatively directly observable data whose meanings can be understood but not necessarily accepted by individuals holding contrary views. For example, hard data may be a tape recording of what people said; soft data may be a recollection of what was said.

Another characteristic of defensive reasoning is that individuals state conclusions, claim the conclusions are valid, yet try to assure that the only way to test the conclusions is to use the logic of the individuals who produced them. "Trust me, I know what I am talking about. So-and-so really meant that he disagreed when he said, 'I agree' " is an example of this characteristic.

Defensive reasoning is self-serving, anti-learning, and over-protective—that is, it has the same features that Model I theories-in-use and organizational defensive routines reward. Defensive reasoning is the way in which individuals assure that Model I theories-in-use and organizational defensive routines will be maintained and rewarded.

At the time of the intervention described in this book, I focused heavily on examining defensive reasoning. To get the directors to examine their own reasoning processes, I might ask them to illustrate, with relatively directly observable data, the basis for their inferences. I might also ask them to make their premises explicit or to describe how they would test their conclusions using logic independent of their own and data that individuals with contrary views could accept as valid. (For a detailed example of diagnosing an organizational practitioner's defensive reasoning, see Argyris, 1987.)

I tried to use productive reasoning in crafting my interventions and recommended that the directors do the same. When individuals use productive reasoning, they supply relatively directly observable data to illustrate the basis of the point being inferred, make all inferences explicit, and craft conclusions in ways that permit others to try to disconfirm them.

The Ladder of Inference

The defensive and productive reasoning processes illustrate that making inferences is a key activity in designing and implementing action. It is important to learn to make inferences explicit and to test their validity externally.

The ladder of inference is a hypothetical model of how individuals make inferences. They begin by experiencing some relatively directly observable data, such as conversation. This is rung 1 of the ladder. They make inferences about the meanings embedded in the words (rung 2). They often do this in milliseconds, regardless of whether they agree with the meanings. Then they impose their meanings on the actions they believe the other person intends (rung 3). For example, they may attribute reasons or causes for the actions. They may also evaluate the actions as effective or ineffective. Finally, the attributions or evaluations they make are consistent with their theory-in-use about effective action (rung 4).

If this model is a valid representation of the way individuals comprehend their everyday world, it should be relevant for designing and implementing research.

I used both this model and productive reasoning in designing and implementing the entire project discussed here and its various parts, from a two-day seminar to interventions lasting only a few minutes. For example, I might begin by collecting relatively directly observable data of the directors' actions. I might also collect their views of the culturally understood meanings of the data as well as the meanings they inferred on rung 2 of the model. From this, I inferred their theories-in-use.

During a microintervention, I often asked a director to illustrate the attribution that he was making. Or I asked him if he had tested it. If he had, I asked him to illustrate the test. If he had not, I asked him what the other person did that led him not to test his attribution.

As a researcher, I tested the inferences I made with them. As an intervener, I tried to help them to develop the same skills I was using, so that they could become leaders who could facilitate double-loop learning.

Concepts of Causality

Concepts of causality are central to conducting empirical research. They are also central in everyday life. Shoham (1990) states, "If causal reasoning is common in scientific thinking, it is downright dominant in everyday common sense thinking. All one needs to do is scan a popular publication [to verify that] causal terms—causing, preventing, enabling, bringing about, invoking, resulting in, instigating, affecting, putting an end to, and so on—appear throughout it" (p. 214).

My objective is to produce valid knowledge that is both actionable *and* testable in everyday life. The possibility that this objective can be achieved is greatly enhanced if the concepts of causality used by the researcher and the practitioner are at least consistent, if not similar. The greater the gap between the concept of causality used by the researcher and the one used by the practitioner, the greater the gap between knowledge and effective action.

The concepts of causality that I suggest using to minimize the gap between knowledge and action follow from the premise I described earlier: that human beings design their actions and, by virtue of that fact, concern themselves with causality and causal inference. They formulate intentions and strive to achieve whatever consequences they intend. Hence, their everyday practice depends on what I call *design causality*, which is the causality implicit in the causal connections between intentions and actions in everyday life (Simon, 1969). This kind of causality has been described by Olafson (1967) as "cause by reason" and by Von Hayek (1967) as "sufficient reason." It is the real reason for an action—the reasoning that actually leads to it, as distinct from the reasoning by which it may be justified (Schick, 1991).

What Von Hayek (1967) calls "efficient cause" is also an aspect of design causality. An efficient cause is the causal connection between an action and its consequences, intended or unintended, and between the first-order consequences of an action and any further consequences.

A second concept of causality arises from my premise that individuals also design the social systems in which they work. The designs individuals begin with for all their actions are their theories-in-use. The designs of social systems flow from the aggregated consequences (for instance, limited-learning systems) produced by the participants' theories-in-use.

All these designs form a larger single pattern of causality; hence, I call this second concept *pattern causality*. I claim that individuals are causally responsible for creating systemic patterns that inhibit double-loop learning and any change in governing values. Once a pattern is in place, it feeds back to cause individuals to maintain and reinforce it. We have a circular process of causation from individual to system and back to the individual. This is the process that appeared in the organization studied here.

Lieberson (1991) states that social scientists, broadly speaking, use two types of causality: deterministic causality (if A, then B) and probabilistic causality (if A, then B with such and such probability). As I will illustrate through my research, pattern causality can be either deterministic or probabilistic. On the one hand, we can predict that actors who use Model I theories-in-use will inhibit double-loop learning. We will see that this prediction of deterministic causality held true in the case study, even though the directors did not wish to inhibit double-loop learning; it held after they had learned how Model I works; and it held after they said they would change their model and their behavior (after all, they were in control of their theory-in-use and they owned the organization).

On the other hand, probabilistic causality comes into play when we predict the specific action strategies people will use or when we are predicting what will happen when an individual responds to an initiating actor's strategies. Here, we can only predict a degree of likelihood.

Much research is needed to be able to specify ahead of time all the conditions under which each type of causality will be relevant. The point that seems certain is that individuals and the behavioral worlds they create are subject to both deterministic and probabilistic causality.

The research I and my colleagues have been carrying out is designed to reduce anti-learning actions and increase pro-learning actions. Therefore, we look for ways to interrupt both deterministic and probabilistic circular causal patterns. One way is to alter the systemic pattern. This will work if the individuals have the skills to implement the new requirements made of them by the new pattern.

The claim of our theory—and the empirical data collected so far support this claim—is that individuals may espouse Model II action strategies but do not have the skills to produce them. They are unable to implement Model II theories-in-use. In the organization reported on here, reeducation processes and experiments that followed the processes were needed to transform Model II from an espoused theory to a theory-in-use. That transformation, in turn, began to transform the organizational defensive routines.

The implication of our research and our studies of the literature on causality is that human designs at the individual and system level cause the behavior upon which we as researchers and interveners focus. This has important further implications for the conduct of research to produce actionable knowledge to change the status quo.

The implications (which are discussed in detail in the Appendix) raise questions about the limitations of the prevailing scientific concept of causality. They suggest that pattern causality may be more appropriate to certain research than variance causality. (Mohr's concept of process analysis, 1982, may be akin to pattern causality, although he may not make his concept as fundamental as I make mine.)

This does not mean that the prevailing scientific concepts of causality are to be completely thrown out. For example, testing the propositions of research by confirming and disconfirming is central to my approach. This means I am an adherent of some features of positivism. However, I also believe that individuals, in order to act effectively, will use a "new" concept of causality as long as it contains features consistent with humanistic, interpretive, and ethnographic approaches. It may well be that, by using a concept of causality that positivists would see as sloppy and insufficiently empirical for research, individuals can become rigorous in their predictions and actions in everyday life.

Unfortunately, positivistic perspectives and interpretive perspectives are polarized in the literature in ways that, I believe, are unnecessary and counterproductive. In the Appendix, I try to show that the moment one takes seriously intervention to produce actionable knowledge, the distinctions between objective and subjective research fade away, as do the assertions that humanistic researchers are somehow closer to and more understanding of their subjects than "objective" researchers are.

The Role of Feelings

Although positivists may, at first, think our approach "sloppy," others may think it too rational. They may believe that an emphasis on such concepts as theories-in-use, action strategies, and reasoning will lead to a perspective that downplays the importance of feelings in human behavior. Is the perspective too cerebral? There are several reasons why this is not the case.

The premise of my perspective is that productive reasoning is required to design and implement actions that are effective and simultaneously encourage double-loop learning. This premise makes sense to most research participants. However, when I and my fellow researchers help them see that their reasoning processes are largely defensive, that they are inhibiting double-loop learning while believing otherwise, and that they are blind to the discrepancy, the participants often feel bewildered, embarrassed, or threatened.

Because our approach activates feelings, progress in using it requires that the participants express those feelings and that we respect them. By respecting feelings, I mean that we empathize with them and genuinely understand why they were generated. Our respect does not mean we agree that the participants' feelings are valid in the sense that they flow from an accurate view of reality. However, we recognize that genuine feelings often arise from highly subjective views of events. We strive not to collude with these feelings, nor should the participants, if we are to help them to learn.

Therefore, our next step is to help the participants explore the reasons for their feelings. As they do so, they often see that the feelings were caused by defensive reasoning on their part, as well as on the part of others. Through dialogue, they begin to test the validity of their views of the reasons for, or causes of, their feelings. For example, if they think another person is purposefully distorting, manipulating, or rejecting their views, they can discover whether or not others can confirm or disconfirm these attributions. If they feel that they are acting in caring, sensitive, and supportive ways, do others agree? This kind of inquiry can lead to experimentation with new designs and new actions, which in turn can lead to further new designs and actions. The inquiry can also lead to new errors, which provide a new basis for further learning.

Most individuals with whom we have worked are able to use their feelings to get a window into their competence for double-loop learning. There are a few who have difficulty. They deal with this difficulty by blaming others or the environment and hence absolve themselves from learning. I did not encounter such individuals in the case presented here. However, I have in other research, and I have suggested a model for dealing with such defensiveness (Argyris, 1982, p. 163).

Ironically, my most frequent experiences with this defensive posture have been with organizational development professionals. They may even develop theories of intervention that legitimize blaming others for the professionals' own defensive reasoning and actions. The typical strategy seems to be to label an inquiry into their reasoning processes as "too cognitive" or "too rational." For example, in a recent study, I examined tape recordings of three different encounters with senior professionals and found some curious results (Argyris, 1990b). First, they were unable to define what is too rational, although they expected others to accept the validity of their views. They also crafted their claims of excessive rationality so that any test of the claims' validity would require accepting the professionals' logic.

Second, they asserted that asking individuals to examine their own reasoning could be too threatening. They advised providing safety. As one professional said, "You've got to give the person some space." I agree that having some space or safety is important. I also believe it is important to see what the individual does with that safety. In the cases of which I speak, the professionals used the space to distance themselves from examining their reasoning processes.

For example, a world-class professional and I did some role-playing. I acted as the chief executive officer (CEO) and he as the consultant. I remember feeling that he was acting caringly toward me and soliciting my feelings and views. When we stopped to examine the role-play, he told me and the others in the group that the "CEO" was clearly being defensive and manipulative. I said, in effect, that his comments surprised me because I had no indication that he was judging me that way during the role-play. I then asked him what I had said or done that led him to keep his judgments secret. He became very upset because he felt the word *secret* was judgmental and punishing. I responded that I was unaware that it would have such an impact on him. I then asked how I could have crafted my inquiry in such a way that I would not have upset him and yet could still have learned from him. He responded, in effect, "There you go, getting too rational. I cannot think well when I am emotionally upset." He then asked for space, and we gave it to him. He did not return to help me learn how I should have crafted my conversation. This happened two other times (over a period of several months).

In my view, this distancing closes off learning. Moreover, it does it in such a way that it is not possible for me to test the validity of my claim (that he closed off learning) nor for him to test his claim (that he cannot learn when he is upset). As a professional, I strive to encourage individuals to express their feelings and take responsibility for them, or own them, in ways that facilitate learning for all in the group.

Design of the Research-Intervention Activities

There are a few simple goals that follow from the theoretical framework described in this chapter and that I used to design the research and the intervention activities in the case study.

- Discover the degree to which the directors' theories-in-use are consistent with Model I.
- Discover the degree to which the directors use defensive reasoning whenever they deal with embarrassing or threatening issues.
- Discover the designs (rules) the directors have in their heads that keep them unaware of the discrepancies among their espoused values, their actions, and their theories-in-use.
- Discover the degree to which the directors discourage valid re-

flection on their actions while they are acting. To put this
another way: discover how the directors create designs for action
that they do not follow but that they believe they do follow,
while they are also being systematically unaware of this discrepancy and are behaving in ways that prevent them from discovering the discrepancy and the causes of their unawareness.

• Discover the defensive routines that exist in the organization
and that inhibit double-loop learning. Develop maps of these
organizational defensive routines, specifying the actions that
lead to limited-learning consequences and cause them to persist
even though the directors wish to be free of them.

In order to reach these goals, I determined that reeducation
and change programs should

• Produce relatively directly observable data about the directors'
reasoning and actions. The directors must accept responsibility
for creating these data, and these data must be in a form from
which the directors' theories-in-use can be inferred (for example,
a recorded conversation).

• Encourage the directors to examine inconsistencies and gaps in
the reasoning that underlies their actions.

• Surface and make explicit the rules that "must" be in their heads
if they maintain there is a connection between their designs for
action and the actions themselves.

• View any resistance, bewilderment, or frustration that results as
further directly observable data that can be used to test the validity of what is being learned.

• Produce opportunities to practice Model II ways of crafting actions that will reduce counterproductive consequences.

Starting Points for Intervention

In principle, the kind of research of which I speak can begin with
identifying either the theories-in-use or the organizational defensive
routines. It does not matter which because one will necessarily lead
you to the other. I usually make the choice on the basis of which
of the two is most likely to generate the participants' internal com-

mitment to the research and to the eventual intervention. For example, in one study, the participants wanted to focus on interpersonal skills; therefore, I began with cases that could be used to infer their theories-in-use.

In the study discussed in this book, the directors' attention at the outset was focused on organizational learning. I therefore began by diagnosing and mapping the organizational defensive patterns that inhibited learning, which, in turn, resulted in the organizational politics they disliked. When the map was fed back to them, they reacted positively in the sense that they agreed that the map captured the complexity they faced. But they asked how they had created such a map when they did not wish to do so. That led to using the case approach to diagnose their theories-in-use.

One word of caution. Our research began with what will appear to the reader to be primarily a diagnostic phase to discover organizational defensive patterns and the directors' theories-in-use. In actuality the diagnostic phase included intervention activities. I used Model II values and action strategies when I was diagnosing, as well as when I was helping the directors to change. During the change activities, I continually used diagnostic research procedures to test the validity and actionability of what was being learned.

One of my students once said that, in order to conduct research and intervention intended to produce double-loop learning at all levels of an organization, the researcher should not only have traditional research competencies; he or she also has to be competent in Model II theory-in-use. I agree. My colleagues and I have written several books on how to learn Model II as a theory-in-use (Argyris, 1982, 1985b; Argyris, Putnam, & Smith, 1985; Schön, 1983, 1987). Although this study will illustrate the use of Model II theory-in-use in conducting research and intervening, I must leave the learning of these skills largely to the books just cited, and to the books that I hope will follow this one.

In summary, there are two types of theories of action: espoused theories, those that people report or describe; and theories-in-use, those that people actually use to design and implement their actions. Most people have the same theory-in-use. We have labeled it Model I. In any organization (or context), the use of Model I leads to the creation of limited-learning systems, such as organizational defensive routines. Once the organizational defensive routines are in place, they reinforce and strengthen the use of Model I theories.

A different theory-in-use, which we have labeled Model II, can help organizations overcome the limited-learning systems, especially the defensive routines. The research and intervention goals are to demonstrate pattern causality and to change the causes and the pattern through the use of Model II. Underlying this strategy of intervention is the concept of design causality. The premise is that patterns are created by the designs human beings have in their heads and by the designs embedded in the patterns once they have been put in place.

Part Two

DIAGNOSING
AND INTERVENING
IN THE ORGANIZATION

The purpose of parts Two and Three is to illustrate how the concepts introduced in chapters One and Two can be used to design and implement research and intervention activities. The emphasis is on the actual activities carried out in a consulting organization during a five-year period in order to help it become a better learning organization.

I focus heavily on describing conversations, which we had tape-recorded. There are several reasons for this. First, conversation is central to understanding reality and operating effectively within it. We perceive reality according to how it is prescribed in our language (Pfeffer, 1992). Eccles and Nohria (1992) write that without the right words, used in the right way, "it is unlikely that the right actions will occur. Words *do* matter . . . they matter very much" (pp. 300–301). According to my research, the effectiveness of an individual's action is understood and determined by the individual's theory-in-use. The theory-in-use is inferred from actual behavior, and conversation is the most frequent behavior. Conversation represents data at the first rung on the ladder of inference.

Second, although I make claims only of illustrating my views, these relatively directly observable data do provide readers with the information to make up their own minds about the validity of my inferences and analysis. Readers may also use the conversations as a basis for trying out their own theories and for developing competing explanations.

Third, at the times when I focus on my intervention strategies, I can provide the reader with a window into my mind by commenting on the conversations and also provide relatively observable data showing how I acted and how others responded.

Therefore, parts Two and Three have a multilevel, nested set of purposes. They describe how I construed reality, how I acted as a researcher-intervener, and how the clients reacted and responded. Finally, they provide conversation and talk that specifies what actually was said and done, thereby informing readers how they might act if they were to follow this approach.

From time to time, I also pause to indicate how my inferences and conclusions can be empirically tested. I do not describe how to carry out these tests because the research methods required are elementary and straightforward, and easily available in textbooks on research methods.

Framing the Problem

The seven directors of the organization in this case study framed the problem in various ways. They said they wanted to create an organization capable of persistent double-loop learning within itself and between itself and its clients. They also wanted to know how to reduce existing politics that they thought inhibited their objective of building a genuine learning organization. And they wanted to discover how to build an organization where double-loop learning not only occurred persistently, but did so under conditions of stress, embarrassment, or threat.

During my first interviews, I tried to determine the extent to which the directors believed that counterproductive activities were occurring and their view of the organizational consequences of these activities. I also sought their causal explanations. As we shall see, most of their explanations were highly inferential (third rung on the ladder of inference) and were not testable because they were not rigorously connected to relatively directly observable data. For example, the directors' explanations included the attributions that "people are not candid," "group decision making at the top is poor," and "coalitions exist that create rivalries."

As a researcher-intervener, I had two major tasks. One was to provide a causal explanation that led to a coherent, holistic, testable explanation of their many multilevel, disconnected explanations. This holistic explanation also had to be usable for designing and executing the intervention program. In turn, the intervention program and its consequences could provide opportunities for further tests of the theory.

The second task was to develop generalizations about how to interrupt and reduce organizational defensive routines and skilled incompetence and then to help the directors (and later consultants at all levels of the organization) develop the skills necessary to spread the learning throughout the organization in such a way that it not only persevered but was enlarged and deepened.

In terms of the theoretical framework described in Part One, I had to obtain the directors' respective causal explanations of the problems through the interviews I just described. These explanations represented primarily the directors' espoused theories (Chapter Three).

Next, I had to translate the directors' espoused theories and observations into individual and organizational theories-in-use. In Chapter Four, I illustrate the organizational theory-in-use for the issue of organizational politics, and I present a map of the organizational defensive pattern on this issue, a pattern that I hypothesized was a partial explanation of activities that were counterproductive for learning.

Then I had to feed back the map to the directors (Chapter Five). One purpose of the feedback was to assess the degree to which the directors confirmed and disconfirmed features of the map or, indeed, the entire map. I placed as heavy an emphasis as I could on encouraging attempts to disconfirm, for two reasons. As a researcher, I wanted to encourage the toughest possible tests of my ideas. As an intervener, I knew that the design and implementation of the change program would rest heavily on the explanatory map. If it was faulty, I wanted to know early so that I could correct it. Also, I did not want the directors to withhold their doubts only to raise them after the change activities began. Seeking a tough confrontation over validity satisfied both research and intervention requirements.

The presentation and discussion of the map also had some additional consequences for the directors. First, it provided the directors with a systemic explanation of the causes and persistence of organizational politics. The directors were able to see how their individual actions, interpersonal relationships, and group dynamics combined to create an organizational defensive pattern that was anti-learning and overprotective. The map also helped them see that they acted to make the defensive pattern persist. Second, the systemic, holistic picture reduced the likelihood of simplistic diagnoses and recommendations. For example, by focusing on their individual and collective responsibility for creating the organizational defensive pattern, the map raised questions about the validity of blaming the CEO, or the CEO blaming the directors, or all of them blaming external factors.

Third, the very presentation of a map about undiscussables and cover-ups blew the cover-up and violated the norm of undiscussability. The feedback process became an important unfreezing experience. Since it had been the researcher who violated the norms, it was easier for the directors to consent to the discussion, because they could hold him responsible for any negative consequences. It also made the intervener more vulnerable, but I saw the vulnerability as an opportunity to create further learning for myself and the directors.

During the feedback session, the directors began to realize that the dire predictions they had made about each other were not being confirmed. Individuals did not "go ballistic" (a favorite phrase of some directors), nor did they react like a blast furnace (another frequently used metaphor). The directors also learned that their cover-ups were not as successful as they had thought. Everyone knew most of what the others were covering up, but, of course, each of them covered up that he knew. The session taught the directors that they were all responsible. The political games they were condemning were caused by them.

In the next step, I had to connect the organizational defensive routines to skilled incompetence (Chapter Six). This meant assessing the directors' theories-in-use to see the extent to which they were consistent with models I and II (or neither). A seminar was designed around cases prepared by the directors. The format they used to write the cases was the one described in Chapter Two. As a researcher, I predicted that all the cases would be consistent with Model I. Individuals using Model II would not produce the organizational defensive routines I had diagnosed initially. This prediction tested the theory of action I was using.

The seminar helped the directors see how their individual theories-in-use were getting them in trouble with each other. They could see how they had produced the individual, interpersonal, and group consequences they condemned, and this made each one's personal causal responsibilities more explicit.

The seminar also helped individual directors examine their defensive reasoning and see how it led them to produce actions that were counterproductive and also led them to reinforce their unawareness of their counterproductive impacts.

Finally, the seminar began the learning process by which each director could examine the rules he used to inform his actions. To put this another way, the directors began to discover their espoused rules, which were inherent in their espoused designs for action. They also discovered the rules they used not to follow their espoused rules, the designs they used to be systematically unaware of not following their espoused rules, and the organizational defensive routines they created to support this pattern of causality, thereby assuring its persistence.

3

Step One:
Interview and Observe
the Players

My relationship with the consulting firm began with my meeting the CEO and another owner-director for lunch in order to get acquainted. They told me what they saw as the problem and what remedies they thought were important. I asked them about the causal reasoning behind their diagnosis and prognosis and followed up by describing the options that seemed relevant.

At the end of the luncheon, the two directors expressed a desire to move ahead, and I recommended a meeting with all the directors so that they could have the same opportunities for exploration that the three of us had had. I also wanted to assess the commitment of all the directors and to tell them about certain conditions that were important to me. For example, the research should someday be publishable (with appropriate disguising of the firm's and others' names), I would not act as a private evaluator for anyone in the organization about anyone else and both sides would have the freedom to terminate the relationship with short notice and the obligation to explain the causal reasoning behind that termination. (A detailed description of the ideas I suggest discussing with potential collaborators appears in Argyris, 1970.)

Publication of results, I would tell the directors, is important, and without such a commitment, I could not take on any long-term relationship. As a scholar and a member of a university faculty, I had an obligation to contribute to the stock of basic knowledge, but in doing so, I did not want to harm the organization. Therefore, they would see the manuscript ahead of publication and were free to suggest revisions. If my colleagues and I did not agree with the revisions, which so far had never occurred with any other client, we would be glad to provide the directors with the space to include their views. However, they would not have the freedom to veto publication. Also, we would not recommend identifying the organization no matter how positively or negatively they might view the report.

I would also suggest that it was in their personal interest to require me to publish the results. The best quality control check they had, outside our relationship, was to know that the results would be exposed to the marketplace of academic and practitioner scrutiny. In my experience, reports that were kept secret often led to mediocre methodology and analysis.

I met with all seven of the directors for four hours. They asked many excellent questions, and at the end of the meeting, we made a joint commitment. Several days later, I sent a letter describing the major conditions upon which we had agreed.

The first step in the project was to interview each director individually. I wanted to provide the directors a second, and private, opportunity to question me and the proposed programs and to express doubts that they might not have expressed during the group meeting. Such a dialogue would also provide another validity check on the nature of the commitment (both mine and theirs) and would help each director make a more informed decision about the program.

I have found that the best strategy for this kind of intervention is always to begin with the top organizational level. Moving from Model I to Model II theories-in-use and reducing organizational defenses are potentially embarrassing and threatening activities. They lead to significant changes in the ways individuals deal with each other. It is important, therefore, that the people at the top develop the internal commitment that will support the program for change, sustain them through the reeducation experiences necessary for the changes to succeed and to persist, allow them to have patience with the organization as it learns, and permit them to allocate the necessary financial and time resources.

Readers may still wonder why I did not interview those below the directors about the directors. I tend to resist that strategy, first, because I have come to question the validity of interviews in which subordinates are asked to diagnose their superiors' performances before they themselves have gone through the process of developing a personal commitment to change and continuous improvement. I have found, for example, that subordinates may evaluate superiors more evenhandedly when they know their evaluations will become part of a joint dialogue. Second, subordinates commonly do not even realize the subtleties of the ways in which they bash their superiors until they too are examining their own performances.

But a joint exploration is not possible if the strategy is to begin at the top. There may be conditions under which one may wish to work, at the most, with two levels. I prefer to have the top realize that they are responsible for the spread of the learning *and* that the design to be used will relate to their behavior. If they have difficulty in learning Model II, then they should have the opportunity to realize the extent of their difficulties and the likely impact on the organization.

As the top executives' theories-in-use actually change, and as their skills are not lost under moderate stress, the intervention can move to the next lower levels. One of the most powerful cues that individuals at lower levels can receive about the depth of the commitment by those at the top comes from watching them struggle to act differently and then reflecting on their actions and respecting the time and energy required to produce lasting changes. It is by watching their superiors take personal and institutional risks in order to create a learning organization that subordinates come to feel free to take similar risks and to develop their own internal commitment.

Conducting the Interviews

In framing the individual interviews, I strove to act in accordance with Model II theory-in-use, because that should facilitate the production of valid knowledge. I knew that the questions I would ask would seek the directors' views, evaluations, and attributions about themselves, their fellow directors, and the organization. I came prepared to have them respond in a Model I manner. I hoped that they would respond honestly, but if they responded consistently with their Model I theories-in-use, they were not likely to illustrate their views with relatively directly observable data or to respond in ways that encouraged inquiry into, and testing of, their responses, especially any that presented inconsistencies.

Therefore, I was also prepared to ask for illustrations, to inquire into their responses and test them preliminarily, and to explore any inconsistencies. As I listened to the directors' answers to my questions, I noted to what extent they answered the questions and to what extent they seemed bewildered, embarrassed, or frustrated by my inquiries. I expected some degree of such feelings, and if they arose I would try to acknowledge them.

I would not find such defensiveness troubling. Indeed, if individuals use Model I and live in a system of organizational defensive routines, defensiveness is to be expected. I would become concerned, however, if the directors' defensiveness took the form of cutting off my attempts to get illustrations, test attributions, and explore inconsistencies, either by blaming others or by acting personally upset. These types of responses would give me some clues as to the likely barriers to change.

I began the interviews with three questions directly related to the concerns the clients had raised at the outset.

1. Would you please give me your thoughts about what kind of an institution you wish to develop? What is your vision or hope for this organization?
2. How would you characterize the effectiveness of the directors' meetings?
3. How would you characterize the relationships outside of the board meetings?

The questions, in effect, asked the directors to state their views about their governing values, make evaluations about what was going on in the organization, and state their attributions, or causal explanations, about what was going on.

I listened to the answers to learn the directors' views about the questions asked, and I also listened to the way the directors crafted their views, evaluations, and attributions. Did they illustrate their views? Did they encourage testing of their views?

As we shall see, the content of the responses and the way they were crafted provided important information about the degree to which the directors exhibited Model I behavior and about the strength of the organizational defensive routines within the directors' group and within the organization.

The same information could also be used to provide a test of the theory. For example, if the responses were crafted to be consistent with Model I, then their content should also be consistent with Model I. I should not observe responses crafted in Model II modes whose content was consistent with Model I. Nor should Model II content be crafted in Model I modes.

Let us examine some examples of the ways I sought to get illustrations, inquire beyond what was being said, test for the validity of responses, and surface any inconsistencies in order to get at organizational and individual defenses that the directors might be taking for granted.

When a Director Said	*I Could Ask*
I want to develop an institution that provides as much value added as possible to our clients and a genuine developmental environment for all of us.	Would you please recall a case that you directed and describe the value that you believe was added for the client?
	What would constitute, in your mind, inadequate or poor value added?
	What would, in your view, a genuine developmental environment look like? What would be some of its features?
	Could you give an example of a successful developmental

outcome and one that was not as successful as you would have wished?

Help us to learn about ourselves so that we can make decisions rationally. [By that I mean that] we do not activate our historical defenses.

Would you please describe an example where directors' actions were influenced by historical defenses?

As I compare successful and unsuccessful organizations in our business, the key differences are not in substantive [technical] areas. The key to success is dealing with political change.

Would you illustrate an instance where political change was key to success?
How effective were you and the case team?

Many of us left other and larger consulting firms because of nasty politics. I also realize that we cannot eliminate something by making pronouncements.

It would help me if you would give me an illustration of nasty politics in the organization from which you came.
Do you see the development of nasty politics happening in your organization? If yes, please illustrate. If no, what is preventing them from arising?

We are all concerned about adding value added. What truly bugs me is to see a technically superior set of ideas become difficult to implement.

As you recall, when did you first realize a technically superior set of ideas was going to be difficult to implement?
What did the clients say? How did you respond?

How does a new, fast-growing organization like ours maintain cohesion and energy that existed in the early days as we grow bigger and older?

Please give me an illustration or two of the cohesion and energy that you experience today.
As you survey the scene today, what do you see, if any-

thing, that could erode the cohesion and energy?

We say that we want to be honest with each other. Yet, at times, we act dishonestly. Why? Because, to be honest, I am afraid that if I spoke candidly it could demotivate and, in some cases, paralyze.

Please think of a relationship where you believe these fears are valid.

What is the other(s) doing that you would see as counterproductive?

If you had the freedom to be candid, what would you say?

What is it about what you would say that you would predict the other(s) would find demotivating or paralyzing?

(A collage of answers about directors' meetings, characterizing the directors as ranging from depressed to highly complacent.)

What do fellow directors say or do that leads you to judge them as depressed or complacent?

How aware do you think they are of this? How discussable would your fears be during the meeting?

[There is a] fair amount of hypocrisy—[the attitude is] "I want honest feedback as long as it is favorable."

When a director says something that you believe is hypocritical, how do you decide that it is so?

What does he say or do? What cues does he give?

[People explain] away failure by pointing to factors not under our control.

Please illustrate.

How aware do you think they are when they place the blame on such factors?

What would happen if you "called" them on what you believe is their projecting?

It is very difficult to be tough on your friends. And we are all

Please think of cues that you get from fellow directors that

friends.   lead you to believe you cannot
                                            be tough on them.

We bad-mouth each other in   Please give me an example
private sessions.   where a director has done that
                                            with you or you have done it
                                            with another director.
                                                    When someone else comes
                                            to you to do some bad-
                                            mouthing, how do you
                                            respond?

Too often when we meet we   Please give me an example of a
take hours to settle trivial issues   discussion around a trivial
and rarely talk about the key   issue.
issues.   How aware are the direc-
                                            tors, in your view, that the issue
                                            is trivial?
                                                    How discussable is this
                                            problem during the meetings?
                                            Can you think of a key issue
                                            that was not discussed? Any
                                            hunches as to why not?
                                                    Why did you not say that
                                            the issue was not being
                                            discussed?

There is a lot of talking about   What do you see or hear that
learning. I question how much   leads you to question the degree
genuine interest there is in   of genuine interest?
learning.

Obtaining Data and Insight

The strategy that informed my questions was related to obtaining
more directly observable data and gaining insight into the directors'
reasoning and their awareness of their personal causal responsibilities. For example, I wanted to understand "value added" as each
director conceived it. What did the directors have in mind when they

spoke of a "genuine developmental environment"? What actions would they have had to take to produce what they espoused? How clear were they about gaps in their own or others' views? How aware were they that what they considered to be concrete answers were at least at the third rung (imposing one's own meanings on observed data) on the ladder of inference?

If the directors were clear that organizational politics existed, how clear were they about the causes of the politics? What was their reasoning about the persistence of the politics, even though they espoused the view that such politics were not desirable?

What were the experiences that led them to realize that sound technical ideas were not self-implementable? How did they feel about this possibility? What was their reasoning about the gaps between the formulation of recommendations and their implementation?

When the directors admitted that they were not acting consistently with their espoused values, how did they explain this important discrepancy? Did they believe, for example, that it was caused by individual characteristics such as personality? Did they believe that group dynamics could be a cause? To what extent were the directors able to spell out the processes that led to these discrepancies?

Answers to these questions also helped me, as the intervener, get at the directors' taken-for-granted views. My asking for relatively directly observable data required the respondents to relive the events as best as they could recall. This often led them to think about something they had not said, not simply because they forgot but because they may have taken it for granted. Insights from these answers could also lead to their becoming more aware of their causal responsibilities for the episodes they described.

Identifying Inconsistencies

Inconsistencies provide insight into the validity of what respondents are saying and an opportunity to get at defenses, at any level, that may be taken for granted. For example, during these interviews, directors might correct inconsistencies by adding information that they took for granted. Or, if the directors had not recognized the inconsistencies, the researcher and the directors could explore the source of the unawareness, again learning about what was taken for granted.

Examples of inconsistencies that I raised are the following:

Earlier, you mentioned that the directors were all friends. Then, during the discussion of _____ , you said that you could not tell Jim [a pseudonym] the truth because he was a close friend. Would you please help me to understand the limits to candidness that you believe exist between you and Jim?

You described the growth of the firm with enthusiasm and confidence. When you described the one client you lost to [a competitor], you then explained the loss by [bad-mouthing the competitor]. Was there anything that you or others did that may have contributed to your firm not being selected?

On the one hand, you describe the good feelings when you add value for a client. On the other hand, you also describe how the same client relationships can be dull and boring. What makes for a client relationship that is dull? What makes for a client relationship that is exciting?

At the outset you spoke of the importance of developmental relationships. Later you described how bewildered and fed up you are increasingly feeling with the demands that your consultants make of the firm. How do you deal with the dilemma of supporting developmental relationships but, at the same time, resenting the demands they make on you?

On the one hand, you say that the firm is getting the best MBAs from the best schools that it wants. On the other hand, you also say how blind they seem to be to client needs? Do you have any ideas as to what causes

their blindness? Any idea of what led the firm to be
blind to these attributes when they hired the MBAs?

Testing Inferences

The researcher is more than a listener when he or she makes inferences about respondents' meanings. These inferences are the researcher's creations. They usually come in the form of evaluations
and attributions; therefore, they must be crafted so that their validity
can be assessed in the same way as the validity of the respondents'
attributions. In addition, a researcher can shift attention to the inferences he or she is creating. For example, during these interviews
I might say:

> When you said such and such, I inferred that what you
> were telling me was _____ . Is that correct?

> I am not clear about the meaning that you are intend-
> ing to communicate to me when you say _____ .

Listening

It is common to advise researchers to listen as carefully as they can
to what respondents say in order to report the respondents' views
accurately. Researchers being trained to become better listeners
often ask, "Listen to what?" One answer is "Listen for the information they are seeking." This answer does specify what to listen
for. However, it may lead the researcher to ignore important ideas
that the respondents are communicating but that are not related to
the researcher's tacit or explicit theory. This is an age-old problem
in research.

Earlier, I advised the researcher to listen to anything that
respondents are advocating, evaluating, or attributing and to note
how well the respondents illustrate their views, how well they encourage inquiry into their views, and how amenable their views are
to testing. These three rules provide an operational definition for
the activity of listening that should be valid under any conditions
and that can be learned by most researchers.

I realize that these guideposts are not all there is to listening. A researcher can also have a psychological set toward respondents, primarily based on feelings, that also facilitates listening. If the researcher has this psychological set, he or she is likely to be communicating—at the level of feelings as well as language—that he or she is grateful to the respondents for their time and efforts; committed to understanding their world as well as, or even better than, they do; and committed to express his or her gratitude by building from the research actions that are likely to help the respondents reach their objectives (for example, reductions in destructive politics).

Governing Values, Relationships, and Counterproductive Actions

Let us turn to what the director-owners said during the interviews about the governing values of their organization and their relationships and counterproductive actions during directors' meetings and outside of these meetings. These are the directly observable data, taken from transcriptions of tape recordings. (I have substantially shortened remarks that were already reported earlier in this chapter.) I will present my categorization of these comments at the end of the chapter.

Constructing categories is the first step in organizing the findings into patterns.

> I want to develop an institution that provides value added to our clients and a genuine developmental environment.

> Help us to learn about ourselves so that we can make decisions rationally.

> The task is to create the next generation of directors.

> As I compare successful and unsuccessful organizations in our business, the key to success is dealing with political change.

Many of us left other and larger consulting firms because of nasty politics.

Many of us are good at the technical stuff we use. What I need help on—and I think others do—is, Why is a valid [technical] argument that is genuinely compelling not implementable?

I think that it is fair to say that several of us are worried about stories and legacies that persist in organizations, often in distorted form, long after they [first appeared].

How does an organization maintain the cohesion and energy that existed in the early days?

I am afraid that if I spoke honestly, it could demotivate and, in some cases, paralyze.

We deal with barriers to implementation in ways that are typical of consulting firms but which, I believe, do not encourage genuine learning with our clients. I mean ways such as easing-in, overpowering with information, showing them where they are wrong, and finessing people out of our way. These ways are misleading and totally without merit.

As I look at our directors' meeting, I see some features that I believe we must change. For example: [directors] swing from being depressed to highly complacent; [directors exhibit a] fair amount of hypocrisy—[the attitude is] "I want honest feedback as long as it is favorable"—[and directors] explain away failure by pointing to factors not under our control.

It is very difficult to be tough on your friends.

We create bilateral discussions for the tough issues. This weakens our discussions.

My desire is to help build an organization that does not have the kind of politics that made me leave _____ .

We have different views of how much we commit to build an organization. I am concerned about how much building an organization can harm my relationship with my family.

We all say that we want to create an honest organization. Yet, when someone is honest, he gets bloodied.

The CEO deals with each one of us differently. I know this because I do it too. Also, he comes to me to get a reaction from me before he goes to the individual in question.

Often, too often, when we get together, we argue about peripheral issues. Why do we take so much time with such an obviously easy decision?

There are several of us [who], if we were honest, would have to say that we are master gamesmen. We would rather rewrite history than admit that we are wrong. On the other hand, some of us are the ultimate conciliators. We hate to be tough and people will take advantage of us.

We can have long discussions, then we wind up postponing. This means that the CEO has to make the decision.

I bet there is some difference in views about the impact of the CEO. But I also bet that all of us would agree that he has our interests at heart. If that were not the case, the place would blow up.

We burn up a lot of equity among the directors. Yet, we also build new equity. It tees me off—and I think that is true for other—yet we'll live with it.

There is too much talking by directors about directors without the relevant directors being there.

There is a lot of talk about learning. I question how much interest there is in learning.

Basically we care for each other. We can go after each other, but we don't give up on each other.

I think that the directors spend too much time reading tea leaves about their impact. People do not worry as much as [the directors] think.

Categorizing Values, Actions, and Consequences

I categorized the directors' responses by using the three categories employed to frame the interviews: institutional governing values, relationships among directors during their board meetings and other encounters, and possible consequences (effectiveness) of their actions and relationships. These categories, in turn, came from the structure of theories-in-use, which I described in Chapter Two as composed of governing values, action strategies, and consequences. Organizing the responses around these categories revealed the foundations for the directors' causal reasoning about the world they were creating.

Institutional Governing Values

• An institution should be built that does not have the counterproductive actions and norms that were true of the firms from which the directors came.

- The institution should be known for high-quality work that adds value for the clients.
- Success depends on having sound technical ideas but, more importantly, on implementing them.

Relationships Among Directors

- Being hypocritical
- Explaining away failure
- Having difficulty being honest with friends
- Asking for honesty; getting bloodied when it comes
- Talking for hours around an issue and not making a decision
- Not genuinely listening to each other's ideas; not respecting them
- Hating to admit that directors are wrong
- Dealing with the important issues in one-to-one discussions outside the board meetings, not during the meetings

Possible Consequences

- Developing coalitions among directors
- Having some directors stronger than others because they have more power and influence
- Bad-mouthing each other privately
- Withholding important information from each other in order not to demonstrate or upset each other
- Having the CEO deal with each director privately and differently

Summary

The initial interviews generated important learning about the directors and their group. The directors were unanimous that they intended to create a consulting firm that would provide high value to clients and also provide an internal culture where the consultants could learn and grow and where clients and consultants would persevere in learning. The directors were unanimous that they were working very hard to produce high-quality service to clients. They were unanimous that they and the others in the firm should continue doing so. There was, in short, a high degree of unanimity about the values and conditions that should govern the firm.

The directors were also unanimous that, despite their strong positive commitment to excellence, they were beginning to act in ways that produced the very organizational politics they decried. They reported that when they dealt with issues that were embarrassing or threatening to them, they acted to protect their individual interests. Their action strategies were defensive, anti-learning, and overprotective. For example, they reported acts of cover-up, dishonesty, bad-mouthing, and overprotecting each other. Not surprisingly, they evaluated their decision making as not very effective.

The candor and honesty that they exhibited was, in my opinion, largely due to their commitment to build a fine organization. The skill that I may have exhibited and the compassion and empathy that I may have expressed were, as they reported, helpful. But, in my opinion, I was working with individuals who were so dedicated to integrity and honesty that they described acts where either integrity or honesty, or both, were violated, in order to learn how to stop such hypocritical actions.

As they were describing their counterproductive actions, I believe they were also communicating the message that they wanted to change their actions and were depending on me for help. By doing that, they also placed me on notice that they were going to be hard-nosed about evaluating my actions.

I entered the next phase of the intervention with the belief that I had joined with a group of individuals who were dedicated to learning and with whom I too was going to learn.

4

Step Two:
Organize the Findings
for Learning and Action

The interviews with individual directors were followed by a feedback session for all the directors.

Purposes of the Feedback Session

The first feedback session had six purposes. First, I needed to describe to the directors what I had learned from the interviews and my early observations of their meetings. Second, I wanted to encourage any disconfirmation or confirmation of the findings. My third purpose was to start building an incremental relationship of trust among the directors and between the directors and the intervener myself. My fourth purpose was to plan actions that would correct whichever counterproductive activities the directors chose to correct. Fifth, I wanted to plan the intervention steps required to implement the correction. And sixth, I wanted to conduct the planning in ways that would facilitate the internal commitment of the directors to those intervention steps. This internal commitment would mean that the directors were motivated to implement the changes because doing so would be intrinsically rewarding. Internal commitment is rarely produced immediately, and I will be describing the actions required to develop it over time.

The Feedback Process

Whatever methods are used to diagnose the situation and whatever data are collected, there are four features that are important to an effective feedback process.

1. The material should be organized to describe the variables that cause the functional and dysfunctional activities of the group being studied. The basic criterion for separating functional from dysfunctional activities is the degree to which each activity facilitates or inhibits the detection and correction of important errors or the production of innovations within the group.
2. The variables should be organized into a pattern that explicitly shows how the variables evolved and how the interdependence among them leads to the persevering of the pattern. The pattern should lead to a prediction about its own consequences.
3. The pattern should make explicit the likely personal responsibility of each director in causing and maintaining the pattern.
4. The pattern should be presented in the form of an action map, and that map should present the data in ways that allow the participants to derive both the abstractions that permit comprehensive understanding and the abstractions that illuminate each unique, individual case. The data must also be conducive to generalizing about the present and the future. In addition to providing the information for all these analyses, the map ought to be generalizable beyond the group to other parts of the organization, as well as to other individuals in other organizations. (See the Appendix for a more detailed discussion.)

    The feedback process should help to provide a more holistic and systemic picture of group or organizational reality. It is holistic in the sense that it can cover a bigger slice of reality than do the existing views of individuals or subgroups. It is more systemic in the sense that it can make explicit the interdependencies that result in a self-maintaining pattern.

Tests of Validity

An action map constructed for a feedback session is primarily a representation of actions, strategies, consequences, and governing conditions and the feedback and feedthrough mechanisms that relate them to one another in a persistent pattern. Action maps are, in effect, hypotheses about what drives learning activities within the organization. Therefore, all action maps have to be tested as frequently and as completely as possible.

There are several strategies that may be used to test a map's validity. The first is to show it to the participants to see what features they confirm or disconfirm. However, the researcher should be aware that certain conditions predispose individuals to provide too easy confirmation. My colleagues and I have found that participants are too easily willing to confirm a map if they believe the end result is only research knowledge. They are unwilling to put themselves, their peers, and their organization on the line for the sake of producing maps for scholars to publish in professional journals. This is not to say that they would confirm glaring errors; if the error is glaring, it is unlikely that they are risking much in confirming it. But in our experience, they are reluctant to *dis*confirm when opinions vary widely, when topics are "hot," and when topics are encased in long-standing organizational defensive routines—precisely the conditions under which researchers would seek a healthy debate.

Conversely, if the participants have agreed at the outset that the research will include intervening in order to change the status quo and to open up the Pandora's box they have feared, as well as the defenses they have created to protect themselves, then they are more likely to surface their doubts about the map.

A second strategy to develop tests of a map's validity is to make predictions based on the map. An especially robust test will occur when the researcher's predictions are made known to the participants, the participants disagree with them, and yet the researcher turns out to be correct. For example, the map I presented to the directors (which is reproduced later in this chapter) described how organizational politics were created and maintained. The directors discussed the map in a lively session, and some felt the session was so productive that they would be able to change their actions immediately. We predicted that they would not be able to do so. We were able to test this prediction because we observed and recorded several board meetings after the feedback session but before the first two-day change sessions. An analysis of the tape recordings confirmed that the defensive routines described in the map were alive and well.

My colleagues and I frequently have such experiences, and that raises questions about the commonly made assertion that any intervention—including asking people to fill out instruments or to be observed—leads to changes. In our experience, this assertion is likely to be true only when the changes are changes in behavior, rather than values—that is, when they are related to single-loop learning. It is possible, for example, to help an authoritarian, aggressive leader behave less aggressively, but that behavior often vanishes when the individual is exposed to embarrassing or threatening conditions. The moment the individual experiences moderate to high stress, he or she reverts to Model I theory-in-use and the defensive reasoning that goes with it, which the individual had never abandoned. Managerial gimmicks and fads are often based on behavioral changes that are not accompanied by changes in governing values.

A third testing strategy is to predict the likely consequences of attempts to change the status quo. These tests will be even more robust if the change requires altering what is taken for granted. The more one can specify ahead of time the conditions of change, the sequences of actions that do and do not lead to change, the individuals or groups that will learn faster, and the conditions under which this learning will occur, the more robust the test will be.

These conditions can be produced by designing reeducational experiences directly from the knowledge embedded in the map. For example, my associates and I could predict that the map we created for the directors was not going to change unless the directors changed their Model I theories-in-use to approximate features of Model II. In moving toward Model II, individuals would have to unfreeze Model I. We could assess the degree to which each director (and later others) would unfreeze Model I and practice Model II. We could also make predictions about the likelihood that the directors would be able to make nontrivial changes in organizational politics. Note that this does not mean that individuals in this situation have to get rid of their Model I skills. Such skills may still be relevant for routine issues requiring only single-loop learning. Nor does it mean that all the new behavior produced will be a pure example of Model II. There will be many instances of hybrids of Models I and II as well as instances of pure Model I behavior. What researchers will observe, if there is genuine movement toward Model II, is that individuals will recognize and reflect on their Model I actions, or be comfortable about such actions, without inhibiting their learning.

Constructing the Action Map

As Einhorn and Hogarth (1987) suggest, an action map helps actors to think backward (diagnose past action) and think forward (take action in the future). It is designed to help the actors to find the relevant variables, to link them in a causal chain, and to assess the plausibility of the chain.

The first step in constructing a map is to identify its components. The second step is to order each component according to the role it plays. What contribution does each component make to the overall purpose of the pattern (in the case of the directors, the purpose was learning), to the functioning of other components, and to its own functioning?

These criteria come from an operational definition of component interdependence as the degree to which each component gets sustenance from and gives aid to the other components, and the degree to which each component facilitates or inhibits the purpose of the pattern.

To identify the components of a map and decide their likely sequence, we depend upon the theory described in Chapter Two. Model I and Model II alert us to examine action strategies and their consequences, as well as governing values. Each model also specifies characteristics for action strategies. Model I action strategies include evaluating actions or making attributions in ways that do not encourage inquiry or testing. Model II action strategies for evaluating and attributing require that they be crafted in ways to encourage inquiry and testing.

The theory specifies that behavior consistent with Model I will lead to defensive consequences (for example, self-fulfilling and self-sealing processes and escalating error). The theory also specifies the nature of defensive and productive reasoning.

Researchers can be taught to score transcripts and observations by using these concepts (Argyris, 1985a).

Causal Reasoning

It is our assumption that all individuals create and act in order to maintain the universe within which they live. Effective actions in this context are those that persistently produce intended consequences. Embedded in this requirement is the following causal reasoning: if I act in such and such manner, the following will occur and the following will not occur. Moreover, this causal prediction will persist under specified conditions. However, Model I theory-in-use will always require a categorically different result from causal reasoning than Model II will. Because Model I requires protective results, it will also require defensive reasoning, while Model II will require productive reasoning to create the result of learning.

If actions are explained by actors' causal reasoning and if our map is a pattern of actions, consequences, and values, then it should contain identifiable causal reasoning. We should be able, for example, to identify the degree to which defensive or productive reasoning has been used in creating and maintaining the pattern revealed by the map.

Governing Values

As we have already shown, effective human action requires some order within which on-line acting in a specific situation is possible. Crucial variables in that order are the master values that are not to be violated. Master values act as criteria for assessing the effectiveness of action. They also define the intention of action. For example, in the case study, one governing value held by the directors was high value added for clients. Therefore, every concept the directors used and every recommendation they made could legitimately be evaluated in terms of their concept of value added. Moreover, the same concept could be used to define what was not acceptable, such as analyses and recommendations crafted in ways that hid significant portions of what was learned.

The Directors' Action Map

An action map was developed from the directors' interviews and our observations of several directors' meetings (Figure 4.1). The map depicts a pattern of interdependence among governing conditions, generic action strategies, and several orders of counterproductive consequences. It also depicts the feedback and feedthrough processes by which the pattern is maintained.

Directors' Governing Values

All the directors agreed that the governing values described in the first column existed. They governed actions in the sense that, whatever actions were designed, those actions would always take the governing values into account. The actions would not violate the values; if they did violate the values, additional actions would be designed to deal with the violations. For example, the violations would be covered up, unless there was an intention to change one or more of them.

The second governing value—low respect and trust on interpersonal issues—requires an explanatory word. The map depicts theory-in-use variables. In the case of the other five governing values, there was a high congruence between the values the directors espoused and the ones that they used to guide their actions. There was a relatively large gap between the values the directors espoused about trust and the values that guided their actual behavior. Thus, it was *low* respect and trust that was the theory-in-use variable.

The next column asked how the directors dealt with wicked problems, which are embarrassing or threatening, as opposed to tame problems. How did they deal with "hot" situations?

Directors' Generic Action Strategies

The generic action strategies describe typical ways of handling wicked problems that were seen to be used by the directors. They made attributions about each other's intentions and motives. For example, they might say, "So-and-so is control oriented," "So-and-so's thinking and actions are dominated by money," or "So-and-so manipulates in order to get what he wants."

The directors also attributed to each other a low capacity to deal with wicked problems effectively. Moreover, they shaped their attributions to predict that changes were unlikely, saying, for example, "I know so-and-so; he'll not change," or "Trust me, believe me, that is ingrained in so-and-so. He'll never change." This reasoning was crafted so as to make the predictions difficult to test. The directors were maintaining that they knew the others would not change, that this prediction was valid, and that it required no further testing.

When they were asked if they had ever tested their claims publicly, the answer was that they had not done so. When they were asked why they had not, their answers were that they did not want to upset the other person, open up a Pandora's box, or create bad feelings. In effect, they stated that the cause, or reason, for not testing the attributions publicly was that they cared for the others and the group.

In these ways, the directors made their attributions and the reasoning behind them undiscussable. They also made the undiscussability undiscussable. The latter action strategy was necessary because, if they openly admitted this instance of undiscussability, they would have to make public all their other attributions and cover-ups.

These seven generic action strategies that the directors engaged in were likely to inhibit detection of any errors as well as correction of the errors. In addition, the strategies reinforced each other and thereby constructed a social reality that was anti-learning and overprotective. This meant that anti-learning and overprotectiveness as concepts were also protected.

Consequences for Group Dynamics (First-Order)

Whenever the directors met to discuss wicked problems, they advocated their positions as persuasively as possible, intending to convince the others of their views. Because they crafted and defended

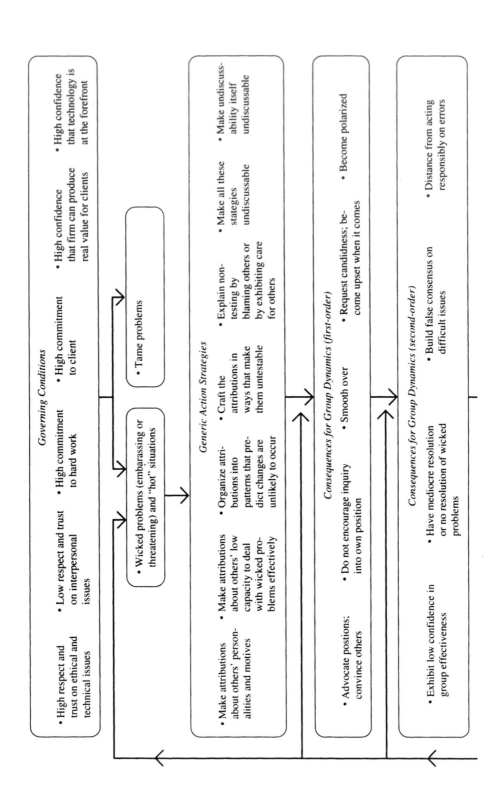

Governing Conditions

- High respect and trust on ethical and technical issues
- Low respect and trust on interpersonal issues
- High commitment to hard work
- High commitment to client
- High confidence that firm can produce real value for clients
- High confidence that technology is at the forefront

- Wicked problems (embarassing or threatening) and "hot" situations
- Tame problems

Generic Action Strategies

- Make attributions about others' personalities and motives
- Make attributions about others' low capacity to deal with wicked problems effectively
- Organize attributions into patterns that predict changes are unlikely to occur
- Craft the attributions in ways that make them untestable
- Explain non-testing by blaming others or by exhibiting care for others
- Make all these stategies undiscussable
- Make undiscuss-ability itself undiscussable

Consequences for Group Dynamics (first-order)

- Advocate postions; convince others
- Do not encourage inquiry into own position
- Smooth over
- Request candidness; become upset when it comes
- Become polarized

Consequences for Group Dynamics (second-order)

- Exhibit low confidence in group effectiveness
- Have mediocre resolution or no resolution of wicked problems
- Build false consensus on difficult issues
- Distance from acting responsibly on errors

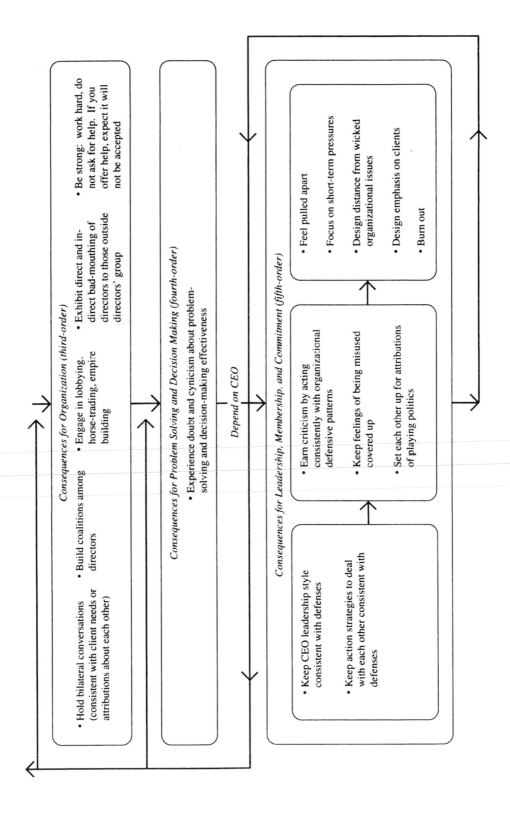

Consequences for Organization (third-order)

- Hold bilateral conversations (consistent with client needs or attributions about each other)
- Build coalitions among directors
- Engage in lobbying, horse-trading, empire building
- Exhibit direct and in-direct bad-mouthing of directors to those outside directors' group
- Be strong: work hard, do not ask for help. If you offer help, expect it will not be accepted

Consequences for Problem Solving and Decision Making (fourth-order)

- Experience doubt and cynicism about problem-solving and decision-making effectiveness

Depend on CEO

Consequences for Leadership, Membership, and Commitment (fifth-order)

- Keep CEO leadership style consistent with defenses
- Keep action strategies to deal with each other consistent with defenses

- Earn criticism by acting consistently with organizational defensive patterns
- Keep feelings of being misused covered up
- Set each other up for attributions of playing politics

- Feel pulled apart
- Focus on short-term pressures
- Design distance from wicked organizational issues
- Design emphasis on clients
- Burn out

their views on the basis of the undiscussable and untestable generic action strategies, they gave little encouragement to others to inquire into the advocated positions.

They acted this way, first, because they believed that as directors they were responsible for expressing their views. Second, as the data in the map show, the directors "knew" that the organizational norms supported anti-learning and overprotective actions and cover-ups of those actions. Under these conditions, directors who opened their ideas to inquiry ran the risk of losing and of being dominated by others. Hence, the directors bypassed these issues and covered up the bypass. The bypass and cover-up were inferred from the smoothing-over actions that were reported during the interviews and observed during the meetings. For example, the directors reported that whenever they had invited others to be candid, they had experienced either "being bloodied" or an awkward silence. Both reactions were upsetting. Neither invited further discussion.

Consequences for Group Dynamics (Second-Order)

The directors' generic action strategies combined with the first-order group dynamics led to at least four second-order consequences.

First, the directors went into meetings with a low sense of confidence that their group would deal effectively with the wicked issues. They did not discuss their low confidence because that was itself a wicked problem.

Second, they evaluated the meetings' resolution of issues as mediocre at best. Again, this evaluation was not discussed during meetings because it too was a wicked problem. After meetings, the directors might meet privately in dyads to discuss their evaluations and attributions with those colleagues whom they expected to hold similar views.

Third, a false consensus was built. For example, the CEO might ask, "Are we all in agreement?" Or he might say, "I think we have discussed this well and have reached the following decision" or "It's time for action steps. Who will do what?" Individuals would sign up or be appointed to take certain actions. The CEO would express pleasure for the "team effort," and they would all go on to the next problem. Weeks later, most of the commitments had not been implemented.

Fourth, in the interviews everyone reported scenarios such as those just described. Everyone also reported feeling that the group members were distancing themselves from detecting, discussing, and correcting wicked problems.

Once again, all the consequences were not discussable and their undiscussability was not discussed. And once again, the consequences reinforced themselves as well as the previous values, actions, and consequences.

Consequences for the Organization (Third-Order)

In this column of the action map were the organizational consequences of the features in the previous columns, ones that could also be observed in settings beyond the directors' group.

The directors developed coalitions among themselves based upon their personal attributions about each other. They reported on or could be observed in bilateral conversations about the wicked problems they saw in clients or in their own organization. The directors used these coalitions to lobby for controversial views, to trade favors ("I owe you one"), and to build whatever empires they believed were just. I did not observe nor was I given reports of one director trying to take over another's turf. The empire building was more akin to building protective walls against penetration by others than to increasing span of control. One especially troublesome issue for some directors was how the CEO distributed leads for new clients. Some felt that the CEO had favorites. The CEO felt that he allocated leads according to his honest judgment of who would best serve the client.

Directors also reported, and could be observed, bad-mouthing other directors within their coalition groups. They acted similarly toward senior consultants if the latter were being pressed by other directors to work with those directors.

Finally, a norm existed as to what it meant to be "strong." A strong director did not ask for help (the protective walls might then be breached). Moreover, if one director decided to offer help to another, the expectation was that it would not be accepted.

Consequences for Problem Solving and
Decision Making (Fourth-Order)

The action strategies, the group dynamics, and the organizational consequences combined in the mind of each director to create a strong doubt about problem-solving and decision-making effectiveness for wicked problems. Moreover, there was a good deal of cynicism about any suggestion that changes could occur without outside help.

The doubt and cynicism seemed sensible. Every action, and every consequence, created and reinforced bypass and cover-up activities. These resulted in the overprotection of the directors and reduced the likelihood that they could detect and correct important errors or create new policies that required discussing difficult issues.

Consequences for Leadership, Membership,
and Commitment (Fifth-Order)

There is a fifth-order set of consequences that arises from the values, actions, and consequences described so far. First, a dependence upon the CEO was created. If a group is not a reliable problem-solving and decision-making body, then the members may turn to one person for leadership. The leader, however, is expected to behave in ways that do not violate the defensive pattern the group would produce on an action map. That creates a double bind for the leader. If his or her acts are consistent with the defensive pattern, they will encourage overprotectiveness and limited learning. The leader's direct reports can then make attributions that the leader prefers their dependence because he or she can unilaterally manage the group. On the other hand, if the leader's acts are inconsistent with the pattern, he or she will create disruptive consequences. For example, if the CEO in our case decided to make discussable what was not discussable, he would have done it in the context of a group where mutual trust on the issues was low. Moreover, the skills the directors had developed were those that served bypass and cover-up. If the directors were required to be candid, it would likely have led to disruptive actions because they would not have had the skills to discuss wicked problems candidly without creating further wicked conditions.

The same would have been true for each director. If anyone had tried to discuss the undiscussable, he would have run similar risks of creating counterproductive consequences and being accused of harming the status quo. If he acted consistently with the defensive patterns, he could be accused of protecting his turf and himself.

Under these conditions, the directors felt misused and the misuse was covered up because it was a wicked problem. The CEO and the directors appeared to be setting themselves up for attributions that they were behaving politically.

These nested double binds, in turn, led the directors to feel pulled apart. They were damned if they did and damned if they did not. It was rational, under these conditions, to distance themselves from the wicked organizational issues and to pay attention to short-term pressures instead. It was also rational to focus heavily on clients, not only because high-quality value added was a governing value but because a client emphasis legitimized the distancing from internal organizational problems.

The ultimate double bind for the directors was that they knew they were responsible for developing a learning organization, and they also knew that every defensive action they took discouraged the development of this learning organization that would reinforce their espoused governing values while increasing trust.

Action Maps as Patterns

Action maps reveal two kinds of causality, which are important for both diagnosing and testing.

Component and Pattern Causality

In Chapter Two, I suggested that when individuals habitually interact in an organizational setting, their designed behaviors, together with the consequences of those behaviors, create complex organizational systems that display pattern causality. Descriptions of pattern causality take the form of action maps such as the one I have just presented, which reveal the pattern-level causes that limit learning and lead to the inability to detect and correct actions that lead to the very organizational defenses that individuals may deny.

Action maps also reveal component causality—the causal connections between the various pattern features, or components. For example, in the case study, the action of making attributions about others was reinforced by the action of making further attributions that stated that directors were unlikely to change their actions. These two components were then reinforced by the participants' crafting untestable attributions. Crafting attributions in ways that made them untestable received reinforcement from making attributions about personalities and about participants' capacities to deal with wicked problems, blaming others, making all these activities undiscussable, and making the undiscussability undiscussable. Thus, all the components identified as generic action strategies reinforced each other.

Component causality also exists between the components in different columns of an action map. For example, the way the directors' generic action strategies reinforced each other discouraged learning in interpersonal relationships. Therefore, individuals advocated their positions in ways that tried to convince and persuade others. This, in turn, meant that individuals crafted their conversation in ways that did not encourage inquiry.

Testing Causal Claims

There are several relatively easy and straightforward methods researchers can use to test the validity of apparent causal relationships, or causal claims.

The first validity test is to show the map to the participants, to see which features they agree with and which features they believe are incorrect. They could disagree about the location of a component, or they could suggest the inclusion of a component seen as missing.

Readers may wonder whether the directors in our study were likely to respond in ways that confirmed the pattern because they did not wish to upset the researchers or get into a hassle with them. There were two reasons why this easy confirmation was unlikely to occur. The first reason was that the map did not present a complimentary picture. It is unlikely that any clients will agree quickly and easily with a map that places them in a negative light.

One might argue that in this case the directors predicted the negative picture. Perhaps they were willing to go along with the map because it was consistent with their predictions. However, this was unlikely because the map was to be the basis for a long-range intervention strategy. The directors were to be asked to spend their scarcest resource, their time, in various change activities. Moreover, these change sessions, if successful, could be passed on to lower organizational layers. It was unlikely that the directors would place their organization at risk for the sake of pleasing an intervener.

A second reason why the feedback activity was not likely to be distorted by the directors' agreeing too easily with the map was that the feedback session was tape-recorded in order to make the discussion the basis for further validity checks. For example, we predicted that the directors would craft their attributions about each other, made during the discussion, so that they were untestable. I confronted such actions during the session, and if the respective directors agreed that the way they had crafted their attributions made them difficult to test, I asked what led them to craft their conversations in this manner. We expected all explanations to be consistent with the features of the map, and the tape recording of the conversations could be analyzed to test our expectation.

In addition, the way the directors explored the pattern was to provide additional evidence on the way they reasoned and acted when faced with embarrassing or threatening information. For example, they might have added new information about hidden attributions, such as fears that they had about making discussable what had been undiscussable.

The second test for the validity of causal relationships is to state predictions and to seek to disconfirm them. For example, the researcher can predict that no actions will be reported or observed that can or will alter the pattern. This prediction should hold over time and for any wicked problem. The only condition is that the participants work within the generic action strategies described in the map. A prediction could also be made that the participants will not be able to change the generic action strategies without assistance from variables exogenous to the pattern (the researcher acting as an intervener, for example).

These predictions should not be disconfirmed even after the participants see the map as a valid representation of their behavioral world. Nor should the predictions be disconfirmed simply by the participants' developing a genuine commitment to change the pattern or using outside helpers who develop intervention strategies that ignore the causal relationships embedded in the map. For example, an intervention that bypasses changing the values and generic action strategies and begins instead with changing the group dynamics or attitudes such as doubting and cynicism will not reduce dysfunctions; if it does, the changes should not persevere.

Changes that bypass the generic action strategies and first- to third-order consequences will work if they alter the wicked problems to simple tame or single-loop problems. For example, it may be possible to develop an information system that reduces the likelihood of topics being made undiscussable, because the system makes them public. On the other hand, reward and penalty schemes to change component parts are not likely to work. In our case study, for example, after a lengthy discussion of the map, a suggestion was made to assess heavy penalties on any director who was shown to have bad-mouthed other directors. The suggested penalty was $500 for each incident. The directors agreed to the fine, but they also predicted that it would not work.

The predictions should be stated without any time limits. Because a defensive pattern inhibits the learning and action that would be required to change it, the predictions are expected to hold as long as the pattern is not altered. Any change that occurs in an action map that does change the pattern causality without an intervention program will be a disconfirmation of the map.

Predictions are not made about the strength of each component in the relationship it has with any other component, because changes in component causality, as I have noted, should not affect pattern causality. If changes in component causality are followed by changes in pattern causality, then once again the causal relationships in the pattern will be disconfirmed.

A pattern of values, actions, and consequences that continually re-creates and reinforces itself is ultra stable because every component receives support from and provides support to every other component, thus inhibiting detection of the errors which, if corrected, would change the pattern causality. Indeed, the pattern in our case study may be said to be causally overdetermined because all the component parts cause and reinforce limiting learning.

Evolution and Description of Patterns

The explicit focus of an action map is to describe a pattern of causality—how it is maintained and how it affects learning—but an action map also serves another purpose. It represents the researcher's hypothesis about how the pattern evolved. It provides a developmental description of how the organizational defensive patterns developed, and I claim that—given the same governing conditions and generic defensive routines—the same consequences will develop every time.

Thus, my theory of organizations provides a conceptual and empirical way to integrate a pattern's development and its form when established. How to combine these two perspectives has concerned researchers for many years. Most organizational perspectives are created primarily to explain the patterning, interdependence, and stability that provide organizational structure. Most of these perspectives assume that there is something "out there," albeit complex, to be described. But explaining a pattern as it exists without explaining how it came about provides only a partial description. A description of an existing pattern is what Quine (1992) calls "to fit"—that is, observed regularity. In the world of practice, "to guide" is also crucial because it focuses on what governs or directs behavior (Bourdieu, 1990).

Latour (1987), for social science in general, and Malave (1991), for organizational studies, have pointed out that a complete theory of organizations requires both perspectives. Malave notes that Katz and Kahn (1966) and Weick (1969) both acknowledge this requirement but neither fulfills it. Malave suggests that one way for scholars to move in the direction of integrating both perspectives is to build on an idea that Allport (1967) called "event structuring." Action maps ccan be seen as a form of event structuring intended

to explain structure as well as the processes by which it comes
about.

It is not simple curiosity that leads scholars who are interested in designing and implementing interventions that create rare
events to deal both with the development and the final form of
organizational patterns. It is difficult to design and implement effective interventions without knowing both. This may be one explanation for the advice attributed to Lewin (1951)—namely, if you
want to understand organizations, change them. Change programs
cannot be implemented without creating new conditions to lead to
new consequences. They require spelling out how to get from here
to there. It is not likely that this can be done without making explicit the processes of organizational development.

To summarize, it is possible to construct action maps from
the values, actions, and consequences as inferred from interviews
and observations. The maps reveal the role of pattern causality,
component causality, and design causality. I also indicate how tests
can be attempted to determine the validity of the claims in the
pattern about what is going on.

5

Step Three:
Conduct Meaningful
Feedback Sessions

Chapter Four presented the theory and strategy for the feedback session and for the map around which the feedback is organized. This chapter describes what actually happened during the feedback session in the case study.

Feedback Session Discussions

As the intervener, I began by describing the governing values that appeared in column one of the map. The directors did not have much difficulty in agreeing that these were their values. When asked if they could think of other governing values, several responded that they could not. They reserved the right, however, to question or add to the list later.

When I turned to the next column, generic action strategies, the directors asked me to describe the action of "explaining nontesting by blaming others" I did so by role-playing what I meant. Providing an answer in the form of recollected conversation is important because it provides clients with relatively directly observable data from which they can get a window into the researcher-intervener's reasoning processes, as well as an opportunity to check their own recollections. Here I was recalling conversation from the individual interviews for the following role-play:

Intervener: Have you ever tested these attributions?

Intervener as a director: No, I haven't.

Intervener: What prevented you from asking [the individual in question]?

Intervener as a director: He'd blow his top. (*Alternative response:*) I like him, and why upset him?

Next came a series of questions about the causes of nontesting and blaming others. I focused on the coerciveness of the system, as well as on the directors' skillful behavior in bypassing and covering up. I wanted to make the point that the directors' actions were predictable from these factors, and not from the untested attributions that they had made, such as saying that someone was power oriented or competitive. These attributions might have been valid, but the data did not directly support them at this time.

In acting this way, I was illustrating actions and rules that I wanted the directors to learn. For example, whenever there are competing causal explanations, select those that are closest to the directly observable data. Also, strive to select causal explanations that require the fewest number of inferences from the relatively directly observable data that are available. Inferences about bypass and cover-up, for instance, can be tested by reference to tape recordings of actual behavior as well as by directors' reports of such incidents. However, inferences about power hungriness or competitiveness require inference processes that are much more complicated and more difficult to test publicly from recordings.

This does not mean that the latter inferences are not valid. It means that it is more desirable if explanations can be made, predictions tested, interventions designed, and changes made with the use of a simple inference structure. It is more desirable in the sense that the simpler the valid explanations, the more likely it is that tests can be crafted to be rigorous, the intervention strategy can be reliable and complete, and the learning required for change can be produced easily.

These rules also have practical value. The shorter the chain of inferences from the directly observable data, the easier it will be for practitioners to test their hypotheses under conditions of everyday life. They can use the ladder of inference, focusing first on the actual behavior, then on the meaning of that behavior, and finally on their explanation of it. For example, focusing either on testing attributions or on determining whether they are testable is less likely to create the communication difficulties that arise when attributions of being "power hungry" or of having "low self-esteem," or a "big ego" are publicly defined and explained.

Inferences connected to what was said and done make it easier for the intervener to educate the clients. For example, when questions arise regarding alternative explanations, the intervener can make his or her views known and illustrate them while modeling the reasoning and the skills that he or she hopes to get the clients to consider. The intervener is not simply feeding back data; he or she is beginning to create the conditions where the clients can choose, if they wish, to learn how to develop new causal framings of familiar issues.

For example, in the discussion I am about to present, as the intervener I focused away from explanations that involved directors' motives and toward the skillful actions the directors used to deal with embarrassing or threatening issues, as well as toward the system they were creating to maintain these skillful actions. The first episode begins with such a refocusing. (The directors' names are pseudonyms. These pseudonyms are reassigned at various points in the book to reduce the likelihood that directors will be identified by internal participants. The directors did *not* ask me to do this.)

David: Is the caring a knee-jerk reaction, or is it more often a legitimate concern about the person's well-being?

Intervener: I think that it is both. The reactions are highly skilled. People are trapped by their own skills.

(*Later.*) These questions are important. I am suggesting that the reason you withhold was not, at the outset, a matter of nasty politics. Your view of dealing with each other in a caring and realistic manner on these issues is to conceal the attributions that you are making and act as if you are not concealing, which makes it difficult to test the attributions in the first place. This, in turn, can lead to the politics that you described as "nasty."

John: I would assume that another reason for not testing is also a fear of confrontation. Just plain, ordinary fear. For example, that the CEO would respond like a volcano.

Intervener: Yes, but note your reasoning. It makes sense not to confront the CEO if you attribute to him that he will react like a blast furnace, the metaphor that I heard often.

Several directors: Yeah, yeah.

Intervener: But that reasoning is self-sealing for several reasons. First, it is not tested. Second, as you will see later on, the system is so designed that the CEO feels that he is in a nested set of double binds. He feels damned if he does and damned if he does not. He tries to control his own feelings of frustration and anger because he, too, is making attributions about what all of you can take. The pent-up feelings may eventually erupt, and hence the blast furnace reaction. Many of you may wonder, Where did that reaction come from? You may feel surprised and bewildered. That is predictable because he has been covering up his views and feelings.

Jim: So these negative behaviors are functional within the system that we create.

Intervener: Yes. What is functional in this system is also dysfunctional in terms of creating an organization that is able to learn, especially learning of the double-loop variety.

In the next episode to be transcribed, the directors ask a series of questions to explore the possibility that the counterproductive features of their actions were caused by factors that were either beyond their control or factors that no one wished to alter, such as those in the governing values. I attempt to answer in such a way that I do not collude in the distancing from personal responsibility that was implicit in their questions.

This appeared to trigger questions about the validity of my position. Did I not have a normative position, and was that not coloring my views? I encourage clients to ask such questions because they are the ones who have to set the stage to test features of the map *and* they are the ones who have to test my reasoning and actions when confronted with embarrassing or threatening questions. It is important for clients to see how I respond. If my actions are consistent with the position that I expect to teach them, then my credibility and that of my normative position are enhanced. This, in turn, can increase the likelihood that the clients will consider designing some change programs. In this episode with the directors, I end up by saying that, ultimately, the choice about the system they wish to have is theirs.

Jim: Is the tension being released due to the nature of the wicked problems or because we are failing to confront these problems?

Intervener: From the data that I have so far, I believe it is more of the latter. I have observed you dealing with wicked technical problems. They appear to be fun for you. I think it is the withholding and covering up that makes the attributions undiscussable, which leads to the pent-up feelings.

Larry: To what extent are these unavoidable in some generic sense in organizations?

Intervener: I would like to give two answers. First, most human beings are educated, early in life, to do what you are doing. So, in this sense, all this is generic. But I believe that it is also alterable.

Larry: But how desirable would that be? Maybe all you are doing is reinforcing your philosophy. Couldn't your thinking also be self-sealing?

Intervener: Yes, and may I add that I want to encourage these kinds of questions as much as I can. I hope that you will be confronting my views all the time. I, too, am concerned about my possible self-sealing reasoning. So we must find ways to test the ideas so that the results are compelling to you.

Yes, I do have a normative position. I believe that any social systems that are anti-learning are dysfunctional to the effective management of the system. For example, they often produce invalid or distorted information. But, again, let's test that.

The decision on how much of this or that should be in your system is your decision. I want to help you make as informed a choice as possible, one that is monitorable and alterable.

Larry: But maybe there are aspects of our reasoning and actions that I, for example, am unable to change. As I hear you, what would be important is for me to be able to discuss it with this group so that I can test how unchangeable things are.

Intervener: Yes. You may even wish to own up that you do not want to change certain actions. Fine. This can be discussed by the group because your decision is not simply an individual one; it is a decision that impacts the whole system.

And by the way, I would like to help you be genuinely accepting of decisions that have your own and your group's approval. One test of your being genuinely accepting is the degree to which others can confront your actions—especially people outside this group—and to which you encourage them to do so.

Ted: Could you talk a little more about your attribution—Am I using the right concept?—that people [in this group] are negative about others' inability to learn with respect to wicked problems.

Intervener: (*Explains.*)

Ted: This perception of a low predisposition to learning about this particular set of issues is a perception shared by a lot of people in this group?

Intervener: Yes.

Ted: Now this question may be unfair, but do you have a comment on the *substance* of that? Is the perception right or wrong?

Intervener: The question is fair. My personal judgment is that, as individuals, each of you is very much learning oriented. But once you are operating as members of this living system, you act more consistently with the anti-learning features encouraged by the pattern describing the system.

Ultimately the answer to your question is to test it in this group. In order to do that, we will have to discuss these issues concretely, focus on actual behavior.

Bill: How much of all this is a function of what's referred to as a siege mentality, which we develop when we're working with clients?

Intervener: I would expect that the siege mentality exacerbates this in two ways. It makes it more likely to occur and it magnifies it.

I also believe that the siege mentality is caused by the way you deal with pressures from clients. For example, you make attributions about them, do not test them, et cetera. And, by the way, your clients may be doing that to you.

Bill: (*Smiles.*) Yes, I think that I do that. You know, "Of *course* I'm right. How could you possibly question my intelligence on the subject?"

(*Later.*) My sense is also that when we get into a political situation with clients, we try to manage it actively.

John: There's a difference, though, in that we're outside agents. Maybe we can be more effective in inherently political environments because we are seen as not being influenced by their politics.

Jim: I think that we try to deal with these kinds of problems by *overpowering* the problem with technical expertise. For example, we prove beyond a shadow of a doubt that so-and-so didn't know what he was doing. We spend no time thinking about how to reeducate him.

David: That's funny. My experience is just the opposite. We bring about changes [in political systems] through private conversations. It's the confidential letter that we send that moves things.

Ted: But I would say that we are better at dealing with technical things than political things. When we break down on the political side, we do overpower clients with our intellectual heavy artillery.

Jim: And to add to the problem, the junior people go into battle with *only* a technical arsenal.

CEO: But maybe some of this behavior with clients is necessary for a company growing at our speed. We don't have time to discuss every problem. Some decisions have to be made in subgroups. We can't get everyone to participate all the time.

The directors' questions about the validity of the theory, the unrecognized distortions that I could be creating, and their alternative explanations illustrated that they were able to ask as tough questions about the theory and the research as scholars with competing views. And the discussion itself illustrated that answering these questions was of important practical value for the directors. It helped them make a more informed choice about the organizational theory and the possible intervention.

As the directors discussed their doubts about the theory itself, they also began to explore the causal explanations, such as siege mentality and not having time to participate in clients' human issues, that they had been using to account for some of their tensions. This discussion provided me with an opportunity to talk about the limits of participation. In my judgment, this was important because professionals like myself are often viewed as recommending unlimited participation. I wanted to establish that participation can be limited, so that the directors could make decisions about the conditions for limiting participation in their own organization.

Intervener: I am not suggesting that you participate on everything. Indeed, even if you had more time, it would not make sense. But in order to make "selective" participation work, you'll have to trust each other much more than you now do. At the moment, if one of you selects to encourage participation on a difficult issue, you may activate all sorts of questions in the minds of the others as to your purpose. And, if this map is correct, the others are likely to cover up their questions.

Intervener and directors: (*The discussion on participation with clients leads to an undiscussable—namely, the lack of genuine participation by some directors on important firm issues. This, in turn, leads to an expanded discussion on what had been undiscussable, especially the directors' relationship with the CEO and each other.)*

Larry: Yes, I want to be involved on the truly strategic decisions. And I want to be involved in defining these. I haven't been involved as much as I would like. (*Gives an example.*)

Intervener: This is an important example. Several of you were not involved [in that decision]. When I asked you about it, you attributed that the CEO kept you out by design. This upset you. But you did not test the attribution.

Bill: And what else is destructive is talking about the decision as if there was a consensus, when there never was one.

Looking back, we can identify a trend that occurs in most groups where the members are genuinely interested in learning and that occurred here as well. The conversations began around concerns that the directors had about ideas and issues related to the intervener's theoretical positions. These concerns centered on how skills can trap people, how it is possible to intend to be caring yet come across as noncaring, how untestable attributions lead to self-sealing consequences, and how these consequences become functional to the systems in which the directors work.

I emphasized that the directors were causally responsible for creating the defensive system pattern and that this occurred even though they did not intend to hurt others or the system.

Then the conversation shifted to an attempt by the directors to define external causes of their counterproductive actions (causes beyond their control). If they could find such causes, they seemed to think, they might be able to develop solutions to their situation without having to focus on such "internal" factors as their theories-in-use and personal causal responsibility. When I suggested that these internal factors were crucial, there followed a genuine confrontation of my views. Maybe what I assumed to be desirable was not? Maybe my argument was self-sealing? Who says that my normative position is correct? Maybe the directors were unable to change the factors that I suggested should be changed? Could not the fault lie in the weaknesses of the technical knowledge? How about the siege mentality developed because of client pressures?

The third phase of the conversation occurred when the directors returned to examining their personal causality. This led to the episode we look at next, in which the directors deal with their own internal politics, such as coalition building.

The CEO's candid reflections on how he built coalitions and how he reacted to certain actions by the directors lead to a deeper analysis of what they are doing to each other. The CEO describes the double bind that he experiences: if he heeds many of the directors' complaints, he could conclude that the firm was in serious trouble and that he was responsible for solving the problem. If he does not heed the directors, he could be accused of being indifferent or rejecting. This leads other directors to explore their feelings about the CEO.

The conversation then turns to problems that plague most consulting organizations, including how to evaluate consultants' performance and how to allocate business leads fairly.

This encourages the CEO to talk about what the directors do that leads him to feel victimized. I add that the directors might also feel victimized by the system. If the map was correct and the system was self-sealing and anti-learning, that system could eventually lead all the people in the organization to feel victimized. The directors support this view.

CEO: I, too, want to discuss [internal politics and coalition building]. I plead guilty to coalition building for a substantive result in some cases. There is also coalition building where you truly want help and discussion.

But I have found that some participants are inefficient participants. Even though I want *genuine* participation, I have learned to bias myself in favor of some of you more than others. Those that I choose do not give me a ten-hour answer. Nor do I get the feeling that they are working out personal problems.

Jim: But isn't that making attributions?

CEO: I agree. I would like to see all this changed. All I am doing is adding more data and asking that we put it on our agenda.

Larry: I have to agree with the CEO's dilemma. I think that I am one of those guys that he avoids, because he does not want to hear about _____ again.

CEO: And the way people react. . . . I get upset, whether I show it or not, with the way people say things. Even when _____ was speaking just now. My temperature went up. (*Explains.*)

When people start their conversation with "So-and-so is out of control," my interest is diminished to zero or negative. My first reaction is "What does he know?" This is not a discussion about so-and-so but [about the complainer's] personal agenda. What am I supposed to say, "You're right. So-and-so is out of control," even though it's not true?

Bill: So you're feeling trapped.

CEO: Yes, and if I disagree, I'm the blast furnace. So I think the way we craft our conversation is important.

Larry: Yes. I agree. You may be guilty of coalition formation. I am guilty of losing my temper. I know that the [exaggerations are exaggerations].

Intervener: (*Gives several examples in which the conversation could have been crafted to deal with the dilemmas described by the participants. Explains the reasoning that informed the way the CEO crafted his sentences.*)

John: (*Later.*) As I listen to all of this, I think that the CEO may be serving as a lightning rod in our group. Whatever decision is going to be made will be unpopular in some way with half of us. He takes the heat as opposed to us.

Ted: Yes. [And to compound the problem,] many of us take positions so that we can tally up whether we were right or wrong. Then we can say to each other, "You jerk, Okay?"

Intervener: And it is unlikely that it will be said openly and even less likely that the evaluation will be tested.

Ted: That's right.

David: Let me add another attribution that many of us make. We will say, "Since the CEO is managing us toward his decision, why the hell are we wasting our time talking? So forget [giving our views]." And we do that to each other about other issues. So we keep quiet and build a false consensus.

CEO: As I listen to this, let me add that half of the time when you come to me with a concern, you craft it as a terrible problem that is not being addressed. The other half of the time is when you feel you have not been consulted. That is crafted as "You are ignoring me."

   If I confirm your fears, I am in trouble. If I say, "I don't know," I also lose. If I have to lose, I'd rather lose by saying, "This is my opinion, and I really believe it very strongly. Unless you have some *really* good reason . . . "[I would rather say that and] appear arbitrary and not participative.

Jim: This is good. I personally think that we should not communicate to you as if you have to solve the problems right away. If we can be more honest about where we are—for example, to say we do not know—then we will know that someone is [working] on it.

CEO: Yes, it is not easy to think straight when someone begins with "Since the firm is going out of business tomorrow, I thought that I might bring up a subject." (*Chuckles.*)

   My predictable defensive reaction is "Oh, my God. He's going to talk about _____ again." If I may say so, _____ is the easiest for *all* of us to communicate with because his is the most facilitative of conversations [and we should explore if this is true, and if so what is a facilitative conversation].

Directors: (*Identify several issues that represent some of the most undiscussable areas of the management of professional firms— namely, the differential competencies of the directors, the impact these competencies have on their compensation, and how competencies and compensation impact on the rest of the organization.*)

Jim: One of our most critical problems is how we measure what each of the individuals in the room is contributing to the value in the firm. This is an [undiscussable] that produces a lot of serious trouble.

Larry: That's a tough issue, but we must tackle it. For my own sanity, I'm glad you brought it up.

David: I think that you assume that John wants to be involved in *every* decision. I think that he, like all of us, has a subset of things that really concern him, and others that do not. If you assume that *every time* you talk with him it will be a two-hour conversation, then that is an attribution about *him* [and that ought to be tested].

Larry: That is why I said it.

David: Which I do not think is right.

Larry: Well, I'm trying to discuss the undiscussable so that we can confront these issues. . . . My attribution about John could be wrong, and you could be right.

John: I think that David is correct that I probably have one of the longest lists of concerns. And I think David is correct in that I do not seek a two-hour conversation.

Also, I would not have some concerns if I were involved. For example, the establishment of a _____ office sort of appeared. It doesn't satisfy what I need to know as a director.

Bill: And that leads to some of the politicking that the model talks about. I've been advised by no fewer than three people to make sure that X, Y, or Z doesn't "take your billing." What a stupid waste of time [to have to think this way].

CEO: This credit hogging bewilders me. I don't think the firm requires it. If there is anything *I'm* doing that's creating that behavior, I want to know because I'm sure as hell not creating that behavior consciously.

Bill: This is not simply "your problem." This is our problem. And I do mean *our* problem. I haven't seen you do that. But the four of us (*names them*), heaven knows, we've been guilty. No question about it.

Jim: Yes, I agree with Bill.

Bill: I absolutely believe that the younger people believe that to be true.

David: One thing that I notice is that the younger consultants have conversations to decide which director is more important than another. (*Describes the cues the younger consultants use to judge the directors.*) I think we should reduce this [because it is political behavior].

Jim: But we peg each other on earnings and billability. This is another subject that has been undiscussable. I think that some of you think that I manipulate this to give some of you better clients.

You know, so-and-so may feel, "I got allocated a *bad* lead. My billings will be lower. *He* saved the easy leads for himself, therefore his billings will be higher."

Ted: We also worry about how the consultants feel about us. Should we worry what they think? Should we care? I don't have good answers for these questions. We never talk about this with each other. We always beat around the bush about it.

All directors: (*Discuss the meaning of money to each director.*)

CEO: I want to take some of the responsibility on these issues. [I would like to make discussable what is in my mind when I have a say about clients and potential clients. I try to make fits that are appropriate. But you may view it differently. I would like to get the whole process on the table.]

Several directors: (*Give examples of questions they wish would be discussed in more detail. All the questions indicate that this has been an important undiscussable area and that the directors wish to make it more discussable.*)

Bill: . . . In a five- or six-month period, I literally almost killed myself to get something done in order to live up to a promise we made to a client. [I feel every day that] if it fails, you will say to me that *I* screwed it up. But if it succeeds, you'll say that *we* succeeded.

David: *We* have never failed. I'm the guy telling you, "Stop saying 'I' in my presentation. . . ."

Bill: Well, I could do the same thing, because when we had our interviews with senior management *last* week, I actually started to keep tallies on the number of times you said "I." . . .

David: But there is a difference in saying, "I think . . ." and "We did . . ."

Bill: You were saying, "I did . . ."

David: Okay. [That's important.]

(*Later.*) I would be *alarmed* if you (because we have worked together) or if *anyone* thought that that was the way I thought about it. It may mean that you were taking a tremendous amount of the responsibility for execution on your back, which is what I love about you (*laughing*), which makes you so valuable to *all* of us, and which is why you're [on the Board] so quickly. But if you felt that *that* was actually my attitude, then I would be horrified.

Bill: I *know* it wasn't. . . . It's all signals. I know it was irrational, I know I shouldn't have gotten upset, and it was childish and all that . . .

Larry: (*Later.*) There are two things that are true here. You *may* be a victim of your own success. We may be looking at you, collectively, the way the Celtics look at Larry Bird. And expecting from you (*explains what was expected*). Maybe that's unfair. Maybe we ascribed to you something that you do not deserve nor should have to deal with.

Two, we all are proud professionals. I can speak for myself, and *probably* for other people in the room, I actually *envy* you. I'd love to be doing what you are doing. . . . [So] when you say something to me, and I happen to be envious, it is likely to create some resentment.

Jim: Yeah. Envy turns into resentment very quickly.

Intervener: [Envy is an important concept for us to discuss in more detail.]

CEO: I hear everyone saying they're underappreciated, and I feel *I'm* underappreciated, and how are we going to deal with that? [It's not in the model.]

The second concern is what is credit. [Is it billings?] If we base the firm on our abilities to sell, we will not be a successful firm.

The third concern is how we can develop mechanisms for giving *real* credit to *real* people. [This is not easy.] I don't know how to do it because there *is* differential performance along different dimensions. On no dimension do we all perform equally. And the final thing is that everyone's performance is changing rapidly. [We must not forget that, although Bill said he was envious of David], David was not performing three years ago.

How do we [give] credit *such that* people are encouraged to continue their improvement, as opposed to credit that locks them into where they are.

(*Later.*) [I acknowledge that I exhibit all the action strategies that are consistent with the organizational defensive pattern,] but I'd just like to know whether, on "flying off the handle," I am perceived as "rare" or "very frequent."

Bill: It surprises me. You have not done so in interactions with me. My perception of you is that you never fly off the handle.

Jim: He flies off the handle if you disagree with him, at least with me.

Larry: [Let me give an example in which we were involved, yet you were not present, Bill.]

Intervener: Do you remember what the CEO said?

Larry: (*Cites conversation.*) And he was yelling. That's what I mean by blowing up.

CEO: I think that some conversations that I have had with some of you would fulfill *any*body's definition of blowing up. (*Gives example.*) Are there other forms of blowing up that I indulge in?

John: There are three possible definitions of "blow up." (*Cites them with examples.*) The third one [is more subtle]. You suddenly disappear off the edge of the earth. You can't be reached. You don't answer things.

David: As a matter of fact, that's what I'm surprised isn't on the list. The CEO, at times, *avoids* a decision or an unpleasantry by *abandoning* the field.

John: Yes, I suspect he is deliberately out of touch.

David: I think the CEO is beginning to fly off the handle much less now.

CEO: I do have a very bad temper. I'll take [things personally].

(*Later.*) Let me tell you guys what I constantly feel. I mean *torn* apart, . . . pulled apart because *one* of the things that just *exhausts* me is the dissonance between the way I *have* to manage the company and the way I would like to behave.

I feel *victimized* by the system *a lot*.

Intervener: Yes, [and I'd like to add] so are the other people in this room victimized by the system. And we have to ask ourselves, Do we want to alter this?

[Does this feature] of the model make sense to you?

Bill: It is pretty descriptive to me.

David: Of course it is. I don't hear anyone saying that they do not believe there's horse-trading, coalitions, bilateral conversations— [they're all there].

Larry: Yes. The one thing that I do not see here is that [others of us are distancing ourselves from the firm as a whole. We get our job done, and stay away from the difficulties described in this model].

Intervener: If I have understood you, you are suggesting that empire building and "nuclear-free zones" are two additional consequences.

Larry: Yes.

David: They represent distancing?

Larry: Yes.

Intervener: And maybe the CEO's nuclear-free zone is produced by dropping out of sight.

Ted: Yes, I too feel pulled apart at times. I'm getting to the point where I feel it is hard to have open conversations about this. You get this designed distancing. I must admit there are times when I like feeling that I can take care of myself.

Jim: Yes, we're not operating as a team.

Ted: (*Later.*) I think that part of the innate resentment . . . is that we don't *discuss* who's got the best characteristics for particular clients. We don't talk about our relative strengths and who fits best.

Bill: As a person who has worked with most of you, I think that I learned more from each of you than you've ever learned from each other. And that's a symptom of the system. And we're losing something if we don't all learn from each other.

Intervener: I should like to repeat that if you all agreed right now that you wished to craft conversations with each other that are more productive, you will have difficulties because of what I have called your theories-in-use. We will have to develop additional ones.

Ted: I know that I have limits. Conversely, I think that I am pretty good at helping people diagnose political realities of clients.

CEO: I think we all have much to learn. I'm impressed with how much all of us have learned today about how we miscraft our talk.

As we have just seen, the CEO began this episode by publicly describing some of the double binds that he felt as well as some of the defensive actions that he takes. In effect, he took personal responsibility for his actions. This led the directors to realize that some of the CEO's "unfair" and "irrational" behavior was rational and fair. It also led them to describe their defensive actions with him and with each other. The discussion produced rich directly observable data about concepts in the pattern embedded in the action map. Such data help to connect the abstractions in the map to the directors' experiences.

The same data also can be used to confirm features of the pattern. Thus, what it is necessary for the directors to say in order to learn is also useful for research purposes.

Moreover, the discussion led to deeper insights into how the directors felt. They spoke of feeling alarmed, angry, victimized, envious, unappreciated, torn apart, and emotionally exhausted. Many of these feelings had been described in the individual interviews, where they were identified as undiscussable. So we saw the directors discussing issues that they had said were undiscussable. Moreover, they did so spontaneously. I believe that this was a sign of their genuine interest in learning and of their commitment to building a firm with minimal defenses. It was also a sign of how the feedback of research can "cause" participants to act constructively.

During the feedback session, there was also an episode where one of the directors disagreed with a feature of the map. When I encouraged discussion of the issue, it turned out that many of the directors had withheld information from him, which could understandably lead to his disagreement. The discussion of the cover-up adds more to the picture of undiscussables.

Intervener: (*Describes his findings that it was a sign of weakness to ask for help.*)

Larry: I do not agree with that. I think that I have gotten help from everyone in this room. And I've given some help. (*The others do not speak up.*)

Intervener: Let's check this out. How do others of you react?

Larry: Am I smoking dope? I don't know how many times every single person in this group has bailed me out.

Ted: I think the problem is greater with the consultants. I know several of them who would feel that it would be a sign of weakness to ask you for help.

Jim: I agree with Ted. I think you feel free to ask us more than we feel free to ask you. I think if I asked for help, people would say, "There goes Jim. He's out of control again."

CEO: I think this is an important point, and we may be sweeping it under the rug a bit right now. I think the "be strong" [attitude] is a big problem in the firm. (*Gives two examples.*)

I also think there is a lot of credit seeking in this group, which is the flip side of asking for help. If you want credit, you cannot ask for help because then you will have to share the credit.

. . . The whole currency is debased, because whenever someone's thanked, they go around and make speeches about how they saved someone's rear.

Remember the motto we created ourselves, "Shut up and get back to work"? This could be interpreted as "Don't bother me with your problems, fix them yourselves."

David: One reason that we are profitable is that we work hard. A work ethic driven out of fear is wrong. A work ethic driven out of a sense of teamwork, that you're achieving something that's worth investing your life in . . . that's positive.

CEO: From my perspective, people working hard is not a problem because people love what they are doing. If we shut up and can't help or learn from each other, that would be a problem. How can we become the learning organization that we say we want to become? How do we help clients become the learning organization that we say we can help them become?

Summary

The topics discussed in the feedback session can be grouped into two broad categories. The first category concerns the characteristics of the pattern and their relationships.

Undiscussables

> Feeling plain ordinary fear of confrontation
> Thinking it is okay to have limited-learning systems and the politics that go with them
> Using a siege mentality to protect oneself
> Putting down clients
> Using technical knowledge to overpower
> Examining what it means to be a director
> Building coalitions, distancing by the CEO, covering up both actions
> Describing the reciprocal distancing
> Haggling over who gets the credit

Perceiving client leads to be allocated in accordance with secret rules and friendships

Needing to be strong, never asking for help

Self-Fulfilling and Self-Sealing Consequences

The CEO feels double binds, bypasses, covers up and becomes upset, which leads him to act like a "blast furnace." The other directors cover up their feelings; hence, these processes become undiscussable.

Directors create discussions that are not helpful and then assign responsibility to the CEO to take action. Then they condemn him for taking unilateral action.

Directors engage in distancing, which leads to more distancing and an increased likelihood that distancing is not discussable and hence is self-sealing.

Directors all feel victimized by a system they created.

System Paradoxes

Bypassing and covering up are functional to the pattern that the directors have created and dysfunctional to the vision of the firm.

Participation can lead to wasting a lot of time and hence can reduce the value of participation.

The second category includes topics that show the directors' reflecting on the total pattern as well as its implications.

Multiple Causality and Circularity

Individuals cover up, and the pattern rewards such actions. There is a circular relationship between individuals' responsibility for dysfunctional behavior and the pattern's rewarding such behavior.

The tension is caused by wicked problems *and* by failure to deal with fear, embarrassment, or sense of being threatened in the presence of these problems.

High-Level Inferences

> Directors make attributions about having nasty motives, and
> about being power oriented, competitive, and money
> crazy.

Questions That Test Hypotheses

> To what extent are dysfunctional consequences true for all
> organizations?
> To what extent are directors able to change their theories-in-
> use and the ways they reason? To what extent do they wish
> to do so?
> To what extent can directors assess their effectiveness as in-
> dividuals and as a group?
> To what extent can directors assess the intervener's norma-
> tive views and values?

The directors provided many illustrations of the way the
pattern as a whole and its component parts functioned, and of the
pattern's possible impact upon the organization's lower levels. The
illustrations were in many cases enriched by explanatory comments.
For example, a major portion of the time was spent talking about
the impact of the CEO's actions upon individual directors and upon
the group.

The feedback discussion also led members to describe how
they felt victimized by the pattern. They, especially the CEO, reported continual double binds and explained how these dilemmas
came about.

As the members discussed the pattern, several things began
to occur that provided important foundations for change. First, the
directors confirmed that they made negative attributions about each
other and that they did not test or encourage others to test them. The
apparent ease and candor with which they admitted their attributions provided evidence, I believe, that the directors' intentions were
not as nasty as the directors themselves evaluated them to be. Moreover, the directors appeared more capable of discussing the undiscussables than they and I originally had thought they would be.

The very act of a thoughtful, spirited inquiry about the map—in the context of a feedback session, managed by an intervener—provided initial evidence that the overprotective features described in the map were valid but alterable. As a result, the directors became optimistic about changing what they had feared was unchangeable. These changes in aspirations, I believe, came from the fact that the directors owned up to "faults" they were attributed to have in such a way that they disconfirmed the attribution that the faults were undiscussable. Moreover, when each director gave the reasons that he acted as he did, the reasons made sense to the others.

At the end of the session, all the directors expressed an enthusiasm for the discussion that had occurred and a cautious optimism for the prognosis for change. There were at least two reasons why the optimism was cautious. First, many directors wondered what would happen after they left the room and especially what would happen when they returned to the pressures of everyday life.

Second, I took every opportunity that arose to point out that in order for the optimism to become credible, new actions must be developed and must persist. In my opinion, the directors did not have the skills to produce the new actions even though they wanted to do so.

I recommended a second seminar to examine the generic action strategies and the theories-in-use that produced them, to learn theories of action that could lead to more productive actions, to practice the espoused theory so that it became a new theory-in-use, and to explore the organizational changes that the new theory-in-use could create. The directors agreed to this seminar.

6

Step Four:
Facilitate the Change Seminar
with Live Cases

I left the feedback seminar with the view that I was working with a group of directors who showed a good deal of courage, a high degree of insight, and keen analysis into their problems. I also felt that with these directors as the foundation for this intervention, it could be one of the most successful in which I had participated.

Interventions in Causality

There were several ways to proceed. The choice was largely a matter of determining which level of causality would be most amenable to change. A focus on pattern causality would suggest that we try to alter the pattern and strive to create holistic change.

I do not know of any published research on how to intervene in a pattern composed of many multilevel, highly interdependent variables that are patterned to inhibit learning. I would not know where to begin or how to manage the intervention processes so that I would not create new and more powerful self-fulfilling counter-productive processes.

A second possibility would be to focus upon component causality. One or two components could be selected with which to begin the change. But which components should be selected? How could the change processes be controlled so that they did not spread from two components to all the components? Again there was the danger of events going out of control.

There was a third possibility that surfaced the moment my colleagues and I asked how human beings created an anti-learning and overprotective organizational defensive pattern when no one required them to do so. How did they create a social system contrary to what they espoused? Attempting to answer this question led us to the concept of design causality that I describe in Chapter Four and in the Appendix. The participants probably had a master design for creating systems that would lead to particular unwanted, counterproductive consequences. This master design was composed of their Model I theories-in-use and the defensive reasoning that accompanied them.

It should not be inferred that because my fellow researchers and I choose to focus on theories-in-use, our approach is primarily individual. Our central focus is on social systems, which means we concern ourselves with group and intergroup factors as well as individual and interpersonal ones. Moreover, theories-in-use are taught to individuals during their early years. Therefore, to focus on theories-in-use is to focus on societal acculturation processes. We cannot alter these societal processes by change programs within organizations. We can, however, begin to alter the theories-in-use by focusing on the individuals who are the agents or carriers of these societally based processes.

It should also not be inferred that we are suggesting that Model I theories-in-use are somehow bad and should never be used. As I indicated in Chapter Two, Model I processes may be functional for routine events that are not innovative, as well as for extreme emergencies such as digging out from a tornado. They are societal phenomena, and indeed, they may exist worldwide, since we find them in studying people in North America, South America, Europe, India, Australia, and Japan (Argyris, 1982; Argyris & Schön, 1978). Individuals become the agents for implementing Model I theories-in-use by following Model I governing values and by being highly skillful in producing Model I actions—performing them quickly and effortlessly.

Individuals also take the actions for granted. They have the actions so internalized that their sense of competence and confidence depends on using them. Finally, individuals develop defensive reasoning processes that help to keep them blind to the action's counterproductive consequences.

It is highly unlikely, therefore, that one can develop Model II espoused theory as a theory-in-use through structural arrangements or by ordering it or even by pleading for it and rewarding it. Our theory of action predicts that one cannot introduce Model II easily even with a highly articulate, learning-oriented set of individuals, such as the directors, who have made a commitment to learn to act consistently with Model II.

Indirect support for this prediction is to be found in this chapter. After the feedback session, the directors wrote cases, which basically illustrated Model I behavior. One could argue that the reason the cases illustrated Model I was that the directors were asked to write about the difficult problems they experienced in the current organization. This focus could have led them to reflect on the recent past; however, there are several pieces of evidence that shed doubt on this possibility. First, some directors chose to write cases about how they would act in the future. These cases were consistent with Model I. Second, an even more powerful set of data came from the discussion about the cases. As we shall see, during the discussion the directors acted toward each other in a largely Model I manner, even though the object of the discussion was to learn Model II behavior. Finally and equally important, even after this seminar to learn Model II as a theory-in-use, the directors still used many Model I actions and only slowly moved toward Model II.

The first step, therefore, to bring about this learning was to help each director assess the degree to which he used Model I to design his actions and the degree to which he was unaware that he did so. At the same time, each director was helped to see how his Model I actions tended to coerce his fellow directors to respond in a Model I mode and to create the defensive pattern already described. Our goal, in short, was to change the elemental designs that were producing the larger, more complicated pattern.

The Case Method

We needed to create learning processes that would allow directors to understand their Model I actions while also giving them opportunities to practice Model II action strategies. To accomplish this task, we chose a case method in which the directors were asked to identify a nontrivial human problem that they had not been able to solve. They typically focused on an episode that had actually occurred and that was frustrating and embarrassing or threatening. We also asked them to state how they would begin to solve the problem *if* they could create whatever situation they wished. This provided insight into their espoused intentions and their espoused action strategies—that is, their beliefs as to the appropriate actions to take in order to bring about the intended result.

Next, the directors were asked to write out a three-page conversation they would hold to achieve their intended consequences. This requirement provided the relatively directly observable data that were needed to get a window into the directors' causal reasoning.

The conversation was to be written on the right-hand side of each page. On the left-hand side of each page, the directors were to write the ideas and feelings that they would not (or did not) express. These data gave us insight into what the directors construed to be the undiscussable barriers to progress. Comparing their feelings with the actual scenario made it possible to see the self-censorship activities of the writers and the extent to which the information in the left-hand columns was bypassed and the bypass was covered up.

Each director was asked to chair a two-hour discussion of his case. His fellow directors acted as consultants to help him analyze his case and redesign it to make his actions more effective. The discussions were tape-recorded. The written cases and the transcripts of the discussions (especially the early ones) can be used to assess the degree to which the written cases and the discussions were consistent with Model I actions and values and with the organizational defensive pattern described in the action map.

A two-day case-discussion seminar was held with all but one of the directors present. (The missing director had to absent himself for personal reasons.) Each of the directors had completed a case to be used for the two-hour discussion the director himself would lead.

Five of the cases were written about the allocation of client leads and the allocation of consultants to implement obligations accepted by the firm. The focus on allocation of scarce resources is consistent with what the research literature describes as a key causal variable in organizational politics (this is discussed in the Appendix). The remainder of the cases illustrated separate but important issues.

I will present two of the cases to demonstrate the degree to which they illustrated Model I and the organizational defensive pattern. The cases are described in their entirety, with light editorial alterations primarily to maintain confidentiality. Although each case was written by a different director, the allocation problems were related to the same client prospect. This gives us an opportunity to see the same problem through the eyes of the director in charge of the case, the director in charge of marketing, and the CEO.

Larry's Case: Allocation of Human Resources

Issue: Planning the allocation of human resources to prospective business has been a constant source of controversy. The CEO has responsibility for allocating consultants to cases. I believe he has an inadequate understanding of what is required to complete much of the work we undertake and has created a process which undermines effective marketing, and encourages unilateral resource grabbing and "black market" deals.

Example: They are myriad; I'll be surprised if you don't receive more than one scenario based on this. The AIR case provides a good example, since it allows us to discuss both the allocation issue and the problem of staffing in the Seattle office.

Strategy: I cannot dignify my historical approach to these issues with the term *strategy.* "Grin and bear it" is a better description.

Larry's Unspoken Thoughts	*Actual Conversation*
There are no resources to get. He doesn't have an answer.	*Larry:* We have to discuss the AIR staffing question. They want to start something soon, and I can't hold them off forever.
	CEO: What is it, and when do they want it to start?

He's really gotten to the high ground with these guys. He doesn't want to blow it.

Larry: The study is on diversification. The head of the group tours business wants to expand and has gotten the CEO involved. They both like us well enough, and our friends are levering us into the arbitrator's position.

Also, we have a shot at doing business unit analysis for their domestic travel business. The corporate thing starts as soon as possible; the domestic thing is more speculative.

CEO: Okay. Well, on the corporate thing we should put some Seattle people on it. How about Burt, Faye, and Clyde?

I'm not surprised by that list. They are all working for John, which means we'll risk simultaneous work peaks, and John eats people's hours alive. How is Faye going to survive a John case *and* commuting from Seattle to Fort Worth, Texas, every week?

Larry: Burt would be great. They liked him a lot last time, and it's the same client team leader. But these guys [the client] are picky. Are those people really available?

CEO: Yes, Newco is uncertain right now, and everyone is going to have to work two cases. Faye is only on Oldco [Fort Worth case].

He feels he can't afford to sell this if no one is going to show up. He'll have to be out there constantly otherwise.

Larry: Are you sure about that? I'm getting mixed signals on that case. First it's on, then it's off.

He doesn't want to get in another one of these "sell it and

CEO: Look, I'm constantly hearing about how this or that

then figure it out" situations.

    If I had a dollar for every time I've heard this speech, *I'd* retire. Why don't you enforce some discipline on people to get them to stop playing wolf?

is going to be sold or go away. If I had dollar for every study that was about to happen, we'd be able to retire. We can count on ACK, so let's get this going.

Larry: I just can't afford to get started and be left holding the bag.

CEO: (*Later.*) Well, why not let Clyde run that?

Larry: That's a bad fit interpersonally. He's not right. And who would replace him on the corporate thing?

The problem really is he doesn't have any confidence in Clyde as a leader. Clyde strikes him as obnoxious a lot of the time, and if we don't manage this right, it'll blow up.

CEO: I don't know. Let him run corporate, and let Burt run domestic.

Larry: Burt knows the corporate people, and they like him. He'd prefer that study, anyhow.

CEO: Well, what are you suggesting? You're eliminating all the options.

No. You haven't presented any options. You just expect me to take care of it. All the options rob Peter to pay Paul.

Larry: The problem here is I need five people now, and I've been holding them [AIR] off forever.

David's Case: Allocation of Human Resources

Issue: For the past two years, the allocation of personnel at the consultant level has been the source of endless turmoil. The CEO has responsibility for it. While he does provide some final arbitration of the process, it is largely an ad hoc system where partners horse-trade and position themselves to preempt others from staffing capacity that, if lost, would jeopardize their ability to meet one of their client's needs. This has contributed to an obfuscation of marketing prospects, overstatement of requirements, underpricing to sell work "now," and a general breakdown of professional development goals.

This is particularly annoying to me since it undermines my ability to control marketing domestically. Moreover, as the largest revenue generator, my cases and prospects are disproportionately affected. (I've had to "un-sell" business.) Also, since resources become the object of jealousy, this encourages a general resentment (an obvious attribution) of me by my colleagues.

Objectives for the Conversation: My short-term objective is to staff a case. I have also endeavored to get the CEO to see that this system is inefficient and breeds some of the dysfunctional behavior he complains about.

David's Unspoken Thoughts	*Actual Conversation*
Here we go again. There is no answer to this question.	*David:* We need to discuss the AIR situation. They want to do some things, and I've stalled them about as long as I can.
	CEO: Great. What's the story?
Not to mention that I've had to troop back and forth to Seattle twenty times a year for two years to get us here.	*David:* There are two things. They want to do a corporate study on a diversification opportunity, and they want to do a domestic-travel strategy study. They'd both probably start soon; I can't hold them off too much longer. I've been stalling for a while, and we definitely have the high ground. We know the CEO, and the EVP [executive vice president] with

responsibility for consultants at corporate is a partisan.

CEO: Well, AIR is certainly a key client for the Seattle office. How many people do we need? When will these start, for certain?

David: Well, I can structure them differently depending on how many people can show up. The corporate thing has got to start almost immediately. We could have billed them last month, but I didn't see any way to staff it. Ideally, we'd have three or four people.

I don't know about the domestic-travel thing. They haven't really committed to it. They're a little price sensitive. But it gets us into FLI [the parent company], and they're describing it as a prototype.

CEO: Well, the corporate thing looks like we've got to do it, and we're right to staff it with people from Seattle. How about Burt, Clyde, and Faye? This would be a second case for all of them.

I'm not so sure about Clyde. Is he a good fit with this client? Is he going to be willing to work for Burt? Will I get any of their time?

David: Well, Burt would be great, since he played a big role on the last study. He should be the leader. But Burt and Clyde are both on Newco [a John case]. And Faye is on BIG, which is John's case too. I hate having two teams working on the same cases. The possibility of simultaneous peaks and valleys in the work loads is great. And John told me that he told the client Faye was 70 percent on BIG.

Besides the fact that it's in Texas. She'll die on that commute.

That's easy for you to say. But if they don't show up, we'll blow this relationship.

CEO: Professionals are supposed to work on two cases. Clyde and Burt are on single cases right now. AIR is key to the office in Seattle, and they'll have to be on it.

David: Well, I'm nervous. John eats the time of his people, and it's showing up in their time sheets and in their performance. The CEO is chairing this effort at AIR. They're an experienced buyer. I can't show up there with a shadow team and survive.

Fine. I agree. But I can't solve it for John, and I can't solve it at the expense of this case.

CEO: [Managing multiple commitments] is a lesson consultants have to learn and John has to learn too. We can't go around saying, "We can't fix that problem." Newco is ending anyway.

And I don't want to be the excuse for why it failed—"AIR siphoned my resources."

David: I know. I agree. John told me he wasn't sure about Newco. Every time I talk to him he's got a different story. First it's going, then it's not.

This again . . .

Except we have a big sunk cost in Newco. I didn't pursue something at AIR because of it. If we're not committed to getting it right there, then we're doing a slash and burn number.

CEO: We'll cross that bridge when we come to it. If I had a dollar for every case that was about to get sold, I'd be worried about things other than selling. We can't count on Newco.

David: Okay. What about Faye?

CEO: What about Fay?

David: John says she's committed to the client 70 percent at BIG.

That's easy for you to say! One of us ends up with a problem.

CEO: Well, she's got to handle two cases. She can have a presence on AIR at least.

I'm resigned at this point. He doesn't have an answer to the problem, and now I have two and a half of the four people I need. Faye is a half, and I'm uneasy about Clyde.

David: OK. What about domestic travel?

CEO: Well, let's stall a little. Then when it's sold, we'll worry about it.

That's classic. I can't get the right people for this one. Why pursue it? It's better to drop it now than take that loss of face.

David: Well, I don't want to pursue it if we can't staff it.

Yes we do. We don't have enough people, but we're still pursuing things with too little discrimination. What's he supposed to do about it? We underhired when FLI had control of the numbers recruiting. We can't grow people overnight.

CEO: We don't know what the situation will be then.

Results: The study is proceeding at corporate reasonably well. The other study has been put off due to my staffing, which may be a long-run mistake. Newco rolled over and expanded (good for John). Now John needs more of Clyde's time, and I'm really understaffed on my study.

Cases as Tests of the Map

The two cases confirmed the component features of the map as well as the features of the pattern as a whole in several ways.

Action Strategies

The action strategies in the cases were consistent with Model I. For example, in both cases, whenever the writers attempted to explain another person's intentions, the following actions were apparent:

Negative attributions were made about the other's intentions and defensiveness.

Attributions were not tested publicly.

Negative evaluations were made about the other's performance.

Evaluations were not tested publicly.

The stated reason for avoiding testing was that the writer was showing concern for the other.

Cover-Ups

The left-hand columns contained the writers' attributions and evaluations of the CEO, of other directors, and clients. They were not communicated to the other person in the conversation, yet these thoughts and feelings were crucial to the way each writer developed his strategies and produced his conversation.

Limited Learning

There was no reflection upon or discussion of the critical issues that were being covered up. Moreover, each case showed that the writer protected himself, that the writer believed that the CEO protected himself, and that the underlying issues with the resource allocation system were never discussed.

Self-Fulfilling and Self-Sealing Processes

Both writers found serious faults with the allocation system and the behavior of the CEO. They entered into the dialogue with doubts that the basic problems would be resolved. The way they crafted their conversations and censored them in order to cover up their thoughts and feelings made it likely that the problems identified in the cases would not be resolved by those conversations. Moreover, given the undiscussability of the left-hand columns and the Model I crafting of the conversation, it was unlikely that the parties would see that they were responsible for creating self-fulfilling processes as well as conditions under which these processes would not be discussed. Hence, their action strategies led to processes that sealed the dysfunctional processes, and these self-sealing processes were not discussed.

Case-Discussion Analysis

All the dysfunctions apparent in the cases should lead to the sense of helplessness and distancing identified in the map; and, indeed, these consequences were actually produced during the discussion of the cases in the two-day change seminar.

Larry: Here are some telling episodes from that discussion. My attitude in this conversation, and in the thirty-five times that I have had it in the last two years, is *not* that the CEO obstructs the solution. It is that there is literally no solution.

CEO: Yes, I agree with the conversation in the case. My thoughts and feelings were something along the lines of "Why are we bothering to have a conversation about something there is no decent answer to? We can solve 50 percent of this problem. But I wonder if we are going to talk about the 50 percent for which there is no answer."

   Several directors openly confirmed their sense of hopelessness. They also admitted that the only strategy left for them was to deal with the CEO individually and hold him responsible for solving the problem. They said they ask for more resources than they expect to get and they act as if this were not the case. The CEO, on the other hand, sensed this but covered up his views.

CEO: My left-hand column is that I will probably be asked to give each of you the eighteen people whose names you've written down.
   (*Later.*) I feel our discussions are useless because there is no flexibility on your part.
   (*Later.*) Everyone tends to use overly dramatic statements; therefore, I have to discount what you say, and of course act as if I am not doing so.

David: (*Tells the CEO that he does not realize how he causes the very problems that he wants to solve.*)

CEO: (*Disagrees that he causes the problems.*) If you all agree that we have too few people, then the majority of the problems are created by you fellows. Why can't you guys manage yourselves?

David: The problem is that each of us has different views of the rules.

CEO: I don't believe that. I have resisted exerting coercive power over you. You are allegedly both adults and my partners. I will never order you to do these things. If you want me [to become coercive], then you can have my letter of resignation.

Larry: What is the nature of the compensation scheme? On what basis are we rewarded?

CEO: I do run the compensation scheme as a political process in order to keep the coalition together. I have had the belief that some of these undiscussable issues would cause so much upheaval that I have deliberately made things vague. The alternative would be collective discussability, which I have always thought would be too disruptive.

Jim: Compensation that is dollars is a minority issue. The issue is self-worth and relative worth. We shouldn't kid ourselves.

Several directors: (*Discuss Jim, who brings more business to the firm than the others do. Some see him as arrogant and self-centered. Others are annoyed because they believe he gets most of the human resources, as well as keeping the best clients. The discussion is candid on all sides.*)

Jim: (*Says he feels he is in a bind.*) If I get the business, I am damned; if I did not, I would be damned. I work my butt off for the firm [and I am not appreciated].

John: I suspect that all of us envy you, and those feelings get in the way.

Let us pause here to examine other explanations that could be offered to account for the difficulties the directors expressed. One alternative explanation is that the directors had not thought through the allocation problems effectively. If they had a successful policy for allocating resources, the interpersonal problems would not exist, or at least would not be as strong. In response to this explanation, the directors would agree that a successful allocation policy would have helped. But the directors would also point out that they had made several attempts to define such policies during the past two years and had failed. They now realize that their Model I theories-in-use lead to the type of discussion that inhibited effective problem solving.

Another alternative explanation is that these problems were caused by rapid growth and fast success and were typical of organizations growing at a fast pace. Again, the directors would not disagree with this view. They stated it often. But, as the CEO noted, holding this view did not help them to manage each other better. Indeed, directors brought in successful plans from other organizations for coping with rapid growth, yet they got nowhere. The point of approaching the problems through learning Model II actions was not to deny these explanations, which were in fact known and accepted by the directors. The point was to find a way of fashioning and implementing policies and practices that would work to solve the problems the explanations represented. These explanations were valid inventions for the directors' problems. The difficulty was that Model I theories-in-use and organizational defensive routines got in the way when the directors tried to implement the obvious solutions of a resource allocation policy and a plan used successfully by others.

Signs of Learning

As the two-day seminar progressed, apparently inconsistent actions were observed. While most of the actions were guided by Model I theory-in-use, others, often little ones, suggested that Model II theory-in-use was being learned. (This imbalance of Model I over Model II is typical of most sessions during the early stages of intervention.)

The context of the episode reproduced here as an example was the discussion of a case in which the problem concerned a director evaluating a senior consultant. Some directors felt the case was not one from which they could learn. They made attributions that the writer chose the case in order to bypass difficult issues about his performance and to look good. The conversation is scored to show which actions are characteristic of Model I.

What Was Said	Scoring the Conversation
Jim: I find this case interesting but not very useful for our learning.	Advocacy; no illustration, no inquiry, no testing
Bill: Well, I checked it out with Chris [the intervener] . . .	
Jim: My left-hand side (*that is, his uncensored thought*) in reading the case is that you picked a bunny.	Evaluation; no illustration, no testing
Ted: I had the identical reaction. I thought it was the ultimate safe topic.	Evaluation; no inquiry, no illustration, no testing
David: I strongly disagree.	Advocacy; no illustration, no inquiry, no testing
Jim: Another left-hand attribution is that you resent being described as mushy or soft or chicken, and you wrote the case to prove you are none of these.	Attribution; no illustration, no inquiry, no testing
David: It does not surprise me at all that he wrote this case because it is a tough one, politically speaking, in the firm and the guy he wrote about is his friend.	Attribution; no inquiry, partial illustration, no testing
Larry: I think that Bill is trying to learn not to be mushy.	Attribution and evaluation: no inquiry, no illustration, no testing

Bill: What do you think
would have been a more appropriate case for me to write?

Jim: (*Answers with an
example.*)

Bill: I didn't remember that
incident.

Jim: My attribution is that [when you raise these issues] it takes the form of "Doctor, I have a friend who has a prob- lem." My read of your tone is that [you are saying to the indi- vidual in the case] "I have a problem with your behavior. I have a lot of anxiety about you." As I read it, my left-hand column was screaming, "This is a cop-out."	Evaluation; no illustration, no inquiry, no testing

Evaluation; no illustration, no inquiry, no testing

Evaluation and attribution; no illustration, no testing |
| *Bill:*   I agree with the first part and not the second. I believe you are wrong. | Evaluation; no illustration, no inquiry, no testing |

Larry: My impression of this
discussion is that we are exor-
cising ghosts again. It's not the
reality today. We are focusing
on ancient concerns.

Embedded in this primarily Model I dialogue were signs of
learning. For example, Jim raised doubts about the value the case
had for learning, and several directors decried the use of "bunny"
cases because a norm was developing that such cases did not provide
much food for learning.

Also, individuals were beginning to make public their un-
censored—or left-hand-column—thoughts, noting that before this

seminar the thoughts would have remained censored. Bill appeared to look for an example of an attribution when he asked them what case they thought would have been appropriate. Later, Jim began to use the concept of attribution, and he also revealed his feelings about Bill's tone in the case and his anxiety that Bill was copping out.

Finally, Larry stated that the discussion was focused on "ancient concerns." This eventually led to a discussion of how the case might represent current issues.

Summary

The cases written by the directors were consistent with Model I. This result was a revelation to each director. Each also expressed surprise by showing how unaware he had been about the extent to which he was using Model I as a theory-in-use.

The discussion of the cases was also based largely on Model I strategies, but there were signs that the directors were moving toward Model II. They began to make their real thoughts public and to use such concepts as evaluation and attribution.

The session concluded with the directors evaluating it positively. They acknowledged that they had a long way to go to develop the competency that they desired. Indeed, several said that they now realized that this program was truly continuous and probably never ending. They ended by committing energy, time, and resources to continue the program.

Part Three

USING KEY LEARNINGS
TO SOLVE
PROBLEM SITUATIONS

The next phase of the continuous improvement was to begin to use the learning developed to date to solve important organizational problems, while sharpening and deepening Model II skills.

The Directors' Experiments

In the eyes of the directors, this began the phase of creating their own experiments. They selected the organizational problems they wished to begin to solve. The types of problems selected varied with the director. The common theme, however, was that they were related to difficult and potentially embarrassing or threatening issues.

I believe that, with possibly one exception, the directors did not delay experimenting with the new ideas because of doubts about their applicability and relevance. The delays that occurred were much more related to finding the "right" opportunity and to developing the courage to try an experiment.

There are several reasons why *courage* is the appropriate word. First, the experiments represented rare events. No one in the history of the firm had attempted to do what was done during these experiments. Even though there had been many informal discussions that such actions were necessary, it had been accepted that they were not likely to occur. Second, none of the directors believed that they had developed adequate skills for acting consistently with Model II. Third, the directors could not predict accurately how others would react. Therefore, they were not confident that they could competently manage all possible reactions. However, they were less worried about their fellow directors than about others in the firm because the directors had developed a norm about encouraging learning.

I served as a facilitator for any director who asked for help. At the beginning all of them did so. I helped them to plan their intervention and participated in the intervention session. My task was to help the directors and others in the organization overcome difficult moments and to reduce the likelihood that events would get out of control.

As the reader will see from the transcripts, I did intervene at times to facilitate learning. These interventions appeared to have at least two consequences. They increased individuals' aspirations about what was dicussable and solvable. They also provided the directors with opportunities to practice their new skills.

There were times when the directors themselves realized they were acting counterproductively. In all these cases, they stopped, reflected on their awareness, and started all over again. Often the others pitched in to help them produce new actions. This led to an increasing sense of genuine collaboration in the service of learning. There were also moments when the directors did not appear to be aware of their counterproductive behavior. During the early sessions, the group relied on me for help in these instances, but as progress occurred, the group members, whether or not they had gone through an introductory session, took helpful initiatives.

My role in this phase raises the question of clients' dependency on the intervener. The directors said that my presence was crucial, even if I did not speak. They felt secure because they assumed that I would prevent the situation from escalating counterproductively if they lost control of it. Thus, it cannot be said that the early successes were accomplished by the directors acting alone.

However, it is also true that, as they gained confidence in their skills over the course of the five years discussed here, as others also learned the skills, and as double-loop learning became part of the organizational norms, I was no longer invited for sessions that years before had been considered important and "hot." Sometimes those sessions were taped, which provided my colleagues and me with data as to what had happened. The directors and others also chose to continue recording some sessions in order to listen to any sections that might be relevant for further learning. I believe that the presence of a tape recorder has a positive influence on learning, and it may well be that it goes with the territory, whether the intervener is present or not. However, meetings that would have been considered hot or dangerous five years ago are rarely seen that way today; hence, they are not taped (unless we ask for a tape for research purposes).

In the eyes of the participants, the experiments were trials of using a new set of skills to produce new consequences. They were not experimenting to test a theory; they were experimenting because they wanted to test and deepen their new skills. They were experimenting in the service of their learning. Nevertheless, if at any time they thought that they had used their new skills correctly, that they had acted consistently with Model II, and Model I consequences followed, then they would indeed question the theory with me and others. In all the cases of which I have direct or indirect knowledge, they learned that they had not acted consistently with Model II. Often they had produced hybrids of Models I and II, and they had focused on the latter.

The Researcher-Interveners' Experiments

In the eyes of the researcher-interveners, experimenting had an additional purpose—namely, testing features of our theory in such a way that fellow scholars would see the tests as valid. A number of factors are relevant to this determination of validity.

All the experiments occurred in settings where the experimenters—that is, individuals in the organization who initiated the experiment—knew that they would not have full unilateral control over the responses of others. Indeed, they did not seek such control, because it would violate the Model II theory-in-use that they were trying to learn and implement.

They also knew that they could not design an experiment

where they introduced one variable and systematically varied it. And, again, they did not seek such a possibility. Individuals designed their everyday experiments in order to accomplish whatever intent they had in mind. They were likely, therefore, to include as many variables as they thought would help. Because they tried to assure their outcomes, their actions may be overdetermined.

The experimenters also knew that they could not cover up their experimental manipulation. They wanted to get something accomplished. If an experimenter did not make that explicit at the outset, it was highly unlikely that the others would pay much attention to figuring out what he or she was up to, and this could inhibit the effective implementation of the experiment. Thus, the experimenters were faced with the challenge of making their intentions explicit while also making certain (as far as they could) that doing so was not the *cause* of whatever followed, because if the explicitness were the cause, the process involved would be Model I behavior.

As we shall see, the experimenters planned their experiments carefully. During the early years, they might spend several hours discussing the experiment with me. They discussed how to design it correctly, how to execute it, and how to react to unexpected consequences.

From my research perspective, in order for the experiments to provide a basis for judging claims about progress toward Model II and toward altering and reducing defensive patterns, they had to be designed to:

> Deal with issues that were nontrivial, that were complex and challenging, and that had the potential for activating embarrassment or threat.
>
> Be consistent with Model II action strategies and governing values. There were a few cases, for example, in which outside clients had given many overt and covert cues that they did not wish to design their relationships to be consistent with Model II. It would be a mistake to use such a setting for an experiment, not because it could not produce valuable information but because the client might discuss the consultants. I should add that there were sev-

eral cases where the consultants took that risk and, in all cases, progress was made.

Allow players to be free to admit that they were novices. In addition to solving the business problem, they wanted to practice their new skills. This meant that each experiment included solving an important problem, practicing new skills, reflecting on the progress of the experiment, and encouraging others to do the same.

Take into account the context in which they were being conducted. Experiments in everyday life are not separable from that life, as experiments might be in university laboratory settings.

Be interrupted and challenged by the participants. Experiments that are not reframable by their subjects are likely to create many difficulties, especially in an organization whose participants are striving to move toward Model II values and action strategies.

The transcripts discussed in Part Three provide illustrations of the types of data that were developed from the experiments meeting these criteria. Once again, researchers with different frameworks can use these transcripts to make their own analyses.

Whatever the limits the experiments may be found to have, they will not be related to some of the more controversial issues about experiments (Greenberg & Folger, 1988). For example, they will not, I suggest, fail to provide informed consent; and they will not use deception, be short on debriefing, ignore possible demand characteristics, or ignore the possibility of explicitly exploring experimenter bias. These experiments could never have been conducted without the consent of the participants. In turn, it was not likely that they would have given their permission to be deceived (indeed, to ask such permission would violate Model II). Debriefing occurred in spades, during and after the experiment. The possibility that the intervener's biases were confounding explanations or learning was continually explored by the participants.

Finally, wherever possible I included descriptions of my behavior as the intervener. I tried to illustrate how an intervener can further participants' learning by modeling the use of the theory of action being taught to the participants. I hope these descriptions will give the researcher and professional a glimpse of the skills required to be a facilitator. (For further details, see Argyris & Schön, 1974, 1978; Argyris, 1982, 1985b.)

7

Explosive Relationships: Stopping Button Pushing

The first experiments I will describe began about six months after the case-discussion seminar and continued for two years. The topic of these experiments was button pushing—namely, producing conversation that upsets another because the content activates the receiver's defenses.

For several reasons, I have selected to focus on the relationship between the CEO and the director I will now call David. First, it represented one of the more difficult relationships, and both had serious doubts that their relationship could be anything but poor and difficult. Indeed, David wondered if he might not have to leave the firm someday. Second, the CEO and David have developed today what they would describe as a very positive relationship. This does not mean that they agree on everything, although they agree on more issues than they did when the continuous improvement program began. I believe both will say that the basis for the positive evaluation is that each can express differences without alienating the other. At the time of this writing, David no longer considers leaving as a serious choice.

The third reason for selecting this experiment is that it represents one of the most frequent types of experiments attempted by the directors. Pairs of directors would meet to work through their

157

respective button-pushing fears. Some directors solved their problems in one meeting, or solved them well enough that they could continue the learning without my help. Others required two to three sessions. I was kept informed of the progress. I, as well as directors who were not involved in a particular dyad, could see the differences during board meetings. The directors who had worked through their problem dealt with each other differently. Also, they would openly continue the learning during the board meetings when they felt that their interpersonal issues were getting in the way of solving business problems. Once in a while, a pair of directors would state openly that they were having a problem, and that the cause or solution was not relevant to furthering the board's problem solving, and they would stop the discussion of their own problem but continue it after the meeting.

The fourth reason is that the directors often learned from their sessions with fellow directors to experiment with similar sessions with their own subordinates, many of whom had not been through case-discussion change seminars. The practice spread when case-team managers held similar sessions with team members. In some instances, many of the team members had not participated in a change seminar although some had. In other instances, discussions of team effectiveness were combined with a case-discussion seminar, for which team members wrote cases related to a particular set of client and case-team issues.

The Experiment

David and the CEO were not satisfied with their working relationship. Each held the other in very high respect regarding key features of his role. David evaluated the CEO as a brilliant strategist, a first-rate analyst, probably the best at attracting new clients, and completely dedicated to the job. The CEO evaluated David as completely loyal and a first-rate director when it came to dealing with certain kinds of technical problems in the industrial world.

Their views as to how to manage professionals differed. The strategies that one evaluated as effective, the other saw as ineffective. What one saw as maintaining control, the other saw as overbearing and unnecessary. What one saw as a diligent audit, the other saw as unbridled mistrust.

For example, David believed that he was good at monitoring and controlling costs. He could see, better than most directors, where money was being wasted. He was ready to be tough and stop "fiscal nonsense." During one of our sessions, he said to the CEO, "Let me tell you, I am a faithful, loyal individual. I'm like your faithful dog. I will be there to protect the company. However, I lack confidence to achieve this on my own. If someone gives me some pats on the back, then my capacity to be faithful is enhanced. But if I do not get rewards [that I believe I deserve], then [I will not be as effective a director as I can be]."

Because of previous conversations the CEO had with me in order to examine his own defensiveness about some of David's actions, I knew that the CEO would agree with David's statement but feared discussing it openly because he did not evaluate such loyalty as an unmitigated good. When the CEO actually heard David's statement, he was able to say, "I am surprised that you are saying this. I am pleased to hear you say this. I think that your diagnosis is correct. But I never thought you would be honest with me. [This frees me up to be more candid with you.]"

David replied that he was pleased to hear that, because he believed that the CEO did not realize how candid and open he (David) could be. He also admitted that he wondered how candid and open the CEO could be when he himself made an error, saying, "I think that you hate to admit that you are wrong."

I intervened to point out that both were making evaluations and attributions about each other. I asked each to illustrate, from his experience, the kind of data he was using to arrive at his evaluations and attributions. This led each to learn that his descriptions of what had happened were not confirmed by the other. Each held different meanings of the problem and—because of incorrect evaluations and attributions—each blamed the other. Each also learned that the other was willing to discuss undiscussables—indeed, was eager to do so. Such learning made both of them more optimistic that problems each had considered uninfluenceable were likely to be alterable after all.

A different level of learning had to do with their practicing

Model II skills. For example, I intervened (consistently with the ladder of inference) to ask them to illustrate their evaluations or attributions with relatively directly observable data. What did they recall about the actual conversation? After one gave his best recollection, I would ask the other if he could confirm the description and to what extent he would draw the same inferences. In other words, I was modeling the behavior that they had begun to learn during the case-discussion seminar. After several such discussions, I rarely had to model such behavior again.

I also focused on the consequences of certain behaviors that I inferred were important yet were not being identified. For the most part, the directors did not discuss them because they required making inferences the directors did not feel competent to make. For example, I told David that I was concerned about the degree to which he needed others to reinforce his self-confidence and self-esteem. His need could make him counterproductively dependent on his fellow directors. The CEO agreed, adding that he did not seek relationships with fellow directors when the relationships would have such built-in dependencies. David had not realized that such a consequence could occur.

I then raised the possibility that his blindness to this possibility could also be operating in his relationships with his subordinates. For example, he might define effective loyalty on the part of his subordinates the same way he defined it for himself, leading his subordinates to infer that he wanted them to be "faithful dogs." David responded that he could understand the logic and found it disconcerting.

Several months later, an opportunity arose that provided a test of what David and the CEO learned in these sessions. A board meeting was to be held where the director of a new office, whom I will call Carl, was to report on progress. The CEO had been a champion of creating this new business activity. David had serious doubts about Carl's performance. He evaluated the office as performing poorly in terms of internal management and attracting new clients.

David also felt that the CEO was not being tough enough on Carl. He felt that, as a director, he had to ask some tough questions. Yet he also felt that such tough questioning would upset the CEO. David talked with me to design his action in such a way that he could communicate his concerns without "turning off" the CEO or other directors. David said to me, in effect, that he did not want to reproduce the counterproductive actions of the past, but he was not confident that he could avoid doing so. We see that David had learned to identify potentially counterproductive actions ahead of time and recognized that he needed help in crafting his conversation to avoid unwanted results.

I recommended a meeting with the CEO to discuss the dilemma. David looked at me with a sense of concern and said, "Are you sure that he won't go ballistic?" I replied that I could not guarantee anything except that the CEO was committed to learning. He could become upset, but I would be there to help transform it into an opportunity for learning if David felt that he could not transform it himself.

I also recommended that David practice how he would communicate his views to the CEO. He agreed, and we worked on crafting various positions for a few hours. Almost half the time, what he crafted would probably have led to the CEO's becoming upset. David then would reflect on the incongruity between the probable results and his intentions. After several iterations, he said, "I think that my biggest problem is not with Carl but with the CEO. I think he is too weak with Carl."

Two kinds of learning appeared to occur. First, David experimented with crafting his views in ways that were consistent with Model II. Second, as he experimented, he began to realize that some of the anger he thought he had toward Carl was anger toward the CEO. He did not condone Carl's poor performance, but his biggest problems were related to the fact that the CEO appeared to condone such poor performance. As we continued our sessions, David began to see that he feared the CEO's behavior could lead the company out of control.

David decided to ask for a meeting to discuss how he could address both Carl's poor performance and his own concerns about the CEO's behavior. He opted to begin by discussing his fears about asking tough questions during the directors' meeting.

David: I want to be free to say the things that are important during our next directors' meeting. I understand that you have some concerns about my potential impact on Carl when he makes his presentation.

My purpose is to understand Carl's performance so that I can posture myself vis-à-vis him in ways that clarify things for all concerned and add value.

I'm afraid, quite frankly, that I may have more incredulous interactions than others, [and if I am not careful] I could act in ways that may be detrimental for everybody [at that meeting].

CEO: I don't understand your concerns.

I recall thinking that the CEO did understand some of David's concerns and that he was trying to get David to be more explicit. I chose not to test this attribution because it would have interrupted the flow of the conversation. My rule is to intervene when I see overt actions that produce self-sealing, anti-learning conditions or when participants have acted in ways that might produce such consequences. I strive to make such interventions when I can illustrate the point by referring to directly observable data.

David: Let me give you a scenario. I would like to ask Carl about his financial performance. I'd like to ask him directly about his marketing objective, . . . successes, and failures.

CEO: [Carl will make presentations on those subjects.]

David: Do you or he object if I ask fairly tough questions?

CEO: I don't know. Help me. Of course, I cannot object to tough questions.

David: My first questions would be (*explains*).

CEO: If you say "profitable," he will get mad because the goal this year is to break even. (*States that David and other directors may have let Carl down by not providing the billings that they promised.*)

David: Are you attributing that we let Carl down?

CEO: Yes, that is a correct attribution.

David: I would have a big problem with that. Could you illustrate that? I do not remember being asked to do that. I have a problem with that.

Intervener: I hear two messages. As far as the next directors' meeting, if you question Carl the way you role-played here, you would get yourself in the trouble that you say you do not wish to produce.

  The second message is that you have made assumptions about Carl's goals that turn out to be not true. [For example, you thought the goals were profitability; the CEO thought that they were to break.] CEO, Would you tell David your concerns about Carl's performance?

CEO: I'm dreadfully concerned about Carl's performance. (*Explains.*)

  The intent of my intervention here was to help David see that the CEO was also concerned about Carl's performance. When the CEO described some of the steps that he was taking with Carl, David would feel, I hypothesized, that things were not as out of control as he feared and that the CEO was not as weak as he had assumed.

David: Do you accept that I am telling you I didn't know about what was really going on?

CEO: I have no reason to disbelieve you. I don't understand why you didn't know about it. . . . It doesn't really matter.

David: To me, it does matter. As a responsible member of the corporate community, I will be happy to [fulfill my obligations]. If I'm at fault, I need to know it.

  (*Later.*) I'm trying to figure out whether they're losing money or not.

CEO: They are not going to make money this year under any circumstances.

David: I'm trying to figure out whether or not they're losing money. Is there something wrong with that? (*Said with increasing feeling.*)

(*Later.*) Aren't we all responsible for making money for each other?

CEO: Yes, but you're not acting that way.

David: What am I doing wrong?

CEO: You want to shoot Carl because he's losing your money.

David: I am asking you a question of fact. You're defending Carl. I don't even know what the facts are.

Intervener: (*Later.*) May I try this another way? Isn't it true, David, that you have doubts about the CEO's leadership?

There were at least two interventions that I could have made. The first was to ask the CEO to test his evaluations and attributions about David. The second was to get to the undiscussable—namely, David's doubts about the CEO's capacity to be tough. Given the conservation that follows, I think that I selected the wrong strategy. The CEO and David were not ready to discuss the undiscussable. Moreover, I think that David was feeling that he was acting consistently with Model II. He was pleased with himself. He was practicing new skills. David confirmed these attributions later.

David: I'm trying to understand if they [Carl's office] are losing money as we speak. I do not think I am being deceptive. Do you think I'm being deceptive? Misleading?

CEO: No, I think you are not being clear. . . . And every time I don't understand, I get into making negative attributions about you (without testing them].

David: (*Later.*) My left-hand side [uncensored] comment is that that's bull.

CEO: My left-hand side is [that you want me to act in ways that will allow you to] go to the directors' meeting and axe Carl. And you want to get my permission to do it.

Intervener: (*Asks David what the CEO said or did that led David to evaluate the action as bull.*)

David: (*Responds by surfacing some of his worst fears—ones that he had not hitherto discussed.*)

Intervener: (*To CEO.*) Where does that attribution about David come from? I hear David saying that he wants to go to the directors' meeting to be constructive. What are the data that you have that say that he wants to axe Carl?

David: Honestly, I'm trying to avoid [creating the same situation that we had several years ago with someone else].

CEO: (*Later.*) I honestly, and I'm going to say this as clearly as I can, I honestly want you to ask any questions you want to ask. I am concerned about how you craft the questions. [For example, Carl is worried that he will be thrown to a bunch of sharks at the board meeting.]

David: [I find this helpful.] I am accustomed that you and I go directly at each other. If you are telling me that Carl is fragile, for whatever reason, I would respect that.

CEO: Yes, I think Carl is fragile.
(*Later.*) But I don't think that his fragility should prevent us from discussing the substance of any question.

David: I will be happy to manage [my actions] in ways that are constructive. That is one of the reasons that I asked for this session.

CEO: (*Differentiates between Carl and the business Carl heads. He feels he is not overprotecting Carl. He has been up front about Carl's limits with Carl himself. I can verify that because I took part in several such sessions. He is concerned about the business performance of the office that Carl heads.*)

David: (*Says he understands the differentiation and that he wants to try to make the business plan work out.*)

Intervener: (*Later. To CEO.*) As I see it, David is trying to tell you that he is trying to change his behavior and the way he crafts his doubts. Also, if I understand it, when David does not get the information that he believes he needs, he easily feels out of control. [Soon he acts like the mistrustful person you wish he would not be.]

CEO: I accept that. . . . Did you hear me saying that he is not changing?

Intervener: I'd like to answer by reviewing this episode. David started by saying that he did not want to be disruptive at the directors' meeting. (*Illustrates.*) I thought that he crafted the introduction well. You responded by, in effect, saying that you did not want David to harm Carl. Moreover, David had wrong data and if he used these data, he would harm Carl.

I was wondering how you knew he wanted to do that? I thought that he said he asked for the meeting to prevent such an occurrence.

CEO: [That's helpful.] I believe [now] that David does not want to screw up the meeting.

Intervener: [And if you recall,] David said that he found it helpful to learn that Carl was feeling brittle.

CEO: There are two things that have been said in this room that are the keys to my nervousness. The first is, as you said, David, that you have lousy data. . . . If you do not have good data, then how can you make a judgment?

Intervener: May I interrupt? I don't find that fair. All of us have the right to make judgments. Is not your problem that, with lousy data, he is likely to make things worse? He could precipitate the very consequences that he (and you) do not want.

David: That's why I need better data.

(*Later.*) Can I stop for one second? We started out this conversation in a highly adversarial fashion.

Intervener: (*To David.*) You didn't.

David: Yes, you're right. (*Turns to CEO.*) I don't know why you went ballistic. I genuinely do not know. I expected that you would, and I was prepared for that. But I wanted it to occur here and not at the meeting.

CEO: You were interested in two things that I can't stand. Office profitability and [judging] a whole new start-up venture by the same standards as an ongoing business.

David: I accept that. . . .

CEO: So I'm really fed up with it. And this is not an attribution to you personally but an attribution to several directors. [You guys are unfair in the way you deal with the new start-up.]

David: And I'm tired of those guys playing off both sides of the street on this office profitability.

Intervener: (*Later.*) I suggest that this issue be discussed at the upcoming board meeting [since this problem is not only David's].

CEO: Yes, I have no problem discussing it.

The board meeting was held. David did ask some of his tough questions. He also prefaced his inquiry by noting that the CEO and he had had a session before this one to provide him the opportunity to practice crafting tough questions in a competent mode. He said that he was going to try to do so, but that he did not guarantee perfection. He invited his fellow directors to intervene if and when they thought he might be acting counterproductively.

Several directors, including the CEO, nodded their heads approvingly. No one went ballistic during the questioning period.

Several months later, David told me that he wanted to continue working on the problem of going ballistic with anyone. He asked about ten consultants and case-team managers to meet with him in order to explore his leadership behavior. In my opinion, the session was open and David handled himself well. He never went ballistic when several consultants accused him of being overbearing and, as several said, rude. David admitted that he acted in these ways and that he had called this meeting to reduce the likelihood of these actions.

He added, however, the fears that he had experienced with some of them. He described how they made promises they did not keep and how they would not help him get ballpark estimates to a demanding client because they needed to run the numbers, which would take several weeks.

According to the CEO and others, David is showing important changes in his actions. However, there is still one area in which he blows up. It is when young consultants deal with their weaknesses by blaming the system and then accusing the directors, for example, of acting in a noncaring manner. David admits that "it blows my mind that I am working long hours, putting myself on the line, struggling to create a supportive world, and then [some people] bitch. Then I think of how much they get paid and I really get upset."

Summary

The CEO and David were able to change a highly dissatisfying and counterproductive relationship—which they, and most of the directors, had considered unimprovable—to a productive one that brought a great deal of satisfaction not only to the CEO but to the other directors. One experiment led to another, and that to another. This example illustrates continuous improvement at its best, because not only was there progress but neither of the participants had to coerce the other into holding these meetings. Both participants felt responsible for designing the meetings and continuing them as needed. These results also held true for the other directors as they dealt with their respective button-pushing problems.

In addition, several directors and consultants who were "near" directors took initiatives independently of each other to explore some of the problems they were experiencing with the younger consultants (Argyris, 1991).

8

Mistrust: Overcoming Resentment and Rebuilding Trust

In this chapter, I will describe a discussion session about button pushing that occurred about three years after the one described in Chapter Seven. This session involved two directors who at an earlier time had not reported any button-pushing problems with each other. However, these problems did arise after the directors experienced certain business-client episodes.

Once each director sensed that they both were having problems, they decided to meet and invited me to attend. However, as the reader will see, the two directors managed the session well, and I was active only twice.

The meetings described in this chapter also illustrate the point that it is not possible to eliminate all problems; new ones will always arise. The challenge is to develop a learning culture in which the new problems can be dealt with effectively.

Directors John and Ted had known each other since the early days of the firm. Recently, John began to mistrust Ted and distanced himself from Ted. Ted noticed the distancing and responded by distancing himself from John. However, neither saw distancing as the appropriate long-range strategy. When both asked if I would meet with them so that they could resolve their issues, I agreed and we met for about three hours a week later.

My role as intervener was once again to demonstrate Model II behavior and interrupt counterproductive behavior. As a researcher, I could check the content of the transcripts in several ways to continue the test of my theories. One check would be the frequency with which the directors advocated, evaluated, or attributed in ways that illustrated their views and encouraged inquiry and testing. A second check would be the degree to which the directors identified self-sealing, anti-learning patterns in their relationship. A third check would be the degree to which the conversation led to the surfacing of causal factors that neither John nor Ted was aware of when the conversation began. All these checks were designed to reveal the practice of Model II behavior.

(Sessions like this one, in which I make a number of brief observations about the conversation, are presented in parallel columns with my remarks on the right.)

The Conversation	*Intervener's Observations*
John: The reason that I have come to this meeting is to discuss our relationship. I do not find myself trusting you. I should like to give you my data and the reasons behind my conclusions. Needless to say, I want your reactions, especially where you believe I may be seeing things incorrectly or drawing the wrong conclusions.	John begins the session by identifying the problem openly; he says he wants to correct it, is ready to provide his data, and asks for Ted's confirmation or disconfirmation.
Ted: I, too, very much want this meeting. I have always felt that I had a pretty good relationship [with you]. I am mystified, and I would like a chance to explain myself.	Ted supports holding this meeting because he wants to correct the situation. Ted says that he is mystified, which could be viewed by John as an invitation to begin.
My attribution to you the last time we communicated was	

that you did not trust me, and I would like to understand why.

(*Later.*) I hope that I can dissuade John of the notion that I'm not trustworthy.

Ted communicates directly that he wants to rebuild trust.

John: I have the same purpose. I want to convince myself to trust you. I want to understand [how all this got created] and correct the situation.

(*Describes several voice mail messages he received from Ted about client Middleco. Ted had told John that he was going to be talking with the CEO of Middleco, who was Ted's client. John began to be concerned because Ted seemed to be making*) twenty-seven apologies for going to see this guy.

(*John says he then learned through another voice mail message that Ted had set up a specific meeting with the Middleco CEO. John began to wonder if Ted was cutting in on his relationship with Middleco.*)

So, I asked myself, why do you send me this apologetic voice mail about the possibility of meeting the Middleco CEO and then go ahead and set a specific meeting with him, and tell me that I need not be there?

What was I supposed to think? Did you really mean to ask me if it was okay to meet with the Middleco CEO? Or were you telling me [in a roundabout way] what you were going to do anyway?

[I have been working hard developing my relationship with Middleco; then to] sort of have somebody, in large part, unauthorized, in a behind-your-

John had brought with him a transcript of the message to present the relatively directly observable data and to show how he made the inference that he did.

John did not include the message as evidence to clinch his case as much as to make available the data that led him to begin to mistrust Ted.

John used the data as the basis from which both could learn. For example, when I read the transcript later, I did find the apologies John described. (I did not read the transcript during the meeting because it was not necessary.)

back style, [take Middleco] in a
direction I am not happy about
is upsetting.

And if you had straight out
told me you were going to do
this whether I liked it or not
[instead of the apologies], then
it would have been out in the
open, and we could have had a
good fight.

You keep telling me that I
am the number one guy in this
relationship. . . . You say
things to seemingly please me,
but your actions are not
consistent.

*Ted: (Responds that he is
finding John's description
helpful. Supplies his version of
the history.)*

My attribution is that you   Ted provides his view of the re-
have historically overreacted to   lationship and concludes with
my conversations with the Mid-   his attribution, which he illus-
dleco CEO, which is why I tap   trates. He also describes
dance around and send you   thoughts and feelings that he
voice mails with fifteen apolo-   had waited until this session to
gies. (*Illustrates.*) I am trying to   describe.
be helpful, [but I do fear that]
I'm going to get my face shot
off. So that's why I tap dance
around. [You know me. I do
not like such conflicts.]

(*Explains that the dialogue
he had with the Middleco CEO
was at the Middleco CEO's initiative, with [Ted and John's]
CEO in attendance. The Mid-*

*dleco CEO raised certain logis-
tical issues, which Ted's CEO
promised him would be re-
solved. After the meeting, Ted's
CEO told Ted to call John to
tell him about the conversation,
but John was not available, so
Ted talked with the case-team
leader.)*

All the conversations that I had with Middleco, [our] CEO was part of. So the notion that I secretly abrogated some arrangements already made [is not correct]. I wasn't trying to hide anything from you.

I had the meeting with your case-team leader since it was low-level logistics stuff. [I have nothing to gain by intervening.] I cannot service Middleco as well as you can; you know much more about the substantive issues of their business.

I guess I resent the attribution that you think that I prompt those meetings with Middleco. I guess that I resent the attribution that somehow I would tell the Middleco CEO that you are not in charge.

The Middleco CEO expressed nervousness [about logistics]. I tried to talk with you. You were in a client meeting so I talked with the case-team leader. [And besides] it was

Ted describes that the CEO (of the consulting firm) was there and that Middleco had taken the initiative.

Ted expresses his feeling of resentment. One could infer a degree of discomfort from his having to preface the expression of these genuine feelings with "I guess."

Note that he did not attempt to escalate this into a demand for an apology or to counter with the assertion that John was not to be trusted.

[our] CEO who took the action steps, and I said that I would voice-mail you.

John: All I know is that when [our] CEO initially voice-mailed me, he included you because he said that you, Ted, were instrumental in developing this client and that I was tending the Middleco CEO over the last couple of years.

    [I was upset that the CEO was describing my relationship with the Middleco CEO that way because it is a much more important one than tending.]

John gives clues that he believes that he is the senior relationship manager and that CEO may be giving Ted unnecessary and unfair credit.

Ted: (*Does not respond directly to John's concerns by assuring him—in abstract terms—that he sees John as in charge. Rather, he gives a long, detailed description of how, in several meetings, he told the Middleco CEO that John was the best officer for the relationship. He provides relatively directly observable data that John can easily check with others.*)

    In a recent telephone call, the Middleco CEO said to me that he was more comfortable talking about certain issues with me because we are old friends. And I said, "Okay, but John's the guy in charge." And he said, "That's fine." He has a great respect for you and your case-team leader.

Intervener: (*To John.*) How credible do you find his description?

John: Well, I don't know. (*To Ted.*) I mean, I guess I have a greater understanding [that you see me in charge].

    [I find myself feeling irritated because several of us have worked hard and racked up

John expresses his fears that because Ted is a friend of the Middleco CEO, John and his group will not get deserved credit for the big payoff.

nontrivial costs over a three-
year period, in order to deepen
the relationship.] And now that
the big payoff is here, it looks
like there may be a big shadow
[over our role].

Ted: (*Asks if John feels penalized for the costs absorbed in order to develop the client.*)

John: (*Responds that he was not penalized but also*) not rewarded. Zero reward. None.

Ted: And you think that you will not get rewarded [for having now developed a victory]?

John: Well, part of the reward is monetary. It's the psychic benefits that are as [important as the monetary benefits, if not more so]. I like having these clients and applying an intellectual agenda that makes things happen.
(*Makes an attribution about Ted's intention.*)

These comments suggest that John may also have concerns that his CEO and partners do not realize the important role he has played in developing the relationship. Being rewarded for this role is more important to him than being the partner in charge of the relationship.

Ted: Why do you say that?

John: Well, because every time I mention it, you just deny it and act like it didn't exist!

Ted: Where have I denied it and acted as if it didn't exist?

Intervener: Can you recollect what Ted said or did that led you to believe he denied your efforts?

I try to focus the conversation on John's recollection of relatively directly observable data.

John: Yes. (*Describes several situations.*)

Ted: All I know is that the Middleco CEO expressed concern about the logistics stuff.

John: [And my fear was that you might unhook the agreement that we had made with Middleco.]

Intervener: (*Later.*) Are you attributing to Ted that he unrealizingly could say things to the Middleco CEO [that would harm your agreements with Middleco]?

John: Yes.

Ted: Realizingly or unrealizingly?

John: I think unrealizingly, I hope unrealizingly.

Ted: [This is helpful.] I'm listening.
   (*Listens to John, then points out that John's concerns stem from the assumption that Ted knew the budget details of the agreement.*) I didn't have a clue.

Intervener: You remember that John began this session by describing your strategy of dealing with difficult issues as being apologetic and "mealy-mouthed" (to use his term). John may feel that when you get into interpersonal conflict, you may hem and haw and, whether you intend it or not, you may give the Middleco CEO the wrong message. I return to the issues of John's worry that Ted could unrealizingly communicate counterproductive information to Middleco.

Ted: I think that I did tap dance in the voice mail. But I do not think that is an illustration of how I normally behave toward him in the event of interpersonal conflict. That's wrong.

John: I guess that Chris [intervener] is on target.

Intervener: A few minutes ago you said that you did tap dance around because you did not want to upset John. Maybe that is the kind of data that illustrates John's fears.

John: Yes, and when I met with the Middleco CEO, he was acting as if he did not make a deal. [Then I wondered what had gone on between him and Ted.]

Ted: [I am still bewildered] that you think that I sent a message to the Middleco CEO that undercut you.

John and Ted: (*Converse about what was said during the meetings at which John was not present.*)

Intervener: (*Listens for any cues that might illustrate John's fears; does not hear any. Asks Ted,*) Is it fair to say that, as best as you can recollect, neither you nor your CEO said to the Middleco CEO something like this: "We want to be of help to you, Middleco, but we want to make it clear that we have no intention of coming between John and you"?	Ted had described several conversations that should be reassuring to John. I felt that none of these were as direct with the Middleco CEO as John would have wished. I tested the hypothesis by asking Ted directly.

Ted: We did not say that. But I have known the Middleco CEO for years. I would not have thought of saying that.

    I was also nervous in that I didn't want to get too much into John's turf. And, I did not ask John about his deal with Middleco because I thought I'd get yelled at.

Intervener: This is an example of John's fears. You dance around something that could upset John. (*Turning to John.*) And he does so, he states, because he worries about you.

John: (*Later.*) Getting the credit and getting the bacon are	We are now beginning to develop the outline of a series of

[important]. I do not want to lose this one. I don't want to get stuff unsold that is sold.

And Ted, it is going to take me a while to get to the point where I do not worry about credit. [Our compensation scheme encourages credit.]

I mean that you live in a different world on that front.

self-fueling processes that lead to counterproductive consequences. The processes are not instigated from competitive win/lose motives. They are created by each director making attributions about undiscussability and influenceability, not testing the attributions, and assuring himself that a test would make things worse.

Intervener: In what sense?

John: Well, he has an older and more mature relationship with [our] CEO.

Intervener: Do you think that this may lead the CEO to favor him on compensation?

We now widen the self-fueling processes to begin to include John's concerns about the CEO and Ted.

John: I think that he has less to worry about.

Intervener: Do you have any data to illustrate these attributions?

Ted: I'd be happy to tell you about my compensation. In 1989, it went down; in 1990, it went down a lot.

John: But why do you say that? I never said that. I never said that you get a great deal. I said you had a great understanding.

Intervener: (*To John.*) Wait a minute. I asked you that. Your response (*recalls the response*) [seemed to say] he might make more money. Because he had a "better" relationship with this firm's CEO, he is more likely to get more favorable treatment.

John: I believe that's what I said. I didn't say that he would get more money.

Intervener: Okay. Fair enough.

John: I chose my words carefully.

Ted: Okay. I apologize, because I read something else into it.

Intervener: [Both of you are clarifying constructively.] I, too, misunderstood.

Ted: [But let me stand this problem on its head.] I've known the Middleco CEO for years. [John wants to act as if] I don't exist. And that reinforces in me a view that he is incredibly paranoid. Well, [that may be too harsh.] But that is why I tap dance around.

Ted introduces a second set of feelings (the first set was the feelings of resentment that he would cut in on the relationship).

Here's what I feel. John never acknowledges that I ever had a role with Middleco. Second, John accuses me of something that I believe the data do not support. I don't know what to do. I'm in a bind. My defensive instinct is to try to stay completely out of it. [But I realize that is defensive.]

Ted begins to define the defensive double-bind consequences of the self-fueling processes as he experiences them.

Ted expresses a desire not to distance himself and not to "give up."

Intervener: I agree that is not going to work.

John: [This is helpful.] I guess now, if I had to do it over again, I would say that this is your relationship. It's not fun for me. It is a chore.

John begins to understand Ted's views but now sees more clearly his own bind. He seeks to be more central with Middleco, something that is not likely to occur because of the Middleco CEO's friendship with Ted. But his solution is one of distancing, and he thinks

that distancing should occur
from the outset.

Ted: May I ask, do you believe that it will continue to be
a chore? Once you guys get going and he sees the quality of
your work, I think I'm going to
disappear into the sunset.

Intervener: John, is there any
way he can be of help to you
with Middleco, without your
feeling that he is trying to take
something away from you?

I wanted to ask John to explore
ways in which Ted could maintain a close relationship with
the Middleco CEO without
John's feeling concerned.

John: Maybe I'm just de-
spondent about it. For whatever
reason, I seek a heightened
sense of being in more control—with the client—over the
agenda. [I've worked for years
to be my own boss, and now
this feels like going backward.]

We are now adding an additional dimension to the self-
fueling processes. John seeks to
document to the CEO and his
fellow directors that he can get
and build client relationships.
He wonders if they see his contributions clearly; hence, he is
concerned about Ted's actions
because they may dilute the others' views of his own
performance.

Intervener: [Your reputation during the last five years has gone
up, and continues to do so.] Is there a point at which you can be
so sure of your reputation that Ted can be of help without your
feeling that he may be robbing you of the fun?

John: Yes. [The more I think of it, it is as much of a problem in
my relationship with our CEO.] I just didn't like to hear on the
voice mail that I was "tending" the relationship . . .

Ted: And my dilemma is that [I have a high respect for you], but

I fear I will say something that [pushes your button]. I don't feel like you're my subordinate.

John: No, I do not feel that, and haven't for a couple of years.

Intervener: Are you [John] interruptible?

John: [Yes.]

Intervener: Maybe you do sound a bit like being his subordinate. If you had your own inner confidence about yourself and how the CEO and your fellow directors evaluate you, then Ted could do anything with the Middleco CEO [that helps] without your worrying.

John: But if he messes it up, I'll get mad. And I've viewed him as coming close to messing up what I had developed.

Intervener: And why not discuss that with him?

John: Well, I was trying to do that in the voice mail. It is just one of these dreaded nasty, wicked issues. When I get mad, I do not mind chewing out someone. But Ted is a colleague.

Intervener: (*To Ted.*) How would you have felt if he had said some of these things to you?

Ted: I would have much preferred it.

(*Later.*) I think I am mature enough not to communicate messages to the Middleco CEO that will undercut John.

Moreover, I'm not getting any credit for this thing.

As to the CEO's description, I think he crafted it badly. I do not think that I developed the relationship and that you "tend" it.

John: It's hard to tell with the CEO. Sometimes his words [pop in, and sometimes they are designed].

But it seems to me that I can test these out with him.

At this point, John returned to the idea that he was acting as if he were subordinate to Ted. He was clear that he did not feel that way, but as a result of the ensuing conversation, he began to see how he could be giving others the impression of acting like a subordinate, because he appeared overworried (too touchy) about Ted's actions.

As the discussions produced a more explicit map of the self-fueling processes, the participants in this session (as well as other participants in other sessions) were able to examine other undiscussable issues or to discuss issues that had been surfaced but could be analyzed further. It was as if they now wanted to test all their hitherto undiscussed fears to see the degree to which they could be connected to the self-fueling processes. Problems that were connectable were no longer explainable by attributing negative intentions—such as mistrust—to others, nor by designing adaptive actions such as distancing. Once these tests were made jointly, it became possible to design new actions, as John and Ted began to do at the conclusion of their joint discussions and testing.

Ted: John, where do we go from here? I don't know what to do next.

John: Well, it's not totally without hope. First, please tell me what is on your mind. [Suspend your tap dancing.]

I will try to counter by being constructive when you are telling me something that you do not think I will agree with. [I will try to act in ways that do not activate your fears.]

(*Describes in more detail what the new relationship could look like.*)

Ted: I'm incredibly comfortable with what you are saying.

John: (*Later. Observes that he feels the Middleco CEO is a*) crafty dog [who might try to pit me against you in order to get what he wants—for example, more services at a lower price].

Ted: (*Presents some supportive evidence.*)

(*Later.*) One thing that I would like to be able to do is to talk to the Middleco CEO without worrying.

John: I agree. [And this conversation has helped me to reduce my concerns and to express any new ones if they arise.]

Ted: May I suggest a few rules of thumb for us? (*Describes them, including ways that he and John would act to prevent the self-*

fueling processes from being activated or, if they are activated, to interrupt them.)

This chapter illustrates that individuals who are learning Model II have not forgotten Model I and may use it when they are upset and angry. Once the anger is expressed, the individuals are able to reflect on the negative impact they are having on each other and to correct it. They become reflective practitioners (Schön, 1983). Episodes like these have become turning points in the relationships of the participants. For example, John and Ted report, two years later, that their relationship continues to be positive and that, in turn, has led to more effective joint relationships with clients.

9

New Team Leadership: Managing the Clash of Expectations and Needs

The case examined in this chapter represents, I believe, a thoughtful discussion by two consultants of several perennial problems in case-team management: educating a new acting case-team leader, reducing misunderstandings due to poor communication under pressure, making attributions that the other person in the relationship is not influenceable, keeping such attributions covered up, requiring the acting case-team member (and others) to be good at analysis yet not being able to define and teach good analysis, and resisting giving A's for performance while the person being evaluated feels that receiving anything but A's means he or she has failed.

The two consultants were members of the directors' firm and had only recently been exposed to a case-discussion seminar, but in spite of their minimal exposure to Model II, they were able to manage the discussion of the critical issues quite effectively. They did not require intervention in order to prevent them from creating self-sealing counterproductive conversation. Instead, most of my interventions focused on helping them explore defensive reasoning and actions of which they appeared unaware. I also was helpful, I believe, in encouraging them to go beyond the learning they reported, by asking how they would continue the learning after the session.

The specific case involves a senior consultant who was assigned to act as a case-team leader for the first time. I will call him Greg. Greg was told that his tasks were to give real intellectual leadership to the team, understand client relationships and provide guidance for the team members, and make the superior case-team leader's life easier and more manageable.

Greg was enthusiastic about his new assignment, but in his opinion, the case-team leader, Steve, acted in ways that made it difficult for Greg to execute his new responsibilities. Indeed, Greg believed that, at times, Steve acted to undermine his role.

Greg told Steve that he would like to discuss the problems. He also asked for me, as the intervener, to be present, as well as the individual who makes case-team assignments. Steve agreed enthusiastically. Both had been through the first phases of the continuous improvement program. The session began with Greg recalling his introduction to his assignment as acting case-team leader.

The Conversation	*Intervener's Observations*
Greg: [When we had our first major meeting, Steve had] a very detailed slide presentation, [and at first in this assignment, I thought that Steve] had done such a thorough work of thinking about what he wanted to do that my primary responsibility was to execute.	
[I continued in this role, but] I realized that I might be in trouble when Steve said, "I don't have any more time to do any more thinking on this case, so, Greg, I expect you to start providing intellectual leadership."	
Okay, but I have never been introduced to the relevant	Greg's reasoning as to how he should act is similar to the rea-

clients. I thought that it was Steve's responsibility to help the transition with the client.

[It created a bind for me.] I was trying to approach Steve. Based on some of his reactions, I was worried that he was thinking that [I was angling for opportunities] to sing and dance in front of clients. And that wasn't the reason. The reason that I wanted [to meet the] client was so that I could figure out what to do.

Steve: [May I give my views on this? I was worried about assigning you to this case because I knew that it was difficult.] I didn't want to dump this on you because I thought you would drown. Now I understand that what I was doing to be helpful was not.

So, it is true that I worked with [another] consultant more closely [and bypassed you] because I knew him. Looking back, that was not a great thing to do. In retrospect, I do not think that you and I had a conversation about this. That was bad.

[Then I got overwhelmed] and dumped the case on you. I didn't give you clear enough directions. You probably overestimated what I wanted. I was

soning described in the action map's pattern. He was willing to provide leadership, but believed that Steve was inhibiting him because he did not introduce him to the clients. Greg bypassed and covered up those views because he created an attribution that, if he spoke candidly, Steve might interpret that as a desire "to sing and dance in front of clients." Greg had never tested this attribution.

Steve was also acting consistently with the defensive action strategies described in the pattern. For example, he made an evaluation that the case was difficult for Greg, but did not test it with him. Then he acted rationally by using another consultant. This bewildered Greg because he thought that Steve, as case-team leader, should go through him, the acting case-team leader. He did not discuss these views with Steve.

We then get an insight into Steve's reasoning when he feels overwhelmed: dump the case onto Greg. Don't worry about not providing clear directions because to do so might take up a lot of time—And Steve can bail him out later, if necessary. Don't say any of this, including

perfectly happy about what you did, but I think I conveyed an impression to you that there was something else I wanted.

Intervener: When did you sense the things you are describing?

Steve: Not until right now. I thought that I was saying to you [Greg] that what you did was fine. Now looking back [and listening to you], I know that that is not what I said. All I can say is that I apologize. [What you thought] wasn't what I meant. And I didn't say [what I did mean].

Greg: [Looking back,] I now realize that the way I asked was not very good.

Steve: Right now, what just popped into my head is that you do not believe me when I say "fine."

Intervener: (*To Greg.*) Do you confirm [his view that when he says "fine"] it is difficult for you to believe him?

Greg: Yes, because "fine" is like a B, not an A.

Steve: That's important. Let's talk about that. [My old mentor in this firm] used to say to me, "Better than I expected," which

the fear that Greg may overestimate what Steve wants.

The responses made by Greg and Steve illustrate the skillful unawareness that was operating during the case-team activities. Both acted spontaneously and both were, at that time, unaware of their counterproductive behavior.

Steve applies the lessons that he is learning by reflecting on what is occurring in this discussion session. He made an attribution that Greg did not believe him when he said "fine," but instead of censoring the attribution, he tested it.

Steve not only found out he was correct; he also opened up a window into how an acting case-team leader (ACTL) reasoned about such grades. This, in turn, surfaced a dilemma that Steve was experiencing with Greg and others that, frustrated the hell out of me. I would just go through the roof. And he would say, "Look, it is not as good as I could do. No, it is not an A."

If you are trying to get me to say [your work] is an A, I will not. It is good work. It is perfectly acceptable. This is competent work.

Greg: Yes, but I think that I am capable of doing more than competent work.

Steve: There's a difference. Are you capable? Yes. Was it an A performance? No.

Intervener: (*To Greg.*) If I were in your shoes, I would have asked, "What is the difference between an A and a B?" Is that fair?

Greg: Yes, that is a good question.

Steve: Yes, that is fair.

Greg: [To be candid,] I think that I know how I could have done an A [job, but I needed some information about the client that I never got]. So to ask you what it would take to get an A would be unfair because I thought I knew.

(*Later.*) [And thinking about what the intervener said,] I actually knew my work was

again, he never discussed. The dilemma was that he wanted to be tough and honest in his evaluations, but doing so would upset an ACTL.

I intervened to help Greg learn to get at the reasoning that Steve uses in his grading. I wanted Greg to learn this before he responded.

Greg surfaces a more difficult problem that can be illustrated by the following reasoning: I know how to get an A, I could get it if Steve introduced me to clients, it is unfair to test my attributions because I know them to be correct.

This is an example of self-referential reasoning that is self-sealing. He "tests" his attribu-

acceptable but not great. I didn't think that it was an A. . . . So I placed the responsibility on you.

Intervener: And you did not tell him?

Greg: Yes.

Steve: [And looking backward], I didn't tell you my thoughts [about] why you wanted to see the client. Which was not fair [on my part].

Intervener: (*To Steve.*) [I would like to suggest another response you could have made.] You could have said to Greg, ["I understand that you would prefer an A. What do you think would be required for you to get an A?" You could learn more about his views regarding getting an A].

Steve: Good point.

tions by using his own logic, whose validity depends upon the untested attributions. This reasoning makes it logical for him to place the responsibility on Steve. If he didn't make Steve responsible, he would have to test his attribution about meeting clients by making it public.

I intervened to ask Steve to explore Greg's views on grading. This led Greg to provide his causal reasoning why he would not get an A, reasoning he now realizes is wrong. This led Steve to discuss evaluations and attributions that he had made about Greg's intellectual performance but that he had not shared with Greg at the time he made them.

Greg: Right. For example, I was saying to myself that the reason that I would not get an A was because I am not meaner and more assertive. [Now I see that attribution is] not fair.

Steve: [I recollect a plane ride with you.] I remember saying to you what is missing here is, What is the nature of competition? [As we] went along with the discussion, [my private conclusion was that you] did not have the insight. You are capable of a solution that goes by the book. But you can't take the next step of [answering the question] What does this all mean? So I'm not going to give you an A.

I never said that to you at that time, yet that was precisely what was running through my mind.

Greg: (Later.) [My request for more client contact] was to get you to spend more time with me. How much time did you spend with me?

Steve: Very limited. [I see now that] I was setting you up for failure. . . . I knew that I should be stopping and spending lots of time with your questions and so forth.

(Later.) [Another problem was that] the client told me that he wanted to work with me alone [for personal reasons]. I agreed, [and that was another reason that I didn't invite you in].

Intervener: The next time that happens to you, I would like to suggest that you say to the client something like "I understand your personal reasons. I would hope that this does not require me to keep Greg, the acting case-team leader, out of our meetings. It is unlikely that I can recall and translate to him accurately everything that went on. As a result, the case may suffer, you may suffer."	My intervention was designed to show Steve (and Greg, if he got into a similar situation in the future) how to deal with dilemmas created by clients who make requests that come between a case-team leader and an acting case-team leader. Steve then surfaced his causal reasoning related to losing the sale. I then suggested ways in which he could make the causal reasoning public.

Steve: That went through my mind. But I was afraid to say that. Basically, I was afraid of losing the sale; so I said yes. (Laughs.) And I felt bad about it.

Intervener: [That is a legitimate fear.] But you might say [to the client], "If you're telling me that this is a condition for the sale, I'll do it. But in order for you to get the value added, we must find a way of keeping the acting case-team leader fully informed and up to date."

Steve: That's fair enough.

There's nothing more that I can say now other than I've got to go back and think about my behavior along the entire front.

[But I'll be honest.] I doubt if I will give out A's until that person can do everything I can do and better. I am resisting [the standard that Steve is implying], but I have to think about that.

Intervener: Are you saying that if Greg does everything in the handbook and truly makes it sing, you would not give him an A?	I tried to get Steve to discuss more about the sources of his doubts and about his newly surfaced ambivalence about grading. His response that he could be feeling threatened was an important reaction that needed to be stated publicly. Doing so, I hypothesized, would make it easier for him to discuss it in the future with Greg or others. It should also make it easier for Greg to discuss these issues in the future. Indeed, Greg followed up with more examples of problems that he had not discussed with Steve.
Steve: That's what I want to think about. I don't know. [If part of the problem is that] I'm feeling threatened, I want to think about that.	
Intervener: And the threat is that he could do it faster than you did?	
Steve: Yes.	

Greg: [If I may, let me add another example of where I got in trouble.] After the _____ meeting you told me that we were breaking new ground. (*Greg and his team had prepared a presentation, which Steve then delivered to the client in a meeting where the team was not allowed to be present.*) You added what we could do better. I voice-mailed the team and told them their performance was "excellent. Steve is really pleased and wants to meet tomorrow."

Well, at the meeting you told them their presentation was okay, but you would never want to stand up and give that presentation. That was, I thought, a mixed message. I felt sorry for the team.

Steve: Okay. Let's talk about it from my perspective. I can see clearly your point.

Greg: Wait, let me finish the example. I came up to you and said that I was worried that I gave the team the wrong impression. Were you really not satisfied? Was I mistaken?

Steve: Good, let me try to explain. The thrust of my evaluation was that the information contained in the presentation was very valuable. What I was trying to convey was that from a technical point of view it was a sloppily put together presentation; it had ragged edges. (*Illustrates.*)

In a hostile client environment, I would have been killed or dead on arrival. [In this environment, I was able to pull it off.]

I hate it when a case team hangs me out to dry with no explanation of what the data point is. And we had several of those.

Greg: And if I could have been in the room, I could have made notes and told the team where [we made things difficult for you].

I observed the _____ meeting and found that helpful. But, I didn't know how to say that to you so that you would understand.

Intervener: What was it about your relationship with Steve that prevented you from saying what you just said at the appropriate time?	Whenever someone gives feedback to another that is abstract, I try to get them to be more concrete. Greg immediately focused on mannerisms such as cutting him off.
Greg: Well, I think it is just his mannerisms. . . . (*To Steve.*) You interrupt me a lot.	
Intervener: Help me to understand. Has Steve ever communicated, in any form, that he does not want your ideas?	Asking Greg to describe examples where Steve acted in the ways that Greg was attributing to him—that is, cutting him off—led Greg to identify his problem as being worried about voicing trivial ideas.
	His causal reasoning began with: Steve intends to cut me off, and progressed to; I attrib-

ute to Steve that he does not
want to listen, especially when I
think that my ideas may be
trivial.

Greg: No. I was worried about saying things that were trivial.
And then the other thing was that I thought it was obvious. I had
never been in a situation where I did not have access to a client.
[Now I realize why Steve kept me out.]

Intervener: To what extent do you find him unreachable, uninfluenceable?

Greg: Well, I think that it is the interruptions. [When he did that,]
I thought that he was getting defensive [and I'd better be careful].
    (*Later. To Steve.*) I recollect that you said to me that you did
not understand why I was making such a fuss over not mentioning
my name. But you continued that you would make sure that you
mentioned my name more often if it would make me happy. . . . I
knew that you did not understand. That, plus the feeling that I was
not doing a good job, led me to shut off.

Intervener: (*Later.*) Do you think that Steve understands now.

Greg: I don't know.

Intervener: What would you want to hear from him or to ask him
to make sure he understands?

Greg: (*Responds.*)

Steve: Let me try to answer. I
think the answer is going to be
convoluted. I might as well do
it that way than edit it.
    I am very confident that
you were left without a natural
client. When the pressure got
high, I instinctively assigned

Steve began to make more of his
causal reasoning explicit. His
reasoning ran: Whenever I feel
pressured, assign the tasks to

the tasks to myself. I don't know if that was the right thing to do. But I do know that it was an instinctual reaction.

If you ask me why did I act as I did, the only answer is that this was incredibly important to me. My behavior pattern throughout my life is that if you want to get it done, do it yourself.

That's how I got to where I am today. If there were troubles, I stayed up all night and fixed them.

Letting go is very hard. [I recollect that example you cited before.] I never thought that [your motives] were to sing and dance in front of the client. But I was not able to tell you that you had to let me do this alone because I was nervous about it.

I said something else. And whatever it was, it was not correct. And you were trying to act on it. And things got weirder. I think the truth of the matter is that I was anxious about it.

[So if you got the signal that I was distancing you,] it was intended. I didn't intend it malevolently. I am not proud of it. I hope that helps.

myself, if I want to get something done (that is not being done according to my standards), do it myself; do not state any of this to others.

Making this reasoning public led Steve to examine possible sources of his defensiveness.

Intervener: Is what Steve saying believable to you?

Greg: Yes, but I came to this meeting because I thought I had some responsibility as well.

Intervener: Okay. But how much faith do you have that this explanation will help him to change his behavior the next time?

Greg: Oh. None; not none, but very little.

Intervener: I think Steve is saying [and let me check this out] that he has learned something and that he will strive to correct it.

Steve: I haven't said that. I've only said that now I understand it is natural behavior on my part.

Intervener: How about the correction issue?

Steve: I don't know. I'm not promising that I can eradicate overnight something that has served me well for years. I'd be lying.

Intervener: And that could make it rational for Greg to think that [all this discussion] will not be helpful the next time. I admire that you do not wish to make promises that you cannot keep. But how about this? The next time you begin a case team, you could include a description of the mixed messages that you may create, especially under stress. You can add (if you believe it to be valid for you) that you want to know when you create such conditions but that you cannot guarantee a change. You are working on it, but it's not easy.	I wanted to make public that Steve's position could cause Greg to wonder about the next time. I then role-played a conversation that he might craft, which would permit him to be genuine yet transfer the learning from this session to other contexts.

Steve: Yes, that makes sense.   The message that I crafted made

But let me tell you a concern that I have. I am aware [of my predisposition to overcontrol]. So in another case team, I have genuinely given them a lot of leeway, [and that team still was not very productive]. So a week ago I said that to them. Then I gave them some ideas.

I acknowledge that I do have a tendency to grab the wheel. To be honest, I do not know how to [get rid of that tendency]. It has served me well.

sense to Steve. But he had fears about how his saying something such as I had said might be misused by case-team members.

Intervener: I believe you have a reputation of being a first-rate technical analyst, et cetera. But I do not see the evidence that it is serving you well as a leader.

I intervened to confirm that Steve has a reputation for being a first-rate analyst. However, I evaluated his leadership actions, in this case, as not serving him well. By that I meant he acted to inhibit his own learning about the management of the case team.

Steve: It is a disaster. And I have been struggling alone to answer . . .

Intervener: I am asking you to consider asking Greg and relevant others to join in that struggle. On the one hand, they could let you know when you appear to be giving them mixed messages.

On the other hand, you want to feel free to do the same. After all, if they tell you to give them some space, [and] if you do and if nothing comes back, they too are producing mixed messages.

Steve: Yes . . . that makes sense . . . I am trying . . . but [it's] not easy. (*Illustrates an attempt to provide more space and provide more client contact.*)

Greg: I have a suggestion. I would like to observe you making the changes, instead of your leaving and bringing back the results. Just let me watch you make the corrections so that I can figure out [how it's done]. That's the fastest way I can learn. . . .

Steve: I'm sorry. Let me interrupt. You've just asked to observe me real time. The problem is that I have no clear idea how [I actually reach a solution]. I worry something to death and then it finally crystallizes. Is it better for you to watch me flounder around or not?

This conversation describes a basic problem that I did not, and still do not, understand. The problem is how to help those who are analytically bright teach others to improve their performance. Steve reacts by distancing himself from Greg. He does not want Greg to look over his shoulder. It is unlikely that he will learn. In addition, he may not know how to ask the right questions in order to learn and, at the same time, help Greg to learn.

Greg: I'd like to observe. To understand how you think. Some people think linearly; some do not. I can learn by observing you. I'd like to see what you do and think and how it eventually crystallizes. Otherwise, when you leave and return with an answer, I feel frustrated. You already knew what you wanted, it seemed like. So [the team's work] was a waste of time.

Steve: Can I stop at that? Your first draft is valuable to me even if it gets torn up.

I sit down and say to myself, I don't like this. What is it that I do not like? [Your draft helps me to think.] I may have done exactly what you did at first. So I find your draft valuable. You don't consider it valuable?

Greg: I do not. When you change things, it is not a further development. It is something totally different.

Intervener: How free would you feel to say that to Steve the next time this happens?

Greg: I could try saying it. But I do not know how to say it without sounding defensive. It makes me sound like I am worried about my own performance . . . and Steve's response then is "Don't worry, don't worry; this is fine."

Intervener: Which does not help you?

Greg: Right.

Steve: I think it would be fine for you to say to me that you do not understand how [I] got from here to there. If you said that, that would be fine. [What would not be fine would be your continuing to communicate] that you were wrong, that you were a failure.

In my experience, people do not believe that I learn from changing their reports.

Greg: What would they believe?

Steve: They believe exactly what you did, which is that this is a criticism of their work.

[As I listened to you I was thinking,] Why is that threatening? I make a lot of false starts. Sometimes I don't. But sometimes I go banging about in a dark room. So you're going to watch me change my mind four times. Do I want to do that in front of the case team? For self-protection, I can go home and do all those dumb things and then I can come back and look smart.

Intervener: How would you feel watching him change his mind? Would it demotivate you?

Greg: No, because [the case-team leader] would be doing it in front of [his or her acting case-team leader] and not in front of the entire team.

Intervener: Why not include the entire case team?

Greg: Because a lot of consultants are not sophisticated enough to follow somebody who's heading in ten different directions.

Intervener: So you have as many fears about them as Steve said that he had about you?

Steve: Yes, your statement is the same as mine.

Greg: No. (*Pauses.*) Okay, I understand it is the same.

Intervener: (*Later.*) I don't understand, as I hear it, why you are cutting off the other case-team members from learning. What leads you to mistrust the five case-team members?

Greg: I do not mistrust them. I would be glad to do it one-on-one.

Intervener: How about one-on-five?

Greg: No, [because it can't be done efficiently in a group].

Intervener: I would like to help both of you and others to experiment with creating these opportunities for learning. One does not have to do it all the time. But one or two in-depth experiences may be helpful to individuals and to the development of more effective case teams.

Steve: And my fear is that they will hear me five different ways and they will not be able to sort things out.

Intervener: And Greg is confirming your fears. What I would like to do is to help set the conditions for periodic, in-depth case-team discussions on these issues. But this would require more development of yourselves and the others. (*Illustrates how continuous improvement program sessions could be used.*)
(*Later.*) How do you feel so far?

Greg: At the end of this case I was attributing negative reasons to Steve. I was getting very angry. This session has helped me to erase a lot of that. I now understand better. I have a new perspective.

But I'm not sure what I would do going forward. For example, Steve has said that when he is under pressure and the case is personally important to his career, he will [take things away from the team and do them] himself. When is a case not going to be important?

Steve: Lots of times. (*Illustrates.*)

Intervener: May I suggest several action steps. First, as you, Greg, have said, you understand Steve better. This means that you may not get as frustrated or angry, which may be helpful.

Greg: (*Nods yes.*)

Intervener: Second, I would like to help you and Steve develop a relationship where both of you can take more risks for learning. For example, Steve will be more open to exploring his dysfunctional actions when he gets anxious. You may be more open to exploring your reactions when you are frustrated with Steve. For example, you went to [the person who makes case-team assignments] and told him that you never wanted to work with Steve again. You also complained to [one of the] directors.

I would like to help you and others to create conditions like this one to test out your evaluations and attributions before you go to the head of allocations or to a director.

Steve: I know that would be helpful to me. Again, I am not promising I will learn easily. I am promising that I want to learn.

(*Later.*) [Up until this meeting] it scared the hell out of me to say what have I said so far, because I didn't know how people were reacting to it.

Greg: Isn't it okay for Steve, or any of us, to have private sessions like this?

Intervener: Yes. But I am recommending that, as your fears are reduced, we raise the ante and try it in a group setting. For example, if Steve and you teamed up in a new case, it might provide opportunities for a group session.

Summary

The dialogue between Greg and Steve illustrates several problems that are generic to case-team management. First is the task of educating a new acting case-team leader. The difficulty of this task was compounded by the fact that this case-team leader did not have the time that was necessary to do a good job. Even if Steve had had more time, the problem would still have existed because he did not fully trust Greg's capabilities, and he made attributions that he could not say so.

At the same time, Greg was making attributions that Steve did not respect his work or his capacities to learn. He, too, believed that these attributions were not discussable. Problems such as these are often framed as problems of poor communication. It is usually recommended that both individuals develop more effective communication skills. Although both could profit from such skill education, it is not clear that it would be adequate or how much of it would be necessary. As the transcript illustrated, both parties in this case were already able to communicate quite effectively. Their major difficulty was that each had been making attributions that bypassed opportunities for effective conversations and covered up the bypass.

This case also illustrates the perennial problem of how to help case-team leaders who are excellent analysts to teach their know-how to others. As far as I could ascertain, Steve knew what good analysis was, but he could not make the features of his own sound analyses explicit and concrete. Moreover, he resisted the idea of permitting Greg to watch him make the sound analyses for which he was famous, because Greg might learn that the process can be incoherent and sloppy. Apparently, Steve felt that if anyone was to observe him, he should exhibit well-organized, coherent reasoning processes.

I believe that younger consultants would profit from observing how elegance can result from nonelegant activities. So far, I have not been able to get Steve to experiment with such a session. At the time of this writing, he expresses a greater interest and willingness but is still not quite ready.

Finally, there were several times when Greg and Steve made important learning explicit. Yet, as we saw, it was not immediately clear, especially to Steve, whether he would continue the learning in a new setting. There were several times when I had to make the importance of continuous improvement explicit by asking each party how free he would feel to use the learning outside the context of the current discussion. Steve was candid about his doubts of doing so in certain areas but promised to think about the issue carefully. He now appears to be continuing his learning by making his hesitancy more discussable by case-team members.

10

CEO's Performance Review:
Getting Feedback
from Below

About two years into the continuous improvement program, the CEO asked that the members of the board of directors give him a review on his performance, just as he reviewed their performances. He recommended that it be a group review because directors might hold differing views on a given issue, making it important for each director to know what the others were thinking. Any recommendations for action would come from the group, and thus the directors' commitment to implementing and monitoring the recommendations would be stronger. Moreover, any hitches in implementation could be monitored and corrected by the entire group.

    The directors would also learn more about the CEO and themselves. For example, the reader will recall that some directors predicted the CEO would react like a blast furnace on certain issues. If they brought up such issues at the review, they could test their attributions. If the attributions were not confirmed, then the directors could explore the reasoning that led them to make incorrect attributions. Also, directors might find it useful to explore the ways they might be manipulating the CEO and the strategies they use to get what they want. Finally, if the process were found worthwhile, other directors might volunteer to have reviews from their peers. Those sessions would have to be designed somewhat differently because not all directors had equal information about each others' performances.

The group agreed to the CEO's recommendation. A five-hour session was held. Although it had been scheduled for all day, the directors ended it early because they felt that the crucial topics had been discussed. The examples that follow illustrate how the CEO and the directors were improving in choosing to use Model II theories-in-use over Model I.

CEO: You have received a copy [of my memo concerning my performance]. I am not going to read it. I'd be happy to answer any questions [about it].

I am most interested in hearing from you about things that you all think I could improve my performance by changing. Also, any things that you believe are important, yet you believe that I do not see. [Intervener, do you have anything to say?]

Intervener: I'd just like to put in a plea to work on the undiscussables.

Bill: [When I have my review with you, you ask me to give my own evaluation first.]

CEO: I would not prefer to do that because in this case there are six of you. I could be talking for hours. Also, I am fearful that the dynamic of the meeting will be that we could go off in all sorts of directions, and you will not get the opportunity to say what you wish to say.

I'd love to see if we can get some interactions going, as opposed to back and forth [dialogue between myself and one other].

Larry: I have a question about the process which I don't know how to resolve. I have a fear that this meeting could become a bilateral . . . conversation rather than a group conversation.

Intervener: One suggestion is that each of you try to begin with an issue that you believe is relevant for the others. If it is an issue that is truly peculiar to the CEO and you, then hold it off until the end. Does that make sense?

Also, I believe that I have your permission to help the group members stay on track. [This is the first time that we have tried to do this. We have little group know-how.] Does that make sense?

Several directors: It does.

CEO: (*To intervener.*) And also help me, because, [as all of us know, I can enjoy listening to myself talk]. My goal is to learn as much as possible from the group.

Chris [intervener] just said that he wanted to make sure the undiscussables were not undiscussables today. . . . I second that wholeheartedly.

Also, I have the fear that maybe some may feel they have to say something positive in order to say something negative. . . . I would just as soon get to the negative or to the areas of improvement.

If I'm hurt or disturbed, I'll let you know.

Ted: [It feels a bit absurd] to be talking about you with your being in the chair. I'd like to have you and us free from any incumbrance arising from your being in the chair.

John: [I agree] as long as we do not create the kind of discussion that might happen if the CEO were not in the room. Maybe the intervener can help on this one.

Several directors: Yes.

Intervener: I'd be glad to be the chairperson. . . . Who would like to begin?

This session began with the CEO setting a high level of aspiration for making the undiscussables discussable. He identified a barrier that he could create (because he enjoyed talking, for example) and invited the directors to help him keep his talking to a productive minimum. The directors also came primed to produce an effective discussion. They had read the CEO's memo sent to them before the meeting, and they too had identified potential barriers and invented solutions to overcome them. Two years ago, the directors would not have paid so much attention to their performance as a group nor, in my opinion, would they have resolved the issues of the potential barriers as quickly as they did.

I believe that I helped to achieve these results. For example, I agreed to act as the chairperson, and I did so because I wanted this experiment to have the greatest possible chance to succeed. I wanted the directors free to focus their attention on evaluating the CEO's performance, and their own, when it was relevant. I also believed that enough directors had experienced identifying their own (as well as others') defensive routines that they could take on the role of monitoring the group process. Finally, I knew that if they began to act dependent upon me, I could surface that issue.

One of the directors volunteered to start the review.

Bill: Let's get the good stuff out of the way. [You are a great teacher and coach.] (*Illustrates.*) [Your writing and communication skills are superb. I can spend more time with you over dinner than anyone else that I know.]

Now, let me get to the other stuff. I have broken it down into areas for continuous improvement. One is old stuff; I do not know if it will reoccur, but it worries me. The other is current stuff. I'd like to start with the current stuff.

I will call the first issue postponement or avoidance or just real discomfort with tough issues. And I'll illustrate. I attribute to you that these things are unpleasant and difficult: stuff like firing people, capital structure of the company, saying no to us as a group [and so you avoid telling us about them directly]. (*Illustrates.*) We need to be told [in no uncertain terms], even if it hurts us.

[Let me pause and see if I have identified an issue that is important for others.]

Intervener: I would like to ask the CEO not to respond as yet. Let's get the views of others. Is this issue an important one for others of you?

Larry: (*To CEO.*) I have long-term and short-term issues. The short-term issue is [getting the best consultants working on my cases]. And oh, yes, now that I am asking you about resources, why not deal with [long-term] issues like overstaffing, restructuring of the firm, et cetera. [We make all sorts of demands.]

Ted: And I agree that you have to discipline us by selecting one or two issues and going at those.

John: (*Later.*) What I object to is that we are holding the CEO primarily responsible. For example, we focus on his management style but not on our own. We make him responsible for these issues, and my observation is that our behavior has consistently disrupted his efforts to delegate. And when he delegates what happens is that nothing gets done.

Second, there is the constant second-guessing that goes on inside this group. (*Illustrates.*) When we have anxieties about the competence of others, we go to the CEO to solve them. For example, a director goes to the CEO and asks, "What's going on in Europe?" Unstated is "I don't trust the people in charge of Europe."

CEO: For the record, such a conversation has occurred in the past eighteen months.

Intervener: I should like to interrupt. (*To John.*) I am ambivalent about what you are doing. On the one hand, the issues that you raise are important. But so far, the way they have been crafted (*illustrates*) could lead members of this group to attribute to you that you are protecting the CEO.

I think that most individual issues about the CEO have a group side to them. We should get at both sides. So let's keep going. I do not think the CEO needs protection, at least not yet. Does that make sense?

John: That makes a lot of sense.

Other directors: (*Agree with John.*)

CEO: I agree.

Jim: (*To CEO.*) I wish that you would be much more clear about your views, especially bad news. I see you hesitating, and the way I explain that to myself is that you are still trying to protect us as a group. My sense is that the group has grown beyond that. There is a real appetite to deal with the tough issues.

Intervener: Larry, I think that you have been trying to get in.

Larry: Yes. . . . It never ceases to amaze me, the games I play and he [plays]. For example, instead of raising [an issue] explicitly, I raise side issues; the CEO responds with side issues, sort of signaling that he is not interested. . . . We sniff around each other as opposed to discussing the real issue.

And I don't know whether it is my fault or the CEO's, but he certainly triggers fantastic defensive routines in me so that I feel that I cannot discuss the real issues. So the communication is zippo.

Ted: Why?

Intervener: What does the CEO say or do that leads you to feel defensive?

Larry: I'm not sure. When we said that the CEO avoids confrontation, [what came to my mind] was that I also avoid confronting. And also [I don't agree with Ted]. I do not expect the CEO to discipline me. I expect his opinion, but I am responsible to act. If he disagrees with me, fine, let him say so.

John: I agree.

Ted: Can I pick up on something that you said, John? Let me see if I can be clear. Recently, I was at a _____ meeting where the CEO made tough decisions. The decisions were uncomfortable [to make with the] people in the room. Yet he made them on the spot. . . . I think that the fundamental challenge the CEO faces is not to get sucked into everything that goes on in the company. He has to figure out the few projects that are key and get on with them.

CEO, there was something telling [in your memo] when you said that your loyalty is first to the employees, second to the clients, and third to the shareholders. I would have had shareholders at the front of the list and not at the back of the list.

CEO: Just a quick distinction. I see all of you as employees and shareholders.

Ted: Right. But many of the problems [on your list] have to do with us as shareholders. . . .

And the second issue is lack of trust [in us].

I also agree that you have a personal loyalty to people who have been loyal to you. (*Illustrates.*)

Jim: I accept that some of the issues [faced by the CEO] are tough. (*To CEO.*) But [I think] that you make them tougher than they have to be.

I'll use myself as a case in point. This is one of the undiscussables. Only recently have I learned about your lack of trust in me in certain areas. And the only way I learned it is by first talking with [the intervener, who suggested that we all meet—which we did]. I felt that I literally had to beg to get you to the point of telling me that you do not trust me. If, on the other hand, we had discussed this earlier, we could have begun to solve the problems [jointly and sooner].

Intervener: I should like to say what I am learning so far. I'm attributing that most of the group believes that the CEO does not show as much strength as they wish he would show on the tough issues.

Then there are two sets of explanations you [gave for the CEO's behavior]. The first set of explanations [ascribes the problem to] personality, . . . largely [the CEO's personality]. The second set is systemic. That is, we [all] create the conditions that cause such actions.

The group is asking the CEO not to hesitate to make choices. Fine. But let us also examine the group's role in identifying these tough choices.

Ted: The CEO does make tough decisions—at least with me. There are a number of people [in my office] that I have not fired. Yet he, on a regular basis, tells me to fire them. [And he gives me his reasoning and his illustrations.]

Bill: I think the undiscussable around this issue is _____ .

John: This is interesting. You wonder how we grew as fast as we did? I can recall meetings where the CEO asked the same question. I know that he cut back our hiring targets during _____ .

Intervener: (*Later.*) May I ask something? What is on the left-hand side of your column when you say _____ ?

Ted: My intention was to say that I'm not sure that we can get a terribly much higher standard of decision making over the life cycle of the firm than we have already.

Yes, we have made mistakes. We must learn from them. But I wouldn't necessarily dump it all on the CEO.

Intervener: I have not heard the conversation as saying that it is all the CEO's fault. I think he even illustrated how he colluded in playing games. . . . Am I communicating?

Ted: Yes, you are.

Bill: (*To CEO.*) I am concerned about where the shareholders' interests fall on your authority.

The second concern that I have [is whether the financial model you have for the firm is correct or not]. I think most of the financial models that we have so far—not only yours—are rubbish.

My attribution to you has been that you do not place this issue on top. You felt that if the models were incorrect [that was less important than hiring the right people, encouraging their personal and professional development . . .]

Jim: I think the CEO understands the current financial model. . . .

Intervener: (*Later.*) Some of you are concerned about the CEO's views on financial models. He can give us his views.

Your other concern I will frame as "How does the CEO learn? How does he detect and correct his errors? How does he involve us?"

Larry: I'd like to make a recommendation for the CEO's actions. (*Does so.*)

Intervener: May I suggest that we not get into recommendations until we have heard from the CEO?

Larry: Fine.

One role that I often take on in sessions like this is to maintain a balance in the flow of the attributions about causality. In this kind of session in this case study, the flow usually went from what the CEO had done to the consequences on the directors. Little attention was paid to the causal flows from the directors to the CEO and from among director to director. In this instance, as I think the transcript illustrates, the group members' feedback is balanced. They identify the CEO's actions that require improvement, but they also identify their own needs for improvement. There is a balance in assigning responsibility.

Because the transcript is highly edited, one feature is not fairly represented. I focused on differences in views, on negative feedback given to the CEO, and on how well the CEO and the group dealt with embarrassment or threat. Although the issues discussed would normally produce defensive routines and self-sealing processes, these actions hardly occurred. The few times they did occur, the participants, including myself, were able to discuss them and reduce them. Thus, the editing does not present a totally valid picture of how hard the directors worked on each issue.

Next, the discussion returned to the issue of the way the CEO made decisions.

John: The CEO makes a judgment based on very strong intuition and then he puts it into practice. He will change his judgment as experience dictates. (*To CEO.*) But it is not easy to get you not to make the judgment [in the first place] or to influence you once you have made it.

Intervener: Could you illustrate?

John: My favorite is (*describes an instance in detail*). I believe that the CEO thought the decision he made was correct and truly appropriate. I believe that sometimes he needs [too much] experience before he can say that his decision was incorrect.

Bill: I guess I would violently disagree.

Intervener: Yes, but let's get this view out in the open.

CEO: (*Later.*) May I make a comment. The decision I made on _____ was a mistake. (*Appears emotionally upset.*) I am now taking corrective actions.

I have edited this episode heavily. The issue is still alive and affects the careers of several individuals. The CEO's emotion, I believe, was partially due to his recalling many feelings he had had during the past year as he tried to correct the problems arising from his decision and to make certain that no participant was treated unjustly. I also believe the record would show that he was patient, in order to give the directors the resources needed to correct the problems. I further believe that expressing the error publicly in this meeting was itself emotional. Up to that moment, the betting was that the CEO would never publicly admit the error and would not permit discussion of it. Acting as he did, however, he disconfirmed that attribution and made such undiscussables more likely to be discussable in the future.

The CEO also chose to make discussable another undiscussable—namely, the firm's managerial and ownership structure.

CEO: I am finding this very helpful. But I would like to respond to several of the points and then we can continue to others.

Our information processing is flawed partially because of the undiscussability or the apparent lack of clarity about who's competent to do what in this group and what the future senior management structure is going to really look like.

[I think that we are reducing the undiscussables, so let me say something about the future structure of the top.] (*Describes his views.*)

Several directors: (*Discuss issues of ownership structures at length.*)

Ted: Are these issues undiscussables?

CEO: Not from my perspective. If you think these issues are undiscussable, please help me see why.

Several directors: (*Give their views of why they thought the issues were undiscussable.*)

CEO: Do you guys believe that we have a relationship with _____ that is wrong?

Bill: Just mystifying and expensive.

Intervener: What is it about the way the CEO is dealing with this issue that causes you to believe that _____'s compensation is expensive relative to value received?

Bill: Okay, good point. I guess [I haven't made that clear]. It comes back to the avoidance of difficult issues. (*Explains and illustrates.*) So what I'm saying is, because this is a tough decision, the CEO is dancing around it. Therefore, I get nervous.

CEO: And do you have evidence that tough discussions are not going on?

Bill: Sure. We've had this issue for several years, and we still haven't had a discussion about the capital structure.

CEO: I am not going to have a discussion with _____ about changing the capital structure until this group's absolutely clear on what it's doing.

Several directors: [That's fair.] (*They ask specific questions about the role of* _____ .)

Intervener: Do some of you distrust the CEO's ability to have that conversation with _____ ?

John: No, distrust [is too strong]. I am concerned about his avoiding the tough issues.

CEO: (*Later.*) I am ready to talk about _____'s role in the firm. [To my knowledge,] we have not had a secret discussion about roles.

Ted: Well, maybe we need some further discussion because it feels secret to me. Let me say how I arrive at that. (*Explains, and others add their views.*)

Intervener: As I hear this discussion, it contains two levels, and the levels are interrelated. (*To CEO.*) One is your capacity to make tough decisions, to learn, et cetera. Individuals now see these issues as partly yours and partly theirs. The other is the financial structure of the firm, its governance, and the role of _____ .

We have talked about the first set of issues but not the second. Would you be willing to discuss, in more detail, issues from the second set?

CEO: That is fine by me. But I will need your help to make sure that this discussion is not a monologue or does not become [a dialogue] of point counterpoint.

In a board like this, there will be a predisposition toward the short term. It is my job, whether I like it or not, to be long term. I have to err on the side of being long term because the group is likely to err on being short term.

There are people who are speaking out of their self-interest. I will test this out to see the extent to which they are speaking for the good of the firm.

There is [the danger in a group like ourselves] to take care of our own and make ourselves feel good. We come closer to meeting our personal financial goals by committing injustices on the rest of the firm. And I'm not talking about survival decisions such as laying people off.

I'd be hard pressed to point to one where we actually committed injustice. There were cases where I felt that people were very comfortable with getting close to committing injustice. I won't say that I stopped it. Sometimes I think other people stopped it, but I feel very strongly that getting comfortable with possible injustice is immoral. (*Illustrates.*)

Jim: Could you illustrate how the use of the rules [you just described play out in a decision process]?

CEO: Yes. Could you say a bit more on what you want to hear?

Jim: Yes. The rules that you delineated, at least in my mind, make a lot of sense. [But they are abstract; I might disagree with how you actually implement them.] For example, take the assumption that people act out of self-interest. . . . I heard [you say] that people cloak their self-interest in other explanations. I think [differently on that subject]. There's nothing wrong with people's being self-interested up to a point. What I heard was that self-interest gets obscured and disguised. . . .

CEO: I have to test whether I'm getting what's best for the firm, which I get sometimes. But at other times I basically get the either well- or ill-disguised "Where's my money?"

The issues discussed here, which the directors will continue to discuss, are critical to the board's effectiveness. The CEO has doubts that the directors, as a group, think beyond their short-term financial gains. Therefore, he takes on the role of protecting the employees, including the directors, from this bias. Some of the directors, on the other hand, are fearful that the CEO will not make certain tough decisions and will rationalize his actions by invoking the firm's long-term interest.

As we will see, the CEO is willing to make explicit the rules he uses to select the director with whom he will discuss particular issues. The key criteria appear to be the anxiety that the CEO thinks such a discussion will activate in the director and the ways the director is likely to deal with such anxiety. If the anxiety is likely to be high and to be projected onto the CEO, then he is unlikely to talk with the director.

The CEO draws a four-box matrix, with anxiety on one dimension and personal financial orientation on the other.

CEO: [People can be arrayed in all four boxes.] Historically, the people that I've been more distrustful of are those who are highly financially driven and [display] high anxiety. Now, there is _____ , who is high on both of these. But [I talk to him anyway because] he has been explicit. I do not have to discount what he says.

John: What I find interesting about the rules is the rule that isn't there. [What are the rules you use to decide] who you involve in decisions, who you look to for advice?

CEO: [I would begin with the obvious,] that I simply do not have the time to talk with everyone. So my rule is to go to the guy who has the best information, the best advice.

It would be a complete cop-out if I stopped then. . . . By far the guy that I talk with most frequently is Larry. He communicates a lot of information quickly. He's proactive in providing the information. . . . Many times I disagree with it, or I don't fully implement it. [He does not fret over providing information; he does not use the opportunity to spend hours on it.] I also have an elimination rule: Don't consult those people who get nervous.

(*Later.*) [I realize the danger in this,] but if you behave anxiously and if you can control it [so that you do not make me responsible for controlling it for you], that's okay. [I seek and need advice from people to whom] I do not have to attribute personal anxieties and [with whom I can talk without our both pretending] that they're not anxious.

I'll tell you the behavior that really drives me crazy. There is some bad financial news. It doesn't matter what the source is. (*Illustrates.*)

I could have actually called up everyone. [But fear would be that the news] would be interpreted by some people as the equivalent of my making an announcement that the firm was going out of business. (*Cites another specific example.*)

I would love not to have negative rules. This gets to my undiscussable of my trust in people. It's not trust such as are they going to steal the petty cash or something. It's can I trust people to bear the strain and not show it on something that will demotivate all the people in the company.

Intervener: [You appear to me to be saying that, if people are anxious, you ask yourself,] can they own up to it and can they manage their anxiety? I've watched Ted, who expresses his anxieties. [Several months ago] he did not do it very constructively. He's now managing his anxieties better. And if I understand you, he does not upset you. . . .

CEO: Ted, I'm [not] asking you this question to be supported in this [but] do I appear to be anxious about talking about [it] if you tell me about one of your anxieties? Does that make me anxious, make it undiscussable?

Ted: No. We've developed a relationship where you know what I'm anxious about, and . . . you're very comfortable dealing with that. . . . And now you are reasonably straightforward in telling me what you are anxious about in me. It took us a while to get there, but we're there. Glory be.

CEO: I'll give you another rule.

Intervener: Before you do, I'd like to check with John [who brought up this issue]. Is this helpful?

John: I thought that it was extremely helpful. Now everybody realizes what they've got to do in their own behavior to earn the right to be consulted.

CEO: And may I add one thing? . . . I'm willing to put on the table all the decisions that I make and discuss openly the amount of control over them I should have. [There are many decisions I would love to off-load or make more jointly.]

But I want to own up that I haven't done that yet. I believe intellectually [that I should do this], yet I haven't, and I don't know why.

Larry: This is useful. Should we spend a minute exploring why?

CEO: I'm not adverse to it.

Bill: [People around this table have views] of who's a real director and who is not. Does anyone care to comment on that?

Larry: I would like to. [I think that this is less an issue since our continuous improvement program started.] If it is still a big issue, then we should confront it. We can no longer afford it.

John: Yes, our risks are getting too big.

CEO: [I should like to take a risk.] You say that we cannot tolerate this any more. In the spirit of making tough decisions, I'll say, okay, let's take some steps to go beyond it.

I'm ready to state a set of decisions and see how they might be made by [others or by others and me].

The CEO asked me, as the intervener, if this switch made sense. I responded that this was a very important topic, but that, before they discussed the list of decisions, I would like to do a bit of role-playing. We could look at how the CEO would now deal with a director who acted as if he were most interested in his own personal agenda and anxiety, and how a director would now deal with his views that the CEO was not acting effectively. The group agreed and some time was spent role-playing difficult encounters. Toward the end of the discussion, the CEO described how he formerly used ambiguity to manipulate some of the directors.

CEO: I will frankly confess to having [used ambiguity] on occasion. If I did it nowadays, I think it would be purely malicious. I don't think that I have done it during the last two years.

John: Before we go to the next topic, I would like to ask you to tell us in our next evaluation session where you put [each of] us in that four-cell matrix.

[Another comment I have] has to do with the degree of involvement in decisions. . . . I don't feel a burning need to be involved in any particular decision as long as [the people who are involved] are held accountable.

CEO: Three years ago, when we started the continuous-improvement program, many of you described my behavior as dictatorial, unilateral, and manipulative.

During the last three years, probably my single biggest priority has been to reduce these behaviors. John just said that I should hold you accountable. How do I hold people accountable without stimulating the fear or the perception [that I'm returning] to a dictatorial method?

Ted: I suggest that the accountabilities be made in open forum, so we can get commitment to the assignment [within the group]. Also, if you (and we) take the attitude that we will make mistakes but they will be discussable, I'd feel comfortable with that.

CEO: [Yesterday I had a meeting with Larry and the intervener.] At one point, I accused Larry of not delivering on what he was accountable for.

[To say] I was stunned is a little bit of an exaggeration, but I was very pleasantly surprised by his reaction. I say this to [publicly acknowledge his actions to change some of the historical views we have about him] and to give him the credit.

After this episode, the group turned to designing a new management schema that might help the CEO genuinely delegate to others. I should note that much time was spent on dealing with important business issues and strategies, many of which I considered privileged information, and therefore I have not included them here.

Summary

Rarely does a CEO bring his or her group together in order to review the CEO's performance. A few CEOs might hold a private review with a close colleague. Few would consider doing it with their entire group, and even fewer would actually implement it. However, this chapter has illustrated that this very rare event can occur with a high degree of effectiveness.

It is instructive to compare the conversations in this chapter with the map presented in Chapter Four. Many of the subjects considered undiscussable at the time that map was drawn (about two and a half years before the session presented in this chapter) were now discussed. The fears about individuals' going ballistic or blowing up did not exist any more. The directors' dependence on the CEO's taking responsibility for effective performance was significantly reduced.

The directors reported that the session was an important one for clearing "old tapes." It was even more important for setting the stage for future progress. In this connection, the CEO, about a year later, recommended a new structure for managing the company. His views had developed from several group discussions as well as individual ones. When he presented the plan, he emphasized that it was a plan and encouraged the directors to confront it. They asked many questions, most of which had little to do with the plan itself but rather with its execution. The concerns raised were related partially to the CEO and partially to the directors. The old bifurcation that saw causality as running all one way seemed gone. The directors were increasingly becoming the coherent, fully functioning team that they had described wanting to be when I first met with them.

11

Managing Exchanges
That Could Go Ballistic:
Discussing and Correcting
Out-of-Control Routines

About the time that I was finishing the final draft of this book, I facilitated a session in which the participants "went ballistic." I have included it to show that even individuals who have learned Model II theories-in-use do become upset, they do have differences with each other, and these differences are discussable and correctable.

The Problem

Directors John and Bill worked together on a large-client relationship. During a dinner meeting with the senior client contact, Richard, they learned that he was not satisfied with the value added; it was not up to the standards he had come to expect from the firm. Richard also said that, in the future, he wanted John to be as active as he had been, or more so.

For several weeks after that meeting, Bill kept hearing reports that John had been bad-mouthing him and a senior consultant in front of other board members. Bill called John to explore the issue. Both described the telephone call as unsatisfactory. Each attributed that the other was hanging on to previously held views and closed to learning.

Bill then wrote a memo to John, parts of which are reproduced here. The excerpts are largely unedited, with the exception of sentences that would identify clients. John, who had a reputation for blowing up, became infuriated after reading the memo. It especially upset him because, in his opinion, he had been a leader in reducing bad-mouthing among the directors. He was deeply angry, not only at Bill but at some of his fellow directors because they had told Bill about John's bad-mouthing. John felt betrayed by Bill and some of his other colleagues. He also felt that Bill was making unfair attributions and evaluations. Bill also was upset; but, as his memo to John will illustrate, he was not certain of the validity of his views. Bill prefers to deal with causes of emotional upsets in as rational a manner as possible.

Both directors agreed to meet face to face. Both asked that I be present. John also telephoned to tell me that, with Bill's approval, he was sending me the correspondence with the client as well as Bill's memo. Before we ended our conversation, John also said that he was finding some features of work dissatisfying and loaded with tensions. He asked that he and I get together someday to talk about these issues. He added that the upcoming session would be a good one for giving me some insight into issues that made him feel unhappy.

Reflecting on the session, I think that I did help the directors resolve their problems with each other. But, as the reader will see, John and Bill—even though they got upset—were able to act in ways that kept the processes from becoming self-sealing. If I was able to help, it was partially because Bill and John were ready to build upon my interventions by using the concepts they had learned and skills they were developing

The session was, in all our views, a success. Feelings were expressed, John and Bill did push each other's buttons, but they resolved the problems. Afterward, both reported that they had worked effectively during a three-day board meeting and in the preparation and implementation of an important presentation with key clients.

Excerpts from Bill's Memo

Let me begin by saying, John, that I have found your behavior throughout to be most caring and helpful.

That is not to say, however, as I will say below, that I feel you should have drawn some of the conclusions that you have. Given your "clean motives," I feel that some of my comments about you might seem not only undeserved but also ungrateful, or even maliciously defensive. For these reasons, I have found this a difficult memo to write.

At this point, let me summarize what I am going to say in this note.

- Some parts of your conversation with Richard (loss of confidence in our firm—or me—because of data errors and lack of rapport with me) make sense to me.
- Other criticisms you have made of our work (lack of ad hoc verification of cost work, no retreading recommendations) also make sense to me.
- However, some parts of your conversation with Richard (I was too pushy in marketing and the poor quality of our work) are puzzling to me in the light of other comments from Richard ("Bill is responsive to our needs"; "This is up to the usual high standard"); another client contact ("It is a shame that we have to finish the relationship just as we were beginning to get to know you and gain confidence in you"); and two other client contacts ("You guys have done a good job; this is just what our company needs").
- I feel that you have been too ready to draw conclusions (*illustrates*) with insufficient data and without testing those data, with the result that they are not accurate.
- You have underestimated in your diagnosis a number of circumstantial points that have had a significant bearing on the case (Richard's dissatisfaction with the case as originally conceived, the early termination of the case, the circumscribed nature of the work).

- Finally, there are a few things that I "attribute" to you which I want to test and discuss with you (that you drew conclusions on scant data and without testing your attributions with me, which would have been very easy, shared these untested attributions and conclusions with a broad group of colleagues, approached the feedback telephone conversation with a desire to make your point rather than to inquire).

My Attributions About You

Whatever the results of our discussions on the above, it is clear that there is still some dispute about the exact data and, as a consequence, some doubt about the conclusions you have drawn. It was evident from our telephone conversation that some of your data were wrong. (*Illustrates.*)

Under these circumstances, I would have very much preferred that you tested those attributions with me. As it turned out, we only had a time-constrained telephone conversation a couple of months after the events. As you will remember, I was very eager to talk to you about it. I understand the constraints on our time, but I do not feel that you made sufficient effort to check your data, perhaps because you felt your conclusions were sound and did not need testing.

I am concerned that you shared these untested and, depending upon our discussion, often wrong, data and conclusions with a wide group of people (indeed, I fear that you shared them with the whole board of the company). I feel that I deserved better than this.

Finally, when we did manage to have our relatively brief conversation over the telephone, I felt that you were unwilling to change your conclusions in the face of contrary evidence. And also I felt that you were going to interpret everything that I said as my being defensive. My evidence for saying this is:

- You began the conversation by saying, "I expect you to push back on some of these things, but I think it important that you try not to."
- You evidently felt quite sure about your conclusions, otherwise you would not have shared them with your colleagues.
- You were reluctant to concede any points. (*Illustrates.*)

Conclusions

Let me reiterate what I said at the beginning—that I believe your motives throughout this affair have been absolutely clean. For instance, I have no doubt that you were/are convinced about your conclusions, and therefore felt sufficiently justified in sharing your conclusions with our colleagues. My view, however, is that not all of the data and conclusions are correct— and that we need to have a constructive exchange of views if we really want to understand what went on, so that we can learn from it. I hope this note begins that dialogue.

The Session

John and I met alone for a few minutes because Bill was a bit late. John asked me my views of the memo. I responded that I thought it provided a good basis for beginning the conversation. John said he was pleased to learn of my constructive reaction because the memo infuriated him. He was especially upset over Bill's attributions that he had spoken negatively about Bill's performance and that of the senior consultant. John, as he himself recalled it, had spoken to several fellow board members because several directors had requested a discussion of the firm's performance. He felt that his description was fair and that he had said only that which he had discussed with Bill on the telephone. I had been present at the meeting with the board members (Bill had been unable to attend), and I was ready to confirm John's views of what he had said; indeed, I did so during John and Bill's meeting.

John told me that he was determined to act effectively during the meeting and that he wanted the session to be a positive learning experience for both himself and Bill. He was concerned, however, that things could get tense. He asked if he could try to craft an opening statement with me. I agreed. Bill entered the room just as John had made an attempt at crafting. After some short pleasantries, John began the session by describing some of his feelings and asking for help, but emphasizing that he felt abused by "the entire system." (Later, I found out that he was referring to several difficult episodes he had with others during the past month or so.) John continued by reminding Bill that he had not asked to work on the joint project. He had done so in order to help Bill's regional billings, which were lower than budget targets.

The Conversation	*Intervener's Observations*
John: Let me start by telling you how perplexed I am. I am genuinely befuddled.	I recall focusing on two themes. One had to do with John's feelings of being hurt. I felt that I should not interrupt the expression of his feelings, but also that I should not agree with John that Bill was the sole cause of his frustration. It seemed to me that Bill was striving to be candid, to be explicit about labeling and seeking to test his attributions, and to be explicit that he thought John's motives were "clean."
I need you to help me explain. . . . I genuinely feel abused by the entire system.	
(*Describes how he was asked by the firm to do consulting in Bill's geographical area.*) I don't enjoy flying that distance. It's not fun for me.	
Bill: Yes, I understand.	
John: But we did it. We all worked hard. It ended prematurely and no one was happy about that. And when I was asked to explain [to several members of the board] why it ended prematurely, I did what I was supposed to do, which was tell the truth.	John, in turn, was striving to communicate his view that he had not violated Bill's confidence. He felt that he had tried to be of help and to be honest, yet all he was getting in return were Bill's unfair attributions. It seemed to me that each

Bill: As you saw it.

John: And I told you everything I said to other people. There is absolutely nothing that I said to others that I had not already said to you.

I know that you and I disagree about whether the work [for the client] was good. As I told you before, I felt that it was pretty average. Did I think it was the worst that I've ever seen? No. Did I think it was the best that I've ever seen? No.

(*Later.*) [As I read your memo,] I came away with the impression that you believed that I was misrepresenting your and others' performance and that I had not discussed my views with you. That is personally troubling to me [because I am committed not to do that].

individual was doing his best to express his respective views and feelings. True, so far some of the actions were not crafted effectively. But each director was working hard at doing so. Moreover, each knew that he had internalized a Model II approach. The two directors might not be able to behave consistently with all its precepts, but they did respect and value the approach. Indeed, John and Bill later stated this explicitly.

My strategy, therefore, was to let the dialogue flow and to intervene when I felt it could go off track or when John and Bill asked for help.

Bill: My position is that you have built a world which I think you believe in. I think that world is flawed. I do not think you have sufficient data for what you've built. But, I have no doubts that you believe [your view of the world].

John: [I am confused with your comments.]
There is no way for me to respond to you.

Intervener: (*Inquires what John thinks is counterproductive about Bill's comments. Tries to communicate, at the same time, to John that he is being understood. Says to Bill.*) I believe that John is saying that your logic is self-fulfilling and self-sealing.

John: Yes, there's no way to respond to you.

Intervener: There is a way. You can ask Bill to help you see [how he concludes] that the world you have constructed is not as accurate as it should have been. Is that request a fair one, Bill?

Bill: Yes. Let me start with my memo. I've tried to put down the data as I see them. [I want to understand] why you're befuddled and feel abused. . . . My memo describes what I believe to be the case. We now have a discussion about whether my data are correct, or the conclusions are right, or whatever.

[If I send you a note with my views] and you tell me that you feel abused or upset, then one response, for me, is to say that I will not do this again.

I did not agree there was no way that John could respond. One way for John to respond was to give Bill a chance to read parts of the memo, thereby giving John an opportunity to show Bill what upset him about the way the memo was crafted. If John accepted this strategy, it would permit Bill to say what he had been trying to say, and it would give John a chance to communicate some of the causes of his unhappiness. Thus, I wanted to express empathy for John's feelings of being hurt, but I did not want to stop there because I felt that John and Bill knew the importance of testing their attributions.

John: There is a part of me that says [I should not have sold this study]. Or, if the study failed, I should have been quiet about it and made it all go away. I simply will not sell [consulting projects] in the future [under these circumstances].

Bill: All this seems irrelevant to what I have written in this note.

John: It is *very* relevant because what I am explaining are my frustrations. What I am telling you is that this type of thing is frustrating.

Intervener: May I interrupt. I hear Bill say that his memo represents his views. The memo

I did not think that John's expressions of feelings and thoughts were irrelevant. He could have important errors in it. [I think that he is asking,] "Before you feel abused, let's check the validity." [If the validity is low,] then you need not feel abused. So I suggest we examine the errors, if any, of Bill's memo.

Bill: Yes!

John: Okay, I'm willing to try. I just want to signal you right up front that I am very frustrated.

Bill: [How is that helpful to me?] I do not have any specifics, any data to understand your frustrations.

John: Bill, you're being highly judgmental [in your memo]. I'm trying to signal you that I don't understand the point. I want you to try to communicate with me in a specific fashion. So when you start to dismiss my emotions as irrelevant or troublesome . . .

was communicating that he felt he had trapped himself by trying to be a team player and help Bill's region out of its financial troubles.

It is true that John's response did not deal with testing Bill's attributions about John. Since John defended the relevance of expressing his feelings, I turned to helping him create a way to test the validity of Bill's attributions.

As I read the transcript, I think my intervention would have been more effective if I had said something like "On the one hand, I agree with John that his expressing his feelings is important and necessary. On the other hand, John, I hear Bill saying that he wants to test his attributions and evaluations."

Bill: No. No. But I never said that.

John: So you're signaling me that my position on this is not that important.

Bill: Well, you're signaling me that my position is not important as well. . . . I feel abused and upset and all those things too.

John: But I do not understand why [you wrote what you did in your memo].

Bill: Well, that's what I'm saying. We both have to understand why. Let's move now from our both saying we're upset and feel abused [to an agenda with which] we can resolve [these issues].

I was getting ready to intervene to help John and Bill examine how each was creating the conditions that the other disliked having imposed on him. Bill's comments here, however, seemed to me to help.

Intervener: Could I put it another way? Both of you feel upset. As I hear both of you, you, Bill, are saying that the first step, in your opinion, is to go through your memo to identify any distortions John may be making in the way that he interpreted it.

I was trying to make explicit how each one's actions were contributing to progress even though each was not seeing the contribution of the other.

Bill: Yes.

Intervener: But John is telling you his feeling, and [before we move to a more rational level] I believe John's feelings should be acknowledged. Does that make sense to you?

John: Sure.

Bill: Yes.

Bill: Well, let me start with your conversation with Richard. It would be useful to me to hear what he actually said.

John: Well, I didn't record it. I did not take notes on what he said. I blazed it into my memory. But, to be perfectly honest with you, I didn't think what Richard said was such a big deal. All of us have experienced times when clients may have negative evaluations of us. It happens to me, to all of us. (*Illustrates.*)

    (*Later.*) You ask me to tell you exactly what was said. I can't. I sincerely doubt that you could tell me exactly what occurred in any conversation that you had had.

Bill: Well, that's not true. [In these circumstances] I ask the client if I can take notes while he is talking. Or I'll sit down afterward and write it down.

John: Then I'm guilty as charged. I did not do that. I probably should have done it, but I didn't.

Bill: [My trouble is that] I have been told that you told your colleagues our conversation with Richard in detail. I also heard that you evaluated the senior consultant negatively.

John: I told them exactly what I told you. [And as far as the senior consultant is concerned,] I evaluated him as the number one consultant in your region.

Bill: But you and I have never discussed the "failure" with Richard.

John: But, Bill, we had no actionable results.

Bill: No. No. We did have actionable results. . . . Don't do the sighing, John. We can all do without that.	I thought Bill's demand that John stop sighing was part of his pattern of negating feelings. Bill appeared to want to get to a rational level of dialogue. Predictably, John reacted angrily.
John: Bill, don't give me that nonsense. I've got a witness (*pointing to me*) who can verify my account. I said positive things about you and the senior consultant. . . . [My conclusion from all this] is don't say anything critical about you, period.	If John had asked me to confirm or disconfirm his account, I would have said, "I do confirm your account. I also want to help you resolve this problem without requiring a witness. I believe that you and Bill are making progress at solving this problem." My instinct was to confirm John's account—but not to suggest that John learn to depend on me (or others) as witnesses—and to communicate that progress was being made.

Bill: No. No. At least brief me first.

John: I did. You and I had a series of long [telephone calls].

Bill: We had a brief telephone conversation which you cut short. I wasn't happy with that. Ted and Jim reported to me that you said [negative comments] about me.

John: Bill, I refuse to be held accountable for what they said.

Bill: No, I hold you accountable for not going through our procedure.

John: But I did talk with you.

Bill: Yes, but there was no closure.

John: Well, Bill, how am I supposed to get closure with someone who doesn't necessarily want me to get closure? How am I going to convince you of something you didn't want to believe?

Bill: When have I ever suggested to you that I did not want to get closure?

John: You are extremely argumentative on points that you hold to be true. You never let go. Never let go!

Bill: Can you give me an example?	John made several attributions about Bill without testing them. I would have intervened, but Bill's request for illustrative data was helpful.
John: Yes. (*Describes a conversation over drinks about the Israeli-Palestinian situation.*)	
Bill: (*Maintains that many at that gathering were slightly drunk.*)	
Intervener: Let's focus on what is happening here. Do you, John, see him as being argumentative here?	When John gave an example that occurred several months ago under conditions that Bill could easily discount, I decided to intervene to ask John if he
John: I see him as now telling	

me to do a series of things that I cannot possibly do. I can't possibly recreate a conversation that I had in the back of a car, nine months ago.

could illustrate Bill's argumentativeness with examples from this session.

Intervener: But one thing that we can do is to try to ascertain the degree of discrepancy between your and Bill's views.

Bill: The only relative direct evidence that I have is that Richard did not like it when we got one of the details wrong. He told me that that certainly soured his view of our work.

The second thing that he said was that he wanted John involved in any further studies.

Both of Bill's comments here confirmed what John was saying was Richard's position. This could have helped John feel that Bill was not only listening but was agreeing.

Intervener: Did you have any sense as to what led Richard to want John to be an active participant in the future?

Bill: (*Describes several reasons beginning with the fact that Richard had felt coerced to do the study by his top management.*)

Intervener: Is it fair for me to say that, after Richard said that he wanted John to be in the relationship, you did not say to him, in effect, "Okay, that will be done. It is important for me and my colleagues to know why"?

The purpose of this intervention was to illustrate how Bill could have gotten Richard to give his reasoning for wanting John involved and to do it in front of John, who was present during the meeting.

Bill: No, I didn't do that. And I regret not having done that.

(*Later.*) I hope that this comes across in my memo. There is nothing that I've seen John do [in this relationship] that is not honorable. But I would like to say to John that there are some things that he does that are dysfunctional.

Both John and Bill are saying things to each other that the other will probably see as building trust. Bill makes it clear that he trusts John's motives. John admits that he can act dysfunctionally and that he is open to examine such behavior.

John: I can give you illustrations of where I have acted dysfunctionally. [I'm open to learning on this.]

Bill: (*Later.*) Why are you getting angry?

John: I'm furious about this. Your memo says that I lied to you. It says that I made a fool of you in the company.

Bill: Where does it say that?

John: (*Responds that the memo asks that they check John's description of what Richard said with someone else. In John's view, that meant that Bill did not trust him.*)

Bill: Let's stop for a moment. Your anger isn't going to make this process work as far as I am concerned. Your anger . . .

John: Bill, you have insulted me in this memo.

Bill: I have not insulted you in the memo. Tell me where I have insulted you.

Intervener: I think John is making inferences . . .

John: [You write,] "I am concerned that you shared these untested and, depending upon our discussion, often wrong data and conclusions with a wide group of people. . . . I feel that I deserved better than this."

Bill: Yes, I am saying these are my attributions.

John: You're saying that I vilified you.

Bill: No, I'm not.

John: You're saying that I embarrassed you.

Intervener: John, you're making a leap. . . .

John: It's totally nuts. I don't need this aggravation for stuff that I didn't do. . . . What possible benefit do I have here, Bill?

Intervener: There is another possibility. Bill could be wrong. He is asking to test out his attribution.	I remember not agreeing with Bill that John's expression of feelings would inhibit progress. I also felt that John was expressing attribution that did not describe Bill's intentions. The moment I had a chance to get back to testing the validity of Bill's attributions, I took it.

Bill: Yes. [What] I wrote here are my attributions. I can either keep them in my head, [which means I'd be thinking] you're a stupid jerk. Or I can do what we want to do in this company; write it down and give you an opportunity to tell me it's wrong. What's wrong with that process? And I'm sorry that I'm getting angry.

John: Help me, Bill, to understand: What would I have to gain by dumping on you to make you look bad?

Bill: I'm not saying any of those things. You're building them into a world of hurt.

John: I am hurt.

Bill: John, let me finish. Because this has happened to me often, it is quite likely those conclusions are wrong. [I said to myself,] I'm going to test them and see if I'm wrong. If he tells me they're wrong, then he'd better believe I'll respond	Suddenly both John and Bill made statements that encouraged features of double-loop learning.

to that. You haven't given me
the opportunity to do that.

John: Let me be honest. The
process that you're going
through to test your attributions is appropriate. I think it's
intelligent, rational. I think it's
the only way that you and I can
have a reasonable relationship.
Let me signal that up front. I
am hurt that you ever came to
this conclusion [in your memo].

Intervener: (*To John.*) Let's
you and I talk. I want to be Bill
for a moment. I understand that
you are hurt. I was unaware
that this would happen as a result of that paragraph. What is
it that you want me to do now?

John: Let me be clear. I have
a set of behavior and conduct
that I hold very dear. I would
not screw a person who I like
and respect as a friend. I just
wouldn't do it. . . . Either Bill
doesn't know me, or somebody
did something wrong, or somebody took advantage of me.

My strategy was to take the
roles of John and Bill alter-
nately and try to communicate
what each would say to each
other if he were not so upset
and not pushing the other's
buttons. These interventions
seemed to facilitate progress.
They led to each director's describing, in his own way, the
difficulties and binds he feels
with the other.

Intervener: (*Being Bill.*) I respect your feelings. [You must be feel-
ing] that I'm really betraying my relationship with you.

    My dilemma is that when I wrote the memo, I did not believe
that I was writing a cock-and-bull story. But I did feel that it could
be wrong. [I wanted to share it with you to test my beliefs.] How
will I learn, if I do not show my views with all their possible warts?

John: (*Talks directly to Bill.*) Here is my problem, Bill. You and

I had a telephone conversation for an hour and a half [and neither of us moved an inch].

Bill: I do not agree.

John: So, when I got the memo, I wondered if it was written to beat me to death.

Bill: (*Later.*) If I have these thoughts, John, how else do I get them out without your saying this is just bull?

John: Let me just say that the process your're going through is intelligent, and [I realize] that I am reacting emotionally to a couple of things which I find hurtful, okay?

Intervener: (*Later.*) I'd like to focus on what is going on here now. (*To Bill.*) You appear to me to be, in effect, asking John, "If you were so upset why didn't you engage rather than withdraw?"

Now let me be John for a moment. [He might say,] "The only way I can stay sane, given my way of blowing up, is to withdraw. That's my way of protecting myself."

Bill: But [he could deal with me a lot more rationally].

Intervener: I am beginning to see a pattern. Early on, several times, you told him, in effect, to be less emotional and more rational. But he is saying, "That's me and I've got to get out those emotions."

I hear him saying that what you have done is in the best of the tradition that we are trying to develop. But he feels hurt. Instead of telling John not to be emotional, I suggest that you encourage him to express his feelings, because you want to build a relationship.

John: Yes.

Bill: Yes. . . . I do not like arguments. I do not like sessions like this. . . . What I see is John getting angry, and that is not going to produce a good result. It is going to get me angry and then we are going to shout at each other. I will think that he can't control himself and that I shouldn't listen to one lousy word he says. Then I'm disengaged [and I do not want such a relationship with him].

Intervener: Saying this is helpful. Now you are not telling John not to get emotional. You are telling him how you deal with emotion; you disengage and you do not wish to do that.

John: And my impression, which may be incorrect, is that you do like to engage [argumentatively] . . . and Chris [intervener] is right: at some level, I get upset. I withdraw because then I just start screaming, or I get upset and I don't get anywhere.

Bill: All I can say is that is not my self-image. . . . In the future, if you see me [engaging argumentatively], please say so.

John: Yes, and may I please ask you to test your image with other people?

Bill: Yes, sure.

Intervener: (*Assures Bill that John did not bad-mouth Bill during that meeting with other directors.*) And Bill, on the other hand, has been a leader in the continuous improvement process. Several months ago, I watched him be confronted by members of his office, and he listened and encouraged the feedback.

Bill: (*Later.*) [I don't think John should have left our telephone conversation as he did.]

Intervener: Now you are telling him how he should act. I recommend that you craft your conversation to include a message, something like, "John, if our conversation ends and you feel I have not learned (or whatever the issue might be), tell me. I will strive to continue the dialogue.

John: If it is important to get closure, then you're going to have to help me because I view you as one of the more difficult people to get closure with.

Bill: (*Describes some of his problems with John.*)

Intervener: (*To John.*) How would you have felt if he had told you that?

John: I would have been mad.

Bill: But John, that creates a bind. If I tell you my true feelings [and say that I want to have an honest dialogue], you see it as my buttering you up. If I do not say the positive feelings and views that I have, you see me as acting negatively.

Intervener: (*To John.*) That creates, I believe, a double bind for Bill. If he keeps his mouth shut, you will get angry. If he levels with you, you will be angry.

John: I'm sympathetic to it. I don't have a good answer.
  (*Later.*) When I read his memo, I said, "How could this guy believe that I would have done any of these things?"

Intervener: And you didn't say [to yourself], "Good, he is being honest and now we can work them through."

John: I understand your point. [I guess if I felt that he would be easier to convince on some points,] I probably would not have leaped to that conclusion.

Intervener: And Bill, maybe the next time you write such a memo, you might alert John that you are aware that he might interpret it as hurtful. That's not your intention. Your intention is to test your beliefs about John.

John: (*Later. Asks Bill to read a particular paragraph from the memo.*)

Bill: (*Agrees and reads.*) "Let me begin by saying, John, that I have found your behavior throughout to be most caring and helpful. . . . Given your 'clean motives,' I feel that some of my comments about you might seem not only undeserved but also ungrateful, or even maliciously defensive."

John: (*To intervener.*) And the way that I interpreted [what Bill just read] was that if he apologized in advance, I will not see it as a problem.

Intervener: You didn't trust him?

Bill: He didn't trust me. He didn't believe me.

John: I read your paragraph and thought you were setting me up.

Intervener: That's helpful. Because I didn't read it that way. I took him at his word.

Bill: Let me say it again. It's a very sincere paragraph.

John: I'm being honest with you.

Bill: I'm in a real bind then. Everything I do to reassure you becomes [for you] a really subtle way of winning a point.

John: Absolutely correct.

Bill: (*Later. Describes receiving many comments from fellow directors that John had been bad-mouthing Bill's performance as well as the performance of others.*) I can't get it over to you how much of an incredible barrage this is, and how offensive it is to hear things like the senior consultant is a poor performer.

John: [As I told you, I never said that about the senior consultant.] Tell me, what do you want me to do? I mean, I don't know what to do.

Bill: Please stop saying all these things.

John: Can I make a suggestion? The next time this comes up, why don't you and I and the third party meet. . . . And I repeat, I never said anything bad about the senior consultant.

(*Later.*) Does that mean you're changing your opinion about this?

Bill: I certainly have changed my view. I now realize that your speech to the board was less inflammatory and degrading than I thought.

John: May I ask you, why should you believe that in the first place?

Intervener: Maybe it is because several years ago you had the reputation of blowing your top and saying things which later you were sorry for. Right?

John: Right. There is no question I had a reputation like that. I guess that I had hoped in the past three years that things have changed.

(*Later.*) I am going to ask you a very specific question. Was there a genuine barrage of data? Because if there was, someone has been behaving inappropriately.

Bill: No, it wasn't a barrage. But it was, I can see [now], sort of fairly innocent.

Intervener: At the outset you held John responsible for the things that others said John had said. . . .

Bill: I changed my mind. You have convinced me otherwise.

John: That's really what I want to know.
     (*Later.*) Again, I agree with the process you went through. I overreacted emotionally. I understand why you [did what you did]. I accept the legitimacy of the effort.

Intervener: (*Later. To Bill.*) Am I correct in inferring that some of your impatience with John is related to what you believe is the bad-mouthing that [goes] on in the firm about your region?

Bill: Yes.

Intervener: I recommend that both of you bring up this problem during the next board meeting.

Bill: Yes, it's important if we are to build a truly global company.

John: I agree.

Summary

During this episode, I felt that I was dealing with two individuals who understood the Model II requirements for an effective dialogue. There was a base upon which they could build to resolve some very difficult problems.
     I went into the meeting quite optimistic that progress would be made. I saw John as being so upset with Bill that he was not seeing the cues in Bill's memo that indicated Bill was open to having his ideas tested. John felt hurt, violated, and abused (to use his words). It appeared to me that he went into the meeting with two objectives. First, he wanted to get Bill to apologize, and he wanted

to announce that he was fed up with the apparent bad-mouthing from Bill and several other directors about his own alleged bad-mouthing. Second, he wanted to learn. During the brief time we had together before Bill arrived, he told me that he was mad and hurt and asked me to help him avoid dysfunctional actions. He seemed to recognize that he was going to get angry, that it was necessary for him to vent his feelings, and that he could do it in ways that were counterproductive.

This episode illustrates, I believe, that individuals can use our approach to express feelings such as anger, for which Model I payoff (catharsis) is counterproductive. Someday John may be able to say, using Model II in a similar situation, that he is angry, that he realizes his anger may get in the way of his listening and his crafting conversation, and that he asks for some degree of patience on the part of others. I have observed two directors use this strategy in two different contexts (although neither was as upset as John was during this episode). In discussions informed by Model II theory-in-use, expression of strong feelings is encouraged; expressing these feelings in ways that inhibit problem solving is to be understood but not condoned.

This episode also shows how individuals can spontaneously create the very conditions they dislike. For example, John perceived Bill as argumentative and closed to learning. John also behaved in ways that could be described as argumentative and closed to learning. When John condemned Bill for vilifying and insulting him and Bill asked for data to illustrate the attributions, John's initial responses were not helpful. Yet he appeared to know that he was venting and that this was not helping problem solving. For example, he told Bill twice that Bill was adhering to the problem-solving process that both valued. During the meeting, John's awareness helped him to admit his own limitations, to reward Bill for his actions, and, I believe, to listen to me.

I also believe I played a helpful role in sensing what John and Bill had intended to say or wished they could say and saying it for them. This strategy was facilitated because John and Bill did have an intention to act as consistently with Model II as they could. They genuinely wished they could do so, in spite of the noise that each created in defending himself. If this had not been their intention, John and Bill could have argued with me and accused me of taking sides. Instead, both reported later that they felt that I respected each of them and that I was going to protect the process as best as I could. Both found that reassuring in the sense that neither director wanted me to side with him at the expense of the process.

This reaction to my role suggests that, if progress continues, I could eventually be replaced by other directors who could act as a third party, or intervener, and focus on the processes for learning in any dialogue or meeting that was hot for several or all of the participants.

12

Conclusion: A Model for Change and Improvement

My conclusions about the value, sources, and implementation of actionable knowledge are presented in five categories: the evidence from existing literature, the theoretical framework, the current state of the intervention activities in the case study, the results of that study, and concepts of causality.

Review of the Literature

The major conclusion of the literature review (Chapter One) was that organizational defensive routines exist in both private and governmental organizations as well as in schools and universities. Although organizational defensive routines appear to be omnipresent, few studies have been conducted about how to overcome them. Indeed, such advice as is given suggests either bypassing defensive routines and covering up the bypass or acting in ways that would strengthen the routines.

The Theoretical Framework

In Chapter Two, a theoretical framework was constructed to explain how defensive routines can result from the theories-in-use that individuals learn early in life to deal with embarrassing or threatening problems and to bypass the behavioral changes required for the double-loop learning that would solve the problems. Since organizations are populated by these same individuals, it is not surprising to find that individuals create organizational conditions that highly limit double-loop learning and protect the individuals from becoming aware of these conditions and from accepting responsibility for creating and maintaining them.

Finally, the theoretical framework shows how theories-in-use and organizational defensive routines combine to teach and reward individuals for using defensive reasoning. Individuals programmed with defensive reasoning make it relatively certain that their everyday interactions will maintain the organizational defensive patterns. Indeed, using defensive reasoning to attack the organizational defenses is a good way to reinforce them. In short, theories-in-use and organizational defenses function together in a self-maintaining, self-reinforcing pattern that is anti-learning and noncorrective.

Many thoughtful and concerned critics have wondered, if this view of organizational behavior is true, then are defensive routines alterable? If they are, could they be altered without harming individuals or organizations? I hope that this research, and my previously published studies (Argyris & Schön, 1978; Argyris, 1982, 1985a, 1990c) indicate that the answer is positive. True, the present study observed individuals who were bright and dedicated to learning. But, as the data illustrated, these characteristics did not mean that the change processes were without stress. Indeed, many of the young consultants studied exhibited a degree of brittleness that I have not found among lower-level, less-educated employees.

Moreover, these early studies can help us build a body of knowledge that could lead to our developing more effective and efficient change programs and programs that will work under increasingly difficult conditions.

However, I, for one, would not seek to produce knowledge that would coerce or manipulate people to change in directions they did not desire. Models II and OII may be my "cup of tea," and as a social scientist, I will strive to make them more and more desirable. But I will also strive to develop knowledge to help individuals openly resist Models II and OII if that is their wish. My desire is to produce con-

ditions in which individuals can produce valid information, make
informed choices, and monitor their implementation.

To meet individuals' needs in this connection, I believe that
the model for change that is in good currency—and which was
originally developed by Lewin (1951)—requires some revisions. The
model is unfreeze, change, and freeze at a new state. My research
indicates two caveats to the model. First, in the study described here,
developing the new state did not eliminate Model I behavior. Model
I remained a valid model for dealing with routine, nonthreatening
issues, although it was used less frequently. Recall the two directors
who used Model I actions when they went ballistic. As I observed
them, I saw that they had not lost their Model I skills. Indeed, they
used them with emotion and energy. But they were able to reflect
on the counterproductive features of these skills and alter their own
actions. It was as if—once they had achieved an emotional catharsis
by venting their feelings freely—they were also able to see the other's
point of view and find avenues for a cooperative dialogue in which
they could talk openly about both the disruptive and constructive
features of their respective actions.

The second caveat is that the new state is not frozen. The
learning in this study occurred in ways that were self-reinforcing.
Indeed, the learning continues at the time of the writing of this
book. The organization has set in motion new policies and practices
that will assure continual change. These policies and practices are
integrated with the technical concepts that drive the practice as well
as with the firm's policies regarding its own governance and the
governance of client-consultant relationships.

For example, the continuous improvement program began at
the top of the organization. As the directors began to act consistently
with Model II values and action strategies, the program was offered
to the entire firm. As consultants, at all levels, and staff were reeducated, they too altered their values and their actions in their
dealings with each other and with the clients. This has made it
possible to develop new modes of governance that encourage individuals to take more responsibility for decision making. New consulting services have been developed that integrate technical and
behavioral aspects of the improvement program. This, in turn, has
led to new internal educational programs. For example, education

about Models I and II is increasingly being integrated with the technical education offered to consultants and case-team managers.

Current Intervention Activities

The trajectory of the intervention activities in the organization I studied may be described as expanding, deepening, and persevering. This does not mean that no one is behaving according to Model I or that no anti-learning activities are to be seen. It does mean that when this activity does occur, it is observable, interruptible, and, if the participants wish, correctable.

The amount of learning by individuals has varied. Some have become quite competent at Model II; some not so competent. I believe that a systematic study of the Model I and Model II activities in the firm would show that the biggest progress has been, and continues to be, made at the top. This result is at variance with the results of many change programs in which the top managerial level is typically at the forefront of espousing change but not of producing it.

Case Study

One of the first steps my colleagues and I took in the intervention program described in this book was to prepare an action map that revealed the organizational defensive pattern and the state of the organizational learning capacities at that time.

The tape recordings and observations of discussions that were presented in parts One and Two illustrate, I believe, that a new pattern is being developed, one that overshadows the old one. As I have mentioned, I do not believe that the old pattern is being eliminated, because I do not believe that individuals who learn Model II will eliminate Model I from their repertoire of theories-in-use and skills. Both patterns now exist as potentials. The change is that the study participants now can choose from two degrees of freedom. They can choose the anti-learning or pro-learning pattern. So far, the data indicate that the participants continue to choose the pro-learning pattern, especially around the tough, wicked decisions that are perceived to be embarrassing or threatening. I think it is fair to

say that the participants feel less free to choose Model II actions
when they are with clients, although they are choosing to act this
way much more frequently than they had predicted at the outset.

The transcripts also illustrate that the participants have reduced the number of anti-learning evaluations and attributions that
they make about each other and the number of actions that made
the attributions and evaluations undiscussable, untestable, and unalterable. The participants are less likely now to blame others for
the existence of the defensive pattern. They have begun to work
hard at building an organizational pattern that facilitates learning
(both double loop and single loop), especially under the most difficult conditions. They have decreased the actions that discourage
inquiry and foster smoothing over, ambivalent responses to candor,
and polarization. There is more encouragement of inquiry, more
facing the issues squarely, and most honesty about ambivalence so
that it is discussable and reducible.

The directors' confidence in each other and in the effectiveness of their group has increased. Board meetings and directors'
reports display significantly less spinning of wheels, polarizing of
views, and biting humor. Not only are difficult topics discussed, but
they are discussed so that decisions are reached and internal commitment is relatively high. For example, during the period of this
study, the directors developed solutions to ownership issues that,
when I began to work with the directors, had threatened the survival
of the institution. They have experimented with ways to appoint
new directors, as well as ways to evaluate their own performances.
They have moved from an organizational structure in which all the
directors managed the firm's business to one in which a smaller
appointed subcommittee manages the everyday but crucial problems. This is not a trivial move because it is this subcommittee that
could spell the difference between growth and stagnation, between
bonuses and no bonuses.

The directors report that horse-trading, covert empire building, political coalition building, and bad-mouthing have significantly decreased. They also report that this does not mean they have
no difficult problems that are embarrassing or threatening. It means
that there is greater confidence that they can work through these

problems with open discussions that will build the cohesiveness of the director group.

The CEO's leadership pattern has altered. He reports that the amount of secret maneuvering with his fellow board members has decreased. Their secret maneuvering with him has also decreased. The pattern of getting resources by screaming that the client is not going to be well served has greatly decreased.

In this book, I have focused on showing that it is possible to produce actionable knowledge for changing organizational defensive routines. I wanted to show that these rare changes can be created in such a way that they will persevere. A natural next step would be for researchers to conduct studies in which they focus on developing quantitative results. I have illustrated how the discussion transcripts can be scored for Model I action strategies (advocacy, evaluation, and attribution coupled with no illustrations and no encouragement of inquiry or testing) and for Model II action strategies (advocacy, evaluation, and attribution coupled with illustrations and encouragement of inquiry and testing). I have also illustrated how organizational action maps can be developed for use in comparative studies.

Concepts of Causality

In the Appendix, I shall examine the relationship of quantitative results to concepts of causality. For example, if our concept of causality is based on variance (Mill's method of difference), then quantitative results can lead to generalizations of the form $Y = f(X)$, which are of value for causal explanations. I shall suggest that these generalizations have limited actionable potential. The concept of causality that I have called design causality may produce knowledge that is more actionable *and* more open to validation. Study designs based on this concept may also produce fewer quantitative results and more specifications for the master programs that people use to design their actions and implement them. However, this concept of causality may allow us to produce both knowledge for action and valid contributions to organizational theory. Both are needed; and they should be linked, not unnecessarily separated.

Appendix

Design Causality:
Explaining, Acting On, and
Integrating Diverse Perspectives

It is possible to develop knowledge that is valid and actionable in everyday life and whose use in everyday life by practitioners or researchers is an opportunity for a valid test of the knowledge. The results of this test, in turn, should add to our understanding of organizations and organizational learning, and especially to our understanding of ways to change the status quo.

Theory of Action

The essential requirement for producing such knowledge is to have a theory of action that can be used to diagnose and understand individual, group, intergroup, and organizational behavior. Such a theory tells the person or group that uses it how to act *effectively*, how to design and implement actions in such a way that the actions achieve the intended consequences, they achieve these consequences persistently, and they do not reduce the actor's present level of effectiveness.

Theories of action are theories of governance; they explain how individuals or groups put their arms around reality in order to manage it effectively. As such, they are normative theories, not theories claiming some objective truth. They specify the action strategies required, the consequences that follow, and the underlying governing values that are satisficed.

Theories of action are at the core of human competence, self-esteem, and self-efficacy. Individuals gain confidence by acting in ways that they and others evaluate as effective. Individuals assure that these effective actions will continue by creating organizational patterns that encourage learning, especially double-loop learning.

Although theories of action are not theories about some objective truth, they do make claims about how to act effectively—indeed, about what is effective in the first place for a particular individual or group. These claims must be subjected to the most rigorous tests available, not only because that is good science but also because we as researchers owe it to the practitioners who may use the knowledge produced by our research and to the people who receive services from those practitioners. All are owed some assurance that we strive to connect practice with testing, action with learning.

In order for theories of action to be tested in everyday life, it must be possible to derive from them the actual behavior required for effectiveness. In other words, theories of action must produce actionable knowledge. The more unambiguous the specification for behavior, the smaller the gap between knowledge and action. Thus, a theory of action must meet three requirements. The same theory should be usable to describe and understand reality, to invent new solutions to problems, and to prescribe what actions are to be taken, how they are to be implemented, and how the effectiveness of the implementation is to be evaluated.

Theories to produce actionable knowledge are, therefore, descriptive, normative, and prescriptive. The research project described in this book was designed to include these three features. For example, my fellow researchers and I described the reality at the client firm's top organizational level (and later at lower levels) by using the concepts of Model I theory-in-use and Model OI limited-learning systems. We were able to show that using Model I and Model OI produced an organizational defensive pattern and the organizational politics that the director-owners did not want because the pattern and politics were anti-learning and overprotective of the status quo.

We then introduced the concepts of Model II theory-in-use and Model OII learning systems as normative inventions to reduce the dysfunctional politics and the limited-learning activities. Finally, Models II and OII were used to prescribe the actions that would be required to produce the desired changes. For example, the directors would have to learn to advocate their positions and make evaluations or attributions in ways that encouraged inquiry and testing, instead of their practice of discouraging inquiry and testing. We designed seminars to help the directors make Model II actions part of their personal theories-in-use. We used the same concepts in all the follow-up business-oriented meetings in order to continue practice and learning.

Every seminar and every meeting was the occasion for a test of the theory's features. For example, we predicted that the directors would not be able to change their theories-in-use or the organizational defensive pattern even after they agreed that the theories were Model I, that the pattern we had mapped was valid, and that they wanted to alter both. We tested the prediction by analyzing the tapes of the feedback sessions and the business meetings to see if we could find Model II actions. We could not.

We also made predictions about what would happen after the seminars. We predicted, for each individual, the likelihood that he would begin to change his behavior, basing our prediction on his pattern of learning during the feedback session or seminar as well as on his commitment to use important business sessions to practice and develop his skills. We made predictions about group behavior by scoring tapes of meetings for Model I and Model II behavior.

When the directors and consultants began to use their knowledge of Model II in dealing with clients, it was possible to assess the extent to which the concepts we used to understand the consulting organization were also valid for their client organizations. Research suggested, for example, that their clients also used Model I theories-in-use and created anti-learning organizational defensive patterns. Thus, the theory used to understand the individual case was relevant to understanding many other cases.

Of course, our "individual case" itself was actually made up of many cases. The theory of action was used to understand each director and the director group. Later, it was used to understand other consultants and various intergroup relations within the firm. Still later, it helped us to understand organizational clients and consultant-client relationships. We developed hundreds of observations and could easily develop literally thousands of scores for each of these units. Each could become the basis of a legitimate study. In short, our theory of action can be used to study units of many different sizes, and it can be used to make generalizations and test predictions about many other settings than the immediate one.

We also developed many opportunities to observe the effect of our intervention upon learning at all levels of the organization. For example, every meeting held after the two-day case-discussion seminar was usually designed to overcome a problem that had previously been considered undiscussable and uncorrectable. The performance of certain directors, the honesty of certain directors, the public evaluation of the CEO's performance, the constructive confrontation of the consultants' brittleness, and the tendency to project blame on others are a few examples.

The sessions were tape-recorded for both our scientific reasons and the participants' educational reasons. We were able to score the tapes to determine the participants' theories-in-use, while the participants often listened to the tapes to reflect on their performances. Some asked for transcripts so that they could reflect with more concentrated attention.

In addition, these kinds of recordings could easily be used by researchers to construct observer reliability and validity tests of any type that they wish. (Much would depend on the kind of information they consider to be a valid test of reliability and validity.) Thus, either dedicated positivists or interpretivists could use this kind of data base.

Another possible use for recordings would be to study the intervener's actions during a session. The questions that could be answered include: To what extent did the intervener act consistently with Models II and OII? To what extent did this lead to the consequences predicted by the theory? If the intervener did not act consistently with the theory, why not? What were the consequences?

A final requirement for a theory used to change the status quo is that it should provide strategies for a researcher to question its veracity, some means for users to step backward to reflect on the theory itself. In researchers' jargon, the researcher must have the ability to "go meta" on the theory. Our theory provides this possibility because it is designed to produce double-loop learning, which questions values. This final requirement is especially important for knowledge that is intended both to be actionable and to be under the control of practitioners, not only with ways to keep testing the theory but to question the theory itself.

The least developed part of our theory concerns how to get from here to there. We believe that we are quite strong at the empirical level in helping people move from here to there. We are less strong in being able to specify a priori what goes on during the intervention and change processes. For example, we can predict quite robustly that individuals using Model I theories-in-use will create organizational defensive patterns that inhibit double-loop learning. Finding one nontrivial instance where this is not the case would disconfirm features of the theory. Eventually, we would like to make predictions and produce robust tests that specify what goes on during the processes of moving from here to there.

Empirical Research Methods

The empirical methods used in our research are simple and, I believe, powerful. They can produce propositions that are as robust as, or even more robust than, those based upon much more sophisticated quantitative techniques. They are also powerful because they are simple enough that practitioners can use them in everyday life.

The research methodology we used was consistent with the ladder of inference described in Chapter Two. If this ladder accurately describes how individuals attribute causes or reasons for actions and evaluate the effectiveness of actions in order to manage their lives, then we should design our research using the same stages of inference, because this will minimize any gap between the knowledge produced by the research and its actionability.

The first step, after some introductory interviews, was to collect data that were as directly observable as possible. The beginning approach was naturalistic and ethnographic. To obtain observations that included hard data, we used tape recordings supplemented by human observations.

Hard data are what individuals and groups actually say and do. Conversations are hard data. They are hard data in the sense that people with different views, agendas, and values can agree on what is said. Our courts strive to produce such data. Recall that President Nixon found out that tape recordings can contain hard data.

Once the data were collected, they were analyzed. We used the categories in Models I and II and Models OI and OII to organize the data. We scored directors' meetings, the feedback sessions, the case-discussion seminars, and many other meetings to categorize participants' behavior during the five years of the study that this book covers. Once we had organized the data, we could begin to make predictions.

One example of the robust predictions we made was that the directors would not be able to create or encourage double-loop learning after the feedback session even though they had confirmed the validity of the organizational defensive pattern. We said the directors would act consistently with Model I even though they aspired to become more competent and knew the action strategies that got them into trouble (for example, advocating their ideas with no inquiry, making untestable attributions, denying that they are doing so, and when confronted, blaming another). If one director changed to Model II actions during the months after the feedback session but before the case-discussion seminar, such actions would have been grounds for disconfirming features of Model I.

We also developed an action map, which depicted the organizational defensive pattern that resulted in anti-learning and over-protective actions, especially around any embarrassing or threatening issues. It was possible to use this map to make further robust predictions. For example, even though the directors confirmed the pattern, even though they wanted to change it, they would be unable to do so. Indeed, it was to their credit that they realized that moving from Model I to II and from OI to OII is not easy, that it requires much practice and, therefore, a long time. Their realistic aspirations not only helped them to deal successfully with their vulnerability but also legitimized time and space for the rest of the organization to do the same. People would have doubted anyone who claimed that he or she had learned to be competent with Model II after attending an initial seminar.

Finally, our claim that the empirical results were generalizable beyond this organization was testable. The directors and consultants often found that they could not help a client organization implement recommendations as effectively as the client wished because of the client's organizational defensive routines. The directors and consultants observed generic action strategies, interpersonal dynamics, group dynamics, and organizational consequences similar to the ones described in their own organizational map. Indeed, several senior and junior consultants used that map to develop maps of client organizations. Thus, Model I and the defensive patterns were shown to be generalizable throughout this organization and over time.

The same concepts are, I suggest, generalizable to other organizations. To be sure, there will be some differences in the components. But the generic action strategies and the first- through fifth-order consequences leading to anti-learning consequences that appeared in our action map will be applicable to all other organizations no matter what their size, age, or technological level. The key condition is that the participants use Model I theory-in-use to deal with embarrassment or threat, which means that they will produce OI limited-learning systems and the defensive pattern described in this book. These claims are testable by future studies. Indeed, the present intervention increases the likelihood that clients of the consulting organization may wish to undergo similar change programs. Thus, this project increases the sample of organizations that may be studied.

Researchers' Interpersonal Skills

Research that combines naturalistic observations and interventions to change the status quo requires interpersonal skills. Researchers and interveners will have to be able to use Model II skills under conditions of mild to high embarrassment or threat to themselves. Some of these Model II skills are similar to the interpersonal skills described in the existing literature, such as establishing warmth, trust, acceptance, openness, and flexibility (Berg & Smith, 1985;

Lowman, 1985). There are other skills identified as necessary, but
less is said about how to develop them. For example, researchers
will be questioning the status quo, and they must not take for
granted what the clients take for granted. Therefore, researchers will
be modeling how to make oneself vulnerable without feeling weak
for clients who might feel that the modeled behavior is dangerous
and could open up a can of worms. There will be many moments
when clients will doubt, become upset, question the usefulness of
demonstrated behavior, or express disbelief. As we have seen, this
was true of the directors as well as of other professionals in the firm.
As Spencer and Cullen suggest (1978), interveners require courage.

There are two ways to develop this courage. One is to be an
expert practitioner of a theory that is sound and actionable. It is
then possible to make interventions that are courageous and do it
spontaneously because the theory tells us what design to use and
what to say. The second way is to practice the skills in an environment where learning is rewarded. Both of these ways are helpful.
The better interveners are at using the theory, the more confidently
they will act under difficult conditions. The more practice they
have, the more likely it will be that they can produce Model II
actions.

Graduate social science research programs do not, I believe,
give adequate attention to educating students in these skills. In cases
where they do, the education tends to be largely experiential and
almost devoid of intellectual content that would help them learn to
test theories. Together, these educational trends make it less likely
than ever that our graduate students will learn the necessary competencies. Indeed, my experience suggests that these trends keep
away the very bright and courageous students because they sense
that their courage and their interest in testing and practicing could
get them in trouble with faculty and fellow students. We have published one model for such education (Argyris, Putnam, & Smith,
1985). Much more needs to be done.

Concepts of Causality

As I stated in Chapter Two, the function of reasoning in everyday
life is to provide a basis for opinion, belief, attitude, feeling, or

action. It is through the act of reasoning that individuals explain or account for facts and go from one set of ideas and actions to a new set.

Donald (1991), in his study of the origins of the modern mind, points out that causal reasoning is a latecomer in the development of the human mind. It has been greatly aided by the development of external memory (any device—such as a book, a memo, or another human being—that helps provide needed information outside the actor's memory). Not surprisingly, social scientists have found that causal reasoning guides action and that the purpose of action is to create and maintain mastery of the causal structure of the environment (Heider, 1958; Kelley, 1967; Weiner, 1986). Causal reasoning influences a wide array of human action (Einhorn, 1986; Forsterling, 1988; Weiner, 1991).

The theory of causality that is dominant in research has its roots in the work of John Stuart Mill ([1843] 1949). At the core of his ideas is the rigorous, objective study of variance among variables. However, a dilemma arises in using Mill's concept of causality when the research intent is to produce actionable knowledge. I have stated that the concept of causality used to produce actionable knowledge through research should be consistent with the concept of causality individuals are likely to use when employing the knowledge in everyday life. Donald Schön and I suggest that Mill's definition of a variable (which is key to his basing causality in variance) leads to a type of distancing and a demand for intellectual rigor that are not practicable for our clients when they are implementing the concepts we teach them so they can produce double-loop learning in everyday life (Argyris & Schön, 1990).

Three scholars who represent Mill's view of causality are Simon (1969); Campbell and Stanley (1963), who show more concern for applicable knowledge than Simon does; and James, Mulaik, and Brett (1982).

Central to this view of causality is a particular way of construing the idea of "variable" (Argyris & Schön, 1990). In the work of Simon; Campbell and Stanley; and James, Mulaik, and Brett, for example, causality is understood as a particular kind of relationship among variables. Variables themselves are understood as named attributes extracted from the complexity of observed phenomena, and they are treated as essentially the same whatever the local contexts in which they occur. So, for example, James, Mulaik, and Brett illustrate their concept of causality with the proposition that "role overload may be thought to cause state anxiety" (p. 28). They define state anxiety, following Spielberger (1977), as "subjective, consciously perceived feelings of tension, apprehension [and] nervousness, accompanied by or associated with activation of the autonomic nervous system" (p. 110). They go on to suggest that role overload may be caused, directly or indirectly, by changes in expected quality or quantity of work (such as increases in demand for product) and that state anxiety may be a cause of "other psychological phenomena, such as performance and withdrawal behaviors."

Variables such as role overload, state anxiety, and withdrawal are considered to have the same meaning in each local context in which they appear. It is this presumed constancy of meaning that allows scientists to speak of variations in the local values and relationships of variables. Otherwise, whenever a variable took on a different value or relationship to other variables, they would have to speak of it as a different variable. This view of causality depends, in short, on an ontology according to which the complexity of observed phenomena is transformed into a collection of simple variables maintaining constant identity across local contexts.

Simon expresses this idea in another way when he says that each value of variables X and Y, standing for cause and effect, defines a class of events and that each variable therefore "comprises a set of classes of events" (quoted in James, Mulaik, & Brett, p. 15). On this basis, it becomes possible to say that the same variable, X or Y, may have the same or different values in different settings, a condition necessary for the discovery of general causal relationships among variables.

According to Simon's view, also adopted by James, Mulaik, and Brett, a causal relation is "a function of an effect (Y) on one or more causes (X's)" and takes the form $Y = f(X)$. Such a function is self-contained, which is to say that "one and only one value . . . of Y is associated with each value . . . of X," or that "the values of Y are determined completely by the values of X" (James, Mulaik, & Brett, p. 170). Self-containment implies independence of context. The researcher employing this view of causality seeks evidence to show that the values of Y can be determined, given the values of X and the knowledge that X has occurred, independently of any other features of the contexts in which X and Y occur.

In this theory, causal functions are usually complex, in the sense that they involve many variables. They are asymmetric, because "it is impossible to reverse the direction of causation and still maintain unique determination" (p. 18). And they must be expressed in quantitative terms, because one could not otherwise establish that one and only one value of Y is associated with each value of X.

Causal inferences are usually expressed in probabilistic function equations, because variations in effects (Y's) may be due to other causes (X's) than those expressed in a given function equation, $Y = f(X)$. Self-containment is preserved in a probabilistic function equation if "the realized values of causes included explicitly in the equation determine the [conditional] probability distribution of the effect variable" (p. 18). The thrust of these qualifications is to treat as noise the temporary, idiosyncratic influences of the local context on variables that are presumed to be causally connected.

According to this view of causality, causal inferences may be made from data provided by either of two principal methods of empirical research. In the first, contrived experiment, the researcher creates a research setting separate from the practice setting (an organizational simulation, for example) and constructs experimental and control groups in order to apply Mill's methods of causal inference. He or she seeks to test whether Y is regularly accompanied by X (method of agreement), whether in the absence of X, Y does not occur (method of difference), and whether variations in the value of Y are accompanied by corresponding variations in the value of X (method of concomitant variations). In this way, the researcher tries to determine whether the values of the effect variables are uniquely determined by the values of the cause variables.

In a contrived experiment, the research setting is protected from the constraints and confusions of the practice setting, although conclusions drawn from the research are held to be transferrable to practice.

The second principal method of empirical research is natural experiment, or "quasi-experimental method," in the words of

Campbell and Stanley. Here, the researcher observes a number of practice settings, identifying and measuring in each case the values of the relevant variables. Observations are distributed across many local contexts so that the researcher avoids being misled by the peculiarities of any particular one. As in a contrived experiment, the researcher analyzes the resulting data to test whether the values of the effect variables are uniquely determined by the values of the cause variables.

I and my colleagues would have had difficulty implementing the requirements I have just described in our study. We would have had to treat the directors and others at a respectable research distance lest we became affected by their biases and lost our status as neutral, objective observers. This would have led either to no interventions or to interventions of quite a different character.

This is not to say that we had no concerns about being infected by the directors' biases. Our strategy was to get close enough to the directors so that any loss of our objectivity would be discussable and influenceable. Indeed, the directors did not want us to think and act as they did. That would have defeated their objective of becoming a learning organization. Moreover, they did not want us to be infected by them because then we might not foresee difficulties arising as a result of the intervention. Worse yet, we might have held them responsible for the difficulties.

We would also have had to define our variables so that they were clearly independent of each other and did not overlap. The problem we would have faced was that the directors and others managed their lives by defining variables in ways that often overlapped. They clustered variables in order to overdetermine causality—that is, to try to make certain that what they intended to occur would occur (Hackman & Walton, 1986). If Mill's methods represent precision as distinct from sloppiness, the individuals in our study appear to have learned how to be precisely sloppy—a concept of rigor alien to Mill's views.

Another limitation of the prevalent scientific concept of causality is what happens when we try to apply research results. The first difficulty is that the concepts of rigorously empirical research are akin to Model I concepts, and implementing the propositions that this research produces requires Model I conditions. The second difficulty is that implementing the results rigorously would require amounts of time and other resources rarely available in everyday life for this kind of endeavor.

In order to illustrate these difficulties, I have selected two examples of social psychological experiments that are held in high esteem by academics (including myself): the work of Barker, Dembo, and Lewin (1941) on frustration and regression and McClelland's work (1985) on motivation. Let us begin with a summary of the Barker, Dembo, and Lewin experiment.

They brought children into an experimental situation without briefing them about the experiment. They acted in accordance with good practice by keeping secret the experimental manipulation—namely, frustration. Nor did the children make an informed decision to participate (although I doubt any were coerced if they did not wish to participate).

They created an unambiguous situation of frustration. They got the children to play with and become attached to some toys. Then they placed a physical barrier between the children and the toys thereby "causing" frustration.

They had several observers behind one-way-vision glass scoring the actions of the children. They used instruments that were pretested.

They maintained the barrier long enough to collect observations that could be used to rigorously test their hypotheses. They controlled the time perspective of the children and the experiment.

The results led to the conclusion that mild frustration could lead to creative behavior. Beyond that point, the children regressed. Regression led to more primitive behavior including aggression.

Now let us turn to using this knowledge in real life. It is, I believe, clearly applicable. For example, managers could be taught that if they frustrate people, those people will regress and a likely consequence of the regression is that they will become angry and aggressive. But how does a manager translate this applicable knowledge into actionable knowledge? For example, a manager goes into a meeting to allocate scarce financial resources. He wants to do it fairly, in line with the objectives of the organization as a whole rather than the parochial views of his different subordinates. He also wants to generate internal commitment on the part of the subordinates to the final results so that the likelihood of effective implementation can be increased. He knows that he must be careful to minimize frustration.

How does he find out what his impact is? One way is to ask the subordinates, but doing so may produce biased replies because they may be playing it safe. Another way is to give the subordinates instruments to complete, but doing so might frustrate the people more, especially those who believe they are "winning." He might use an instrument the researchers used by having an observer present, but how would the observer feed back the data? Would she give it only to the leader? Would she include the subordinates? Could not the feedback exacerbate the feelings of frustration for some? If so, how would the manager find out?

How would the manager create clear conditions for reducing frustration? What behavior might lead to frustration even though the manager wishes to prevent it? For example, the manager will have to deny some requests, but how unequivocally clear must the denial be? If he did it with anger, it could lead the subordinates to see him as ruthless and insensitive as well as unilateral. Would not such beliefs have an impact on the feelings of frustration? For example, what if the subordinates said to themselves, "Okay, you're so sure of yourself, you take responsibility for the consequences," and then psychologically withdrew, but covered it up. Such withdrawal could ameliorate any feelings of frustration. It is not easy to create an unambiguous barrier in real life without its producing consequences that go beyond the generalizations related to frustration.

The researchers had it easy compared to the manager. They had the power to create an experimental setting, to round up some children to be subjects, to keep secret the purpose of the experiment, to cover up the secrecy, and to make repeated observations until they were sure they had all the data they needed to produce valid propositions about the impact of frustration.

In other words, while the propositions as stated may accurately describe the impact of frustration on human beings, they say very little about how a manager could make use of the propositions in real life. The propositions are not instances of actionable knowledge.

My second example of this difficulty is McClelland's expectancy value model of motivation (1985). Its fundamental proposition is that the decision to perform specific behavior is a multiplicative function of underlying motive, expectancy of success or failure, incentives, and availability of needed response. Let's go back to a manager in a meeting trying to make a decision on how to act. How will she ever collect and process all that information about what is in her mind regarding motive, expectancy, and so forth, as she strives to lead? How will she ever discover and process the information in the minds of the others that could influence her expectancy of success or failure, the incentives to act, and the availability of the response? Moreover, even if she could collect all these data, how does she produce the multiplicative function under real-time conditions?

There is another problem present in these experiments that is troubling from the point of view of producing actionable knowledge. It stems from the enormous amount of unilateral power the researchers had over their subjects and over the amount of time available to conduct their research.

Having and exercising unilateral power to create a setting and keep individuals in it is not a neutral or benign act. It can influence the ways adults act, learn, or commit themselves (Argyris, 1980). Having all the time that is needed and being able to repeat an experiment until they get it right is a luxury rarely available to actors in real life.

Enormous amounts of unilateral power and unrestricted time are taken for granted by researchers conducting rigorously controlled experiments. If practitioners are to reproduce or mitigate the consequences found in these experiments, they will have to have the same conditions and instruments the researchers had. In short, managers—if they are to re-create, not simply understand, experimental results—will require similar unilateral authority over their subordinates. The theory-in-use of these two experiments (and many others) is Model I. Any attempt to use the propositions rigorously in real life would require managers to create Model I conditions.

Pattern and Component Causality

There are three concepts of causality that are relevant to our research. Two of them, pattern and component causality, are consistent with the prevalent scientific concept I have just described. The third one, design causality, has a different foundation and will be described in the next section.

Pattern causality is illustrated by the organizational defensive pattern described in Chapter Four. The pattern illustrates a defensive limited-learning system in which individuals use defensive reasoning. The causal claim is that dysfunctional organizational politics are caused by this pattern.

This explanation is based on descriptive research. Its logic is that organizational politics existed in the organization studied because individuals created a social system that required them to produce politics.

It is difficult to use Mill's methods to study causality that inheres within a pattern—that, in a manner of speaking, *is* the pattern. As Churchman (1971) has stated, "The differentiating feature of systems is that they can be separated into parts and that these parts work together for the sake of the whole" (p. 49). Thus, in a pattern, variance is presumably limited by a tight interdependence among the variables, an interdependence in the service of the whole.

If variance that varies primarily beyond the whole is to be studied, researchers would have to study a sample of different wholes, different systems or patterns. Once the pattern becomes the unit around which to observe variance, then it is difficult to use rigorously the concept of causality associated with Mill's methods without comparing an appropriate sample of patterns. Moreover, the patterns would have to be defined in such a way that they could be shown to be fully independent of each other yet be causally influenced by each other.

Component causality is related to pattern causality in that it focuses on the empirical relationships between and among variables in the pattern. For several reasons, I did not focus much on component causality. Let us assume, for the moment, that the components that form the organizational defensive pattern can be rigorously defined as independent of each other and their empirical interdependence can vary widely, so that they can be studied with the methods based on analyzing variance.

The first difficulty is that the organizational defensive pattern revealed in the action map is composed of thirty-two multilevel coexisting variables. In order to conduct empirical research with independent variables, we would have to decompose the pattern into many different subunits. Even with the help of sophisticated computer technology, we would have difficulty in varying the variables systematically in order to establish causality in the mode required by Mill's methods. Moreover, would not the result of such an analysis be a complicated set of propositions spelling out precisely the empirical relationships among and between the variables? How could such a map be used in everyday life? There is also a more profound problem that faces us because we seek knowledge about producing a new status quo, one in which Models II and OII are routinely used.

Let us assume, for the sake of illustration, that we set out to study the empirical relationships between high and low frequencies of untested attributions or between high and low frequencies of untested evaluations. We could predict that if our organizational pattern is valid, anti-learning consequences and organizational politics would exist whatever level of variance is observed. The reason this should be the case is that low frequency of untested attributions or evaluations is consistent with Model I and the organizational defensive pattern. The untested attributions and evaluations are observed to be low because they are often censored; they are, to use our jargon, kept in individuals' left-hand columns. The low frequency is the equivalent of "easing-in," or the opposite of Model I. Easing-in, as our theory predicts, also leads to limited-learning systems. Easing-in appears less controlling than confronting does, but is experienced as highly controlling. This nondirective behavior is in the service of Model I governing values, and hence it too leads to defensive consequences (Argyris, 1982).

To put this another way, low frequency of untested attributions or evaluations is *not* equivalent to low frequency of tested attributions or evaluations. Comparing individual instances of these actions does not produce a direct correlation that describes the change in which we are most interested. It is a step-function change to go from untested to tested statements. Both low and high frequencies of tested attributions and evaluations require individuals who can use Model II as a theory-in-use and can create pro-learning social systems. It took the directors and others in their organization several years to learn Model II and to create a learning-oriented pattern.

The variance among the components in a pattern is restricted by the pattern. The variance would be restricted even if we took the directors out of the organization and placed them in a laboratory setting. In the laboratory, we would still have to teach the "subjects" to act consistently with Model II, and we would have to create an experimental context in which double-loop learning could occur. This means the subjects would have to know about the experimental manipulation and be able to confront it, so that subjects reeducated to apply Model II could be compared with subjects who were not reeducated. To understand more fully why this is so, we must turn to the concept of design causality.

Design Causality

Design causality is more fundamental than pattern or component causality. First, it explains how the pattern and its components arose in the first place. Second, it explains why changes within the pattern or its components are not likely to lead to double-loop learning that perseveres. Third, by introducing another theory of action (Models II and OII), it suggests ways to change the pattern itself and its components with it.

At least one other researcher had described an approach that, I believe, assumes design causality. In presenting his "method of specimens," Runkel (1990) seeks to define invariants—as I do with such concepts as Model I and organizational defensive routines. However, Runkel appears to aspire to produce models that may be closer to "the real thing." For example, a specimen model is a model of a railroad or an airplane. Such models purport to be so close to how the phenomena behave that tests of statistical inference are not necessary (pp. 136–137).

One way to illustrate how my associates and I arrived at our concept of design causality is to review our premises and reflect on our research-intervention activities with the directors.

As I stated in Chapter Two, our perspective assumes that human beings are designing organisms. We developed this premise from the studies of such scholars as Lewin (life space) and Simon (design) and from the clinical-personality-cognitive studies premised on the idea that humans strive to achieve their intended consequences (Lewin, 1951; Simon, 1969; Argyris, 1982, 1985b). The more success they have in these endeavors, the stronger their sense of efficacy, competence, and self-esteem. Embedded in this clinical-personality-cognitive literature is the notion that human beings have reasons (conscious or unconscious) for acting as they do and that the reasons are related to mastery and self-regulation (Locke, 1991). Examining these reasons can provide a basis from which to infer the designs that individuals create in order to actualize, or implement, their reasons.

Therefore, the actions, or designs, of the directors and the other participants in this study were hypothesized to be based on conscious or unconscious reasons related to mastery and self-regulation. The directors believed they were beginning to create organizational politics that were counterproductive to building the kind of learning organization they intended to build. The action map we compiled (presented in Chapter Four) confirmed their beliefs.

What would have caused the directors to produce a pattern they did not intend? It could be that they had inherited the pattern, but that was unlikely since they had created the organization only a year or so before I arrived. It could be that someone or some group had more power than they did and had coerced them to comply with the pattern, but in this case no one was above them. Moreover, they owned the organization.

It could be that pressures from clients had caused the pattern. I believe that pressures from clients did exacerbate and reinforce the pattern but did not produce it at the outset. The directors had clients who pressured and those who did not. Yet the defenses existed. There were some directors who managed the pressures more effectively than others, yet they too were involved in creating the defensive pattern. Also, the directors re-created the pattern during the early workshops I held, where they were away from the office and from the everyday client pressures. Additionally, the transcripts reproduced in chapters Four and Five, which contain dialogue from the initial interviews and the feedback session, illustrate that the directors often acted to create their own pressures, which were then partially blamed upon the clients.

Finally, the dysfunctional features of the pattern were reversed, and the reversal appears to have persisted for five years; yet the pressures on the directors from clients—and, indeed, from their own consultants—have increased. Our analysis suggested that the causal responsibility did lie, at the outset, with the directors. The directors agreed. They invited us to help them because they believed they were nontrivially responsible.

This example of design responsibility leads to another puzzle. If it is true, as we maintain, that individuals design their actions, if their actions are designed to achieve the consequences they intend, and if the defensive pattern is a result of their designed actions, then it is possible to infer that they intended to produce the pattern. But the directors denied this; they maintained that their intentions were the opposite.

To begin to solve the puzzle, we introduced the concepts of espoused intentions versus the intentions inherent in a theory-in-use. The directors espoused intentions were to produce productive consequences, but the intentions of their theories-in-use were to produce defensive strategies, which produced counterproductive consequences. If no forces outside the control of the directors required them to act as they did, we reasoned, then the forces must be within their control. Our hypothesis was that they created the organizational defensive pattern by their Model I actions. As these actions, or designs, became routine, they led to the organizational defensive pattern. As the pattern evolved, it fed back to reinforce the Model I theories-in-use. Once these self-reinforcing and self-sealing conditions existed, they created the politics and other anti-learning consequences.

The organizational defensive pattern is indeed composed of individual, interpersonal, group, intergroup, and organizational variables. But since there is no evidence to suggest that the pattern was forced on the directors, we concluded that the causality began with the Model I theories-in-use. The directors (and later all the other consultants) brought the theories-in-use with them to their new organization.

The concepts of pattern and component causality could also

be used to explain what caused the directors' counterproductive actions. However, I do not believe that these concepts can explain how the directors created a pattern they decried. The concept of design causality not only explained the existence of the pattern to us; we also used it to begin to change the pattern and, in so doing, alter the components of the pattern. Thus, pattern and component causality were altered by a change program that was based on design causality.

The reader may ask why human beings have selected Models I and OI. I do not have a systematic answer to that question. So far, the research suggests that the answer (or answers) will require a more complete historical analysis of human beings as designing systems, as well as a more comprehensive knowledge about the designing process. The most that can be said about the present state of our knowledge is that Models I and OI are alterable, and the alterations in one case can be shown to have persisted for five years, as well as to have expanded and deepened. In another case, the results have continued for fifteen years (Argyris, 1982).

To summarize, using rigorous research methods that are consistent with the concept of causality related to variance may lead to the following difficulties when the objective is to produce actionable knowledge for changing the status quo.

Prevalent Scientific Concept of Causality Advises	Actionable Knowledge for Changing the Status Quo Requires
Variables that are defined as autonomous and are as separate from each other as possible	Variables that are differentiated but whose differences are functions of the variables' connections with other variables in a pattern
Consistent and generalizable meanings that are disconnected from the concrete and specific	Consistent and generalizable meanings that are explicitly connectable to the concrete and specific
Causal relationships that are expressed by the use of	Causal relationships that are expressed by reference to

analytical-quantitative techniques that depend upon variance	pattern and design causality
Generalizations that describe the status quo	Generalizations that describe the status quo in ways that can lead to changing the status quo generalizations
Generalizations that are produced under Model I conditions	Generalizations that are produced under Model II double-loop learning conditions

Positivistic Principles and Our Research Perspective

The characteristics described in the left-hand column of the preceding list are typically associated with positivism. Although I differ with the positivistic perspective in regard to the necessity of using these five characteristics, I do not differ with some of the fundamental concepts of positivism related to testing the validity of hypotheses and explanations. For example, I adhere to the four checks on causal reasoning that Lee (1989a, 1989b, 1991) places at the core of positivistic thinking regarding causality. The first check is to craft reasoning and actions in such a way that the reasoning can be falsified by observing the actions of both the reasoner and others. The second check is to show that the causal reasoning is logically consistent and contains minimal numbers of unrecognized gaps. The third check is to craft causal reasoning with a relatively high explanatory power and minimal concepts and premises. The fourth and final check is to create reasoning that can survive falsifiability and comparison with competing reasoning.

I hope the empirical material in the book and the analysis in this appendix indicate my commitment to my hypothesized theory of action and my profound commitment to subjecting it to continual, robust tests.

The research in this book illustrates three features of robust tests. First is the specification of what will and will not happen. The intent is to subject predictions to disconfirmation as well as confirmation. For example, we predicted that Model I governing values and action strategies would lead to anti–double-loop learning systems and not pro–double-loop learning systems.

The second feature of a robust test is that it predicts the conditions under which the hypotheses will hold, *and* it predicts that this particular cause–and–effect relationship will always be the case. For example, we predicted that the directors' Model I theories-in-use would lead to the organizational defensive pattern, which, in turn, would feed back to reinforce the Model I theories-in-use. This prediction should have held as long as the directors' theories-in-use and the defensive pattern were not altered. A six-month or so gap between the first feedback session and the two-day case-discussion seminar occurred, which allowed us to test the prediction. During this time, even though the directors had committed themselves to changing the organizational defensive pattern, they were unable to do so. They required theories-in-use reeducation, which took the form of the seminar plus relevant follow-up experiments.

Recently I met a senior executive who, in another organization ten years ago, had led a successful fight not to enter an intervention change program of the kind I describe here. He felt that changing theories-in-use and organizational defensive routines was too dangerous. He told me that he now wishes that he had supported the program. He is now the firm's CEO and spends countless hours dealing with organizational defenses with his brand of bypassing and covering up.

The third feature of robust tests, or predictions, is that they are not influenced by the indeterminacy principle. For example, knowledge of the intervention and of the measures used to assess the change program did not lead the directors to alter their theories-in-use, even though they wanted to do so.

Subjecting theories to robust tests is consistent with our aspirations to produce propositions that show deterministic causality rather than probabilistic causality. So we saw in Chapter Two, Lieberson (1991) defines deterministic causality propositions as those that take the form: if A, then B. Probabilistic causality propositions take the form: if A, then the probability that B will follow is _____ . For example, deterministic causality appears in our prediction that, given Model I governing values, then Model I action strategies (specified ahead of time) will lead to defensive consequences that inhibit double-loop learning (also defined ahead of time). We predict not a probability but a surety that certain governing values and action strategies will lead to certain consequences. The specific behavioral consequences are not described in advance because the prediction is that, under the conditions just specified, one will find all the behavior to be defensive and anti-double-loop learning. Conversely, one will not find behavior that leads to double-loop learning.

Positivistic and Humanistic-Interpretive Approaches

Humanistic-interpretive researchers assert, I believe correctly, that positivists strive to be objective. In being objective, they tend to ignore meanings held by their human subjects, because a consideration of those meanings would require an intuitive, subjective, and empathic grasp of the subjects' consciousness (Giddens, 1976). They also tend to ignore the processes by which their subjects construct their realities (Rosen, 1991).

This results in positivistic researchers' distancing themselves from their subjects. Humanistic-interpretive researchers get close to their subjects, according to Van Maanen (1982), because they live among their subjects. I agree with this conclusion up to a point. The point can be defined by asking, How close is close?

Van Maanen certainly had close relationships with his subjects. Witness the rich dialogue that he reports, including candid comments by some policemen about their behavior toward the citizens they arrest. I think it is fair to say that Van Maanen documents that police expressed a nontrivial amount of hostility and prejudice toward the citizens they serve. He also documents how this hostility can become internalized by individuals (appearing, for example, as constant swearing) and can be the basis for a police culture that protects such individual defenses.

Van Maanen does not, as far as I can tell, conduct research to explore the causes of these individual and cultural defenses in more depth. This could be done, for example, by developing an intervention program, intended to surface and reduce the defenses. I believe Van Maanen would not disagree with this possibility but would maintain that intervention to change taken-for-granted behavior is not part of his research practice. The point that I am making is not that he must change. The point is that he and other ethnographers ought to specify the distancing that they create, just as they specify the distancing the positivists create.

Van Maanen limits his ethnographic research in ways that respect the distancing the police exhibit toward the citizens they serve. If he could help the police explore the causes of this distancing, he could help them get closer to themselves. Indeed, ethnographers themselves might benefit by exploring the meaning of their collusion with subjects' distancing. One might say that some humanistic-interpretive, or naturalistic, researchers get close enough to know when they are getting too close.

Therefore, Rosen's (1991) assertion that naturalistic researchers deconstruct the barriers between themselves and their subjects requires more careful specification. The same is true of his assertion that since naturalistic researchers deconstruct barriers, their instruments are necessarily flexible and less rigid than those of the positivists. Again, much depends on the meaning of rigidity. For example, if rigidity means the directions for using the instruments are not to be altered, then the cases that we ask our clients to complete *are* rigid. We do not permit deviance. Indeed, any deviance is seen as possible data about either individual or organizational defensive reactions.

I suggest that a bigger problem with questionnaires, a type of instrument that Rosen queries, is not that they are rigid but that the kinds of data they collect make it difficult to infer subjects' meanings (Argyris, 1976). Questionnaires are typically composed of questions that stimulate answers from the third rung on the ladder of inference (imposing meanings), answers which have been obtained by using the fourth rung (theories-in-use). Neither is sampled by the instruments. Recently attempts have been made to correct this problem by Axenn, Fricke, and Thornton (1991) and Rentsch (1990). If I understand them correctly, I do not believe that they deal as yet with action. But this limitation can be corrected with further research.

Another position often taken by field researchers who focus on naturalistic observations is that such research goes deeper than does research that is designed to be distant in order to be objective.

Again, this position seems plausible. However, there are gaps and inconsistencies to be found, which are illustrated by Dyer and Wilkins's critique (1991) of Eisenhardt's position on how to conduct research (1989).

Dyer and Wilkins favor using stories to generate theory. They believe that single case stories can deliver deep insights, while those developed from comparative case studies are likely to be "thin." The difficulty is that they craft their position so that it is not disconfirmable; indeed, it is not producible. For example, what are the properties of a story? What are the properties of "thin" insights? Dyers and Wilkins state: "Although it is difficult to determine how deep a researcher must go to generate good theory, the classic case study researchers certainly went deeper into the dynamics of a single case than Eisenhardt advocates" (p. 616). But the authors do not define what an appropriate depth is. Until this is done, how can we judge Eisenhardt's position to be wanting?

One could argue that in-depth insights can come from experiences lasting only a few hours. For example, Lewin and Barker were highly skilled at observing children at play and immediately relating what they saw to concepts of field forces, life space, gate-keeper, frustration, and regression. They had the skill to observe action and connect it to theory (Wheelan, Pepitone, & Abt, 1990). They could also learn from lengthy experiences, as Lewin learned about democracy and prejudice by being a Jew in Nazi Germany.

Dyer and Wilkins assert that in multicase studies the focus is on the construct to the detriment of the context. I am in favor of focusing on the context, as I believe the research in this book illustrates. But those of us who support contextual research are, I suggest, responsible for defining context in a way that is not self-referential, which makes testing features of it difficult. Dyer and Wilkins approvingly cite several classic case studies that tell a story (for example, Whyte, 1991). Yet, as Eisenhardt shows in her reply, those studies had features that were consistent with her view of context as much if not more than with Dyer and Wilkins's view. I can personally attest that Whyte spent several years trying to find more rigorous ways to test features of his theory. He had Elliot Chapple measure me to see if could carry around a midget interaction chronograph. The chronograph was a massive gadget that would count interactions in an objective manner; it represented positivism with a vengeance.

Rosen (1991) emphasizes that ethnographers typically collect qualitative and not quantitative data. However, in the study described in this book, the qualitative data could easily be translated into quantitative data. One could count, for example, the frequencies with which human beings advocated, evaluated, and attributed in ways that encouraged inquiry and testing. One could count the number of self-sealing nonlearning episodes, such as the self-fueling processes described by Hackman (1989) and his associates. I think that the standards for explanation and internal validity can be met with these simple quantitative procedures because our theory permits robust predictions, because tests can be conducted in changing the status quo, *and* because changing the status quo is such a rare event that, if it is done, you do not need sophisticated quantitative procedures to document it. For example, the dialogues between the CEO and the directors and the evaluation of the CEO's performance by the directors were rare events. Three years before they occurred, the participants unhesitantly predicted that such activities were not likely to occur; and, as one director said, " 'not likely to occur' means until hell freezes over."

Finally, Rosen (1991) also suggests that ethnographers do not allow any theoretical preoccupations to decide whether some facts are more important than others. I agree that competent ethnographers focus on the relatively directly observable data. For example, we used observations and tape recordings. Both, but especially the latter, could be used by any researchers with significantly different theories to test our generalizations or to develop tests of their own.

It is difficult to agree, however, that ethnographers do not allow any theoretical preconceptions to decide whether some facts are more important than others. As I see it, by eschewing interventions to change the constructed world they describe, they ignore, or do not permit to surface, the data that would arise if anyone tried to change that world. They may not let their preconceptions decide which facts are and are not important. But they allow their preconceptions to create conditions under which crucial facts will never arise.

Kunda is quoted by Rosen (p. 21) as saying that "ethnography is the only human activity in the social sciences . . . [that] is not divorced from the modes of experience that I consider human." I do not question that Kunda considers ethnography to be connected to what it means to be human, but the validity of the assertion is, in my judgment, doubtful. Kunda's study, which in my opinion is an excellent example of ethnography, misses the core of what it means to be human, according to *his* standards. Being human means to act, to construct a world, and to engage the world in ways that engage the actors.

Kunda observed human beings "being human," but he never became human in the sense of taking action to help his subjects in the struggle of being human. It was possible for Kunda to become as human as his subjects by developing interventions. Interventions are human experiments that have the intention of constructing different virtual worlds.

The Limits of Pluralism

There is another trend in the research literature that may also inhibit the development of actionable knowledge. This trend is to advocate pluralism in theoretical approaches (Bolman & Deal, 1991; Burrell & Morgan, 1979; Gill & Johnson, 1991; McGrath, Martin, & Kukla, 1982; Morgan, 1983; Schein, 1987a; Scott, 1981; Van Maanen, 1982). The suggestion seems sensible, especially for the younger social sciences. The difficulties surface when one compares the advice that flows from the pluralistic approach with the approach illustrated in our research, which is intended to produce actionable knowledge.

For example, Morgan and Smircich (1980) describe two researcher paradigms, interpretist and functionalist. They describe each paradigm's assumptions about ontology, human nature, epistemology, metaphors, and research methods. The interpretist and functionalist paradigms are placed along a continuum ranging from subjectivist (for the former) to objectivist (for the latter). The result is a thirty-box table describing the different assumptions that accompany the different degrees of subjectivism and objectivism.

A first reaction to the table is that it makes good sense. There are indeed paradigms that are primarily subjectivist and others that are primarily objectivist. However, a second reaction is that the table does not accurately characterize the assumptions regarding ontology, human nature, epistemology, metaphors, and research methods embedded in the theory and research described in this book. The problem is not that only some of the categories in the table are relevant; the problem is that almost all the categories are relevant. The research described in parts One and Two incorporates many characteristics of both the subjectivist and the objectivist approach as described in the table.

For example, the pattern of the director group's defensive routines represents reality as a social construct. It is implemented in a realm of symbolic discourse. It is a contextual field of information. It is a representation of concrete processes and structures in the sense that these processes and structures exist "out there." It coerces different directors to behave in similar manners.

The assumptions about human nature illustrated in our research also range from the extremes of subjectivism to those of objectivism as presented on the table. For example, the participants were symbol creators, symbol users, and actors using symbols. Our research depended heavily on understanding them as information processors with limited capacity to deal with environmental complexity. We described many examples where the same individuals were primarily adapters and responders before and after the interventions.

Finally, our research methods ranged from explorations of pure subjectivity, to script and symbolic analysis, to contextual analysis, to historical analysis of the director group, and to the design and execution of many experiments. Moreover, the entire research project occurred over a period of five years before publication and it continues. History became increasingly important as the interventions became cumulative, but so did the testing and experimenting used to assess the extent to which the new pattern contained processes and structures that "coerced" action in the service of learning and of reducing defensive routines at all levels.

When individuals, groups, intergroups, or organizations are studied under conditions where interventions are an integral part of the activity *and* where the interventions involve double-loop learning, I suggest that both subjectivist and objectivist assumptions will always be relevant. It is only in theoretical applications that they can be treated as antithetical. For example, we had to help the directors become aware of how they constructed reality (subjectivist). We then helped them see how these constructions led to a pattern that was "out there" because they had placed it out there, through actions designed to inhibit. This, in turn, required that we map contexts and study systems and processes. Finally, this led us to help the directors see how they had created a world where a positivist stance was both necessary and counterproductive.

When we helped them begin a new pattern, we had to help them learn new metaphors and to keep side-by-side the metaphors of theater and culture and the metaphors of cybernetics and organisms. We also helped them design and implement many experiments in order to create over time a new pattern that was "out there" and that "coerced" Model II behavior. Moreover, through the analysis of transcripts, we could become as quantitative as we wished in order to assess the impact of the new actions and the patterns the directors were building. Both the old and new realities produced contexts composed of concrete processes and structures. However, the new pattern included processes and structures to monitor and question those processes and structures.

I believe that the reason our empirical observations about organizational politics are consistent with the major published perspectives on this subject is that our research was guided with the intention of producing actionable knowledge. For example, the directors defined organizational politics as influence activities to obtain ends not sanctioned by the organization and as activities to obtain sanctioned ends through nonsanctioned influence means (Mayes & Allen, 1983). The directors' behavior was often self-serving (Sander, 1990) and in opposition to the formal organization; it was intended to get scarce resources and to build power. Conflict and uncertainty were frequently observed and reported. All these features were consistent with the definition of organizational politics by Drory and Romm (1990). The directors did bargain, negotiate, and jockey for position, especially around the allocation of scarce resources. Although they espoused a lack of enduring differences in values, beliefs, and perceptions of reality, their theories-in-use encouraged these differences. This led to the formation of coalitions within the director group and, later, between members of the directors' group and of several groups below the directors. These features are consistent with organizational politics as defined by Bolman and Deal (1991), Daft (1983), Eisenhardt and Bourgois (1988), and Kumar and Ghadially (1989).

Because we aim for actionable knowledge, our strategy is not consistent with the pluralistic strategy of using several different perspectives relatively independently of each other. For example, Hassard (1991) has described a study in which four different paradigms (functionalist, interpretive, radical structuralist, and radical humanist) were used to study features of an organization. Each study was conducted consistently with each perspective's assumptions regarding ontology, epistemology, human nature, and methodology. Each produced different descriptions of different features of the organization.

Moreover, there was no attempt reported to produce actionable knowledge relevant to changing the status quo. The exercise met the needs of the researchers, who wanted to see what the different perspectives would produce, and the subjects' interests were subordinated to the researchers' interests. The same is true of the analysis made by Allison (1971) of the Cuban missile crisis.

The researchers also produced, by design, defensive routines in their relationships with the subjects. They withheld their interest in conducting the research with four different paradigms, because they feared that they might not gain access if they revealed their intentions fully. In our view, they bypassed embarrassment and threat and covered up the bypass.

Donaldson (1985) suggests that integrative research, which allows paradigms to be used conjointly, is necessary because integration can lead to increasingly comprehensive theories, a consequence favored by science. Those in the pluralistic camp disagree. They claim that such approaches are, in, effect, a succumbing to the dominant paradigms, such as the functionalist-positivistic. Jackson and Carter (1991) defend paradigm incommensurability because doing so expands "dramatically the scope of organization studies, the interests represented, and those empowered to speak" (p. 111). I support the expansion. My argument is that when guided by pluralism, it does not go far enough or deep enough. One way to go further and deeper is to focus on producing actionable knowledge, especially of the variety that leads to double-loop learning. Research that produces such knowledge must, by necessity, be interventionist and must combine reeducation of individuals with change in the social units in which the individuals are embedded. Paradigm incommensurability inhibits production of actionable knowledge. Therefore, the plea for incommensurability, which is intended to avoid domination by any one approach or combination of approaches, may have the unintended consequence of becoming a plea for merely a different kind of scientistic authoritarianism.

Basic and Applied Research: The Role of a New Type of Consulting

Historically, researchers have differentiated between basic, or scholarly, and applied research. For example, Cronbach and Suppes (1969) separate "conclusion-oriented research" (basic) from "decision-oriented research" (applied). Coleman (1972) continued and expanded the distinction by calling the former "discipline research" and the latter "policy research." Many scholars accept this distinction. An excellent compilation of their positions can be found in Stringer (1982). Basic research is designed to test theories and to produce generalizations, is open to scrutiny by the scholarly community, and does not begin with an intention to be of help or to produce implementable knowledge (Coleman, 1972).

Action or applied research, on the other hand, seeks to solve client problems and to produce workable solutions that are usually not abstract (in order to be relevant to the concrete problems of practice), that are rarely subject to scholarly scrutiny, and that are intended for implementation. Some would go as far as saying that it might not be necessary or useful for such researchers to be concerned about truth. Indeed, they might find that being helpful requires ignoring truth (Ellis, 1982).

McGrath and Brinberg (1984) have developed a model that attempts to show why many of these differences between basic and applied research may be symptomatic of researchers' defenses. Using the validity network schema, they are able to show that basic and applied research may have different pathways but that both are centrally concerned with the validity and generalizability of propositions. They suggest that both camps show an interest in each other's biases but that they tend to deal with that interest by mentioning it last. I believe that there is much wisdom in McGrath and Brinberg's perspective. However, I hesitate to agree with their proposition that basic researchers are primarily concerned with the conceptual domain and applied researchers with the substantive domain. I hope I have shown in this book that their conclusion that these different concerns lead to different and apparently contradictory paths of research practice is not necessarily the case.

Peters and Robinson (1984) describe a view that is closer to the one I take. They differentiate between weak and strong versions of applied research. Our perspective fits the strong version domain, where applied research becomes truly action research and where the intent is to link this action research to social science theory—indeed, to test such theory's features.

Peters and Robinson conclude that both versions of applied research espouse involvement-in-change and organic research processes heavily influenced by collaboration between researchers and subjects. They also conclude that the researchers who advocate the strong version tend to place a heavier emphasis upon constructivist/ interactionist epistemology, which stresses that our understanding of the world is both social and constitutive and that social actors create their own histories and are capable of reflection-in-action in order to change the world as it is. The strong version, they conclude, is emancipatory.

I believe that the processes that led to the weak version of action research (that is, away from Lewin's original emphasis) arose from the view that scientific knowledge cannot be produced from social science research to resolve practical problems, because practitioners place constraints and apply pressures on researchers that inhibit valid understanding and disconfirmability. I believe that this does occur. I also believe that it does not have to occur.

For example, in conducting research where helping a client and producing actionable knowledge is an objective, one often will be pressured by time, practitioners, and organizational politics. However, I believe that these can be dealt with so that the researcher

does not have to comply with them. It is true that, in not complying, the researcher runs the risk of being asked to leave, but it is also
true that researchers can be educated in action strategies that reduce
the likelihood of such rejection (Argyris, Putnam, & Smith, 1985).

In the type of research that I have described, I recommend
that the researcher leave a client, or never accept an invitation in the
first place, if staying or accepting will necessitate a serious compromise on the requirements of sound research. My colleagues,
many of whom are much younger than I, have found that when it
is necessary they are able to alter deadlines set by practitioners; they
can also show how the parsimony and elegance that is the hallmark
of basic research is value added for practitioners.

I also believe that it is possible for researchers to connect
practical problems to basic theory. Lewin (1948), for example,
showed that practical research on how mothers can get their children to eat wholesome food, how to sell defense bonds, or how to
produce more effective leaders could be guided by the theoretical
concept of "gatekeeper." I am willing to go as far as saying that if
a practical problem cannot be connected to basic concepts of the
discipline, then it may be best for researchers to choose not to study
it. So far, I have not been faced with such a choice.

I believe further that research to produce actionable knowledge can and should be exposed to self-correcting procedures. It may
be, as Coleman (1972) suggests, that much of the self-correcting
activity in present policy research is best conducted by independent
studies. I am recommending that self-correcting procedures should
be designed into studies because these procedures protect the human
subjects, as well as foster the production of valid basic knowledge.

Rothschild (1971) recommends that, when researchers cooperate with practitioners, the researchers should not have a heavy
impact on formulating the objectives, should not decide that the
objective requires research for its achievement, should not decide
that the research should be done, and should not decide to change
the objective of the research in midstream.

If this is to be interpreted to mean that researchers should not
take these actions unilaterally, then I would agree. For the research
that I have described, however, I believe the researcher should have
a significant influence on all those decisions. I hope I have shown

that I did have a substantial impact on many such decisions. I hope I have also shown that my impact turned out to be in the interest of the clients. Indeed, they would not have me act otherwise. I do use a fifty-second/four-hour contract in all my research relationships. Either side can terminate the relationship in fifty seconds. Both sides commit to provide up to four hours to discuss the termination decision, for the purpose of understanding what happened not for the purpose of changing the decision. So far, those that I have studied have not exercised the option. I have done so in two studies. In one, I began to realize that the clients were producing unethical activities. In the other, the clients did not wish to conduct the research as rigorously as we thought was necessary for their sake, as well as for the sake of contributing to knowledge. I believe that a focus on producing actionable knowledge in the service of improvability will lead to a more intimate connection between consulting and scholarly research. As knowledge becomes more mature in the social science disciplines, it is to be hoped it becomes more actionable and likely more salable. As knowledge becomes more salable, the pressures for it to be rigorous will likely increase. Thus, I foresee the day when the fading away of the distinctions between scholarly research and salable knowledge that is happening now in biology will also occur in social science. This will require a much more rigorous practice in consulting because consultants will, I believe, take on the role of the universities' and the public's go-between. In their activity to facilitate organizational health, they will be like medical professionals in their activity to facilitate physiological health. This makes it urgent that the highest standards be set for the practice of consulting. The medical profession began to achieve its high standards when its members developed an intimate relationship with research universities. As a result of this interdependence, medical schools cooperated with faculties of arts and sciences regarding basic disciplines. Many medical schools developed their own research activities producing knowledge of the highest quality.

I agree with Seashore (1985) that consultants are a rich natural resource for building usable knowledge. I would like to go further by creating a niche for consultants who are action researchers conducting basic research. I also agree with Simon (1976) that consulting can be an important source for knowledge. However, I disagree that consulting and research should be separated. I understand, I think, the basis for their position. When they think of consulting, they think of solving practical problems in ways that do not contribute directly to theory. That view is the dominant one in the current practice of consulting. But, it does not have to remain so. The objective of this book is to describe research activity that adds value to practice and, at the same time, to scholarly theories.

I would like to see consulting firms and universities begin to develop cooperative relationships. If the cooperative work is carried out at the highest levels of quality, everyone involved will gain. But this means nothing less than that the standards for research in both institutions should be the same. The distinction between basic and applied research should be reformulated by showing how the latter can contribute to the former.

Seeking Truth and Improvability

The underlying assumption in my views is that seeking truth in the service of improvability is a valuable purpose for science and for practice. Seeking truth is an ongoing activity—never fully achieved, always approximated. It has always been regarded as the ultimate purpose of research. The major test of how well we are doing in seeking truth (with a small "t") is to formulate statements of truth as hypotheses and then strive to disconfirm them, not simply confirm them (Popper, 1959). The reason we should strive to disconfirm instead of simply confirm is that people tend to rely on confirming. They seek out instances in which the hypothesized property is known or expected to be present rather than absent (Klayman & Ha, 1987). They are biased toward seeking instances that confirm their hypothesis rather than instances that are inconsistent with it (Kunda, 1990).

I should like to emphasize combining the activities of seeking truth with seeking improvability. Why? Because the universe that we are studying is created by humans. It is a virtual world constructed by the players, who then live within its requirements. The likelihood that the worlds we create are perfect or near perfect is low. They are more likely to be imperfect, with gaps that we slowly fill by living in our worlds and trying to make them more effective. The constitutions of most countries are living examples. In the United States, we have been trying to improve our Constitution and its implementation continually for more than two hundred years. Few people doubt that we have a long way to go.

References

Abt, W., Magidson, P., & Magidson, J. (1980). *Reforming schools: Problems in program implementation and evaluation*. Newbury Park, CA: Sage.

Adelson, J. (1985). Four surprises, or Why schools may not improve at all. In J. Bunzel (Ed.), *Challenge to American schools: The case for standards and values* (pp. 17-28). New York: Oxford University Press.

Alderfer, C. (1977). Improving organization communication through long-term intergroup intervention. *Journal of Applied Behavioral Science, 13,* 193-210.

Alderfer, C. P. (1992). Changing race relationships embedded in organizations: Report on a long term project with the XYZ Corporation. In S. Jackson (Ed.), *Working with diversity* (pp. 136-166). New York: Guilford Press.

Alderfer, C., & Brown, L. D. (1975). *Learning from changing*. Newbury Park, CA: Sage.

Alderfer, C., Tucker, R., Alderfer, C. J., & Tucker, L. M. (1988). The race relations advisory group: An intergroup intervention. In *Research in organizational change and development* (Vol. 2, pp. 269-321). Greenwich, CT: JAI Press.

287

Allison, G. (1971). *Essence of decision—Explaining the Cuban missile crisis.* Boston: Little, Brown.

Allport, F. H. (1967). *Theories of perception and the concept of structure.* New York: Wiley.

Allport, G. (1969). *The person in psychology.* Boston: Beacon Press.

Arendt, H. (1958). *The human condition.* Chicago: University of Chicago Press.

Arendt, H. (1963). *On revolution.* New York: Viking Penguin.

Argyris, C. (1957). *Personality and organizations.* New York: HarperCollins.

Argyris, C. (1964). *Integrating the individual and the organization.* New York: Wiley.

Argyris, C. (1970). *Intervention theory and method.* Reading, MA: Addison-Wesley.

Argyris, C. (1976). Problems and new directions for industrial psychology. In M. D. Dunnette (Ed.), *Handbook of industrial and organizational psychology.* Skokie, IL: Rand McNally.

Argyris, C. (1978a). Is capitalism the culprit? *Organizational Dynamics,* pp. 21–37.

Argyris, C. (1978b). *Organizational learning.* Reading, MA: Addison-Wesley.

Argyris, C. (1980). *Inner contradictions of rigorous research.* San Diego, CA: Academic Press.

Argyris, C. (1982). *Reasoning, learning and action: Individual and organizational.* San Francisco: Jossey-Bass.

Argyris, C. (1985a). Making knowledge more relevant to practice: Maps for action. In E. E. Lawler III, A. M. Mohrman, Jr., S. A. Mohrman, G. E. Ledford, Jr., T. G. Cummings, & Associates, *Doing research that is useful for theory and practice* (pp. 79–106). San Francisco: Jossey-Bass.

Argyris, C. (1985b). *Strategy, change and defensive routines.* New York: Harper Business.

Argyris, C. (1986). Skilled incompetence. *Harvard Business Review, 64*(5), 74–79.

Argyris, C. (1987). Reasoning, action strategies, and defensive routines: The case of OD practitioners. In R. W. Woodman & W. A. Pasmore (Eds.), *Research in organizational change and development* (Vol. 1, pp. 89–128). Greenwich, CN: JAI Press.

Argyris, C. (1990a). The dilemma of implementing controls: The case of managerial accounting. *Accounting, Organizations, and Society, 15*(6), 503–511.

Argyris, C. (1990b). Inappropriate defenses against the monitoring of organization development practices. *Journal of Applied Behavioral Science, 26*(3), 299–312.

Argyris, C. (1990c). *Overcoming organizational defenses: Facilitating organizational learning.* Needham, MA: Allyn & Bacon.

Argyris, C. (1991). Teaching smart people how to learn. *Harvard Business Review, 69*(3), pp. 99–109.

Argyris, C., Putnam, R., & Smith, D. (1985). *Action science: Concepts, methods, and skills for research and intervention.* San Francisco: Jossey-Bass.

Argyris, C., & Schön, D. A. (1974). *Theory in practice.* San Francisco: Jossey-Bass.

Argyris, C., & Schön, D. A. (1978). *Organizational learning.* Reading, MA: Addison-Wesley.

Argyris, C., & Schön, D. A. (1990). Two conceptions of causality: The case of organizational theory and behavior. Working paper, Harvard Business School and Department of Urban Planning, MIT, Cambridge, MA.

Argyris, C., & Schön, D. A. (in press). Conceptions of causality in social theory and research: Normal science and action science compared.

Axenn, W. G., Fricke, T. E., & Thornton, A. (1991). The microdemographic community-study approach. *Sociological Methods and Research, 20*(2), 187–217.

Bailey, F. G. (1988). *Humbuggery and manipulation.* Ithaca, NY: Cornell University Press.

Bandura, A. (1989). Organizational application of social cognitive theory. *Australian Journal of Management, 13*(2), 275–301.

Barber, J. D. (1977). *The presidential character.* Englewood Cliffs, NJ: Prentice-Hall.

Bardach, E., & Kagan, R. A. (1982). *Going by the book.* Philadelphia: Temple University Press.

Barker, R. G., Dembo, T., & Lewin, K. (1941). *Frustration and regression* (University of Iowa Studies in Child Welfare 1, pp. 1–43). Ames: University of Iowa Press.

Berg, D. N., & Smith, K. K. (1985). *Exploring clinical methods for social research.* Newbury Park, CA: Sage.

Blake, R. R., & Mouton, J. S. (1961). *Group dynamics—Key to decision making.* Houston, TX: Gulf Publishing.

Blumberg, A. (1989). *School administration as a craft.* Needham Heights, MA: Allyn & Bacon.

Bolman, L. G., & Deal, T. E. (1991). *Reframing organizations: Artistry, choice, and leadership.* San Francisco: Jossey-Bass.

Bourdieu, P. (1990). *The logic of practice.* Stanford, CA: Stanford University Press.

Boyer, E. L. (1985). *High school.* New York: HarperCollins.

Brodsky, N. A. (1989). *Professional excellence in action: Process and barriers.* Unpublished doctoral dissertation. Graduate School of Education, Harvard University, Cambridge, MA.

Broudy, H. S. (1972). *The real world of public schools.* Orlando, FL: Harcourt Brace Jovanovich.

Brown, R. H. (1978). Bureaucracy as praxis: Toward a political phenomenology of formal organizations. *Administrative Science Quarterly, 23,* 365–382.

Brunsson, N. (1989). *The organization of hypocrisy.* New York: Wiley.

Bunzel, J. H. (1985). Introduction. In J. Bunzel (Ed.), *Challenge to American schools: The case for standards and values* (pp. 3–13). New York: Oxford University Press.

Burns, J. M. (1978). *Leadership.* New York: HarperCollins.

Burrell, G., & Morgan, G. (1979). *Sociological paradigms and organizational analyses.* London: Heinemann.

Campbell, D. T., & Stanley, J. C. (1963). *Experimental and quasi-experimental design for research.* Skokie, IL: Rand McNally.

Cartwright, D. (Ed.). (1951). *Field theory and social science.* New York: HarperCollins.

Chance, W. B. (1986). *The best of educations.* Chicago: John D. & Catherine T. MacArthur Foundation.

Churchman, C. W. (1971). *The design in inquiring systems: Basic concepts of systems and organizations.* New York: Basic Books.

Coleman, J. S. (1972). *Policy research in the social sciences.* Morristown, NJ: General Learning Press.

Cronbach, L. J., & Suppes, P. (Eds.). (1969). *Research for tomorrow's schools*. London: Macmillan.

Daft, R. L. (1983). *Organization theory and design*. St. Paul, MN: West.

De Charms, R. (1973). Intervention is impossible: A model for change from within. In W. L. Claiborn & R. Cohen (Eds.), *School intervention* (pp. 243-258). New York: Behavioral Publications.

Deci, E. L., & Ryan, R. M. (1991). A motivational approach to self: Integration in personality. In R. Dienstbier (Ed.), *Nebraska symposium on motivation: Vol. 38. Perspectives on motivation* (pp. 237-289). Lincoln: University of Nebraska Press.

Donald, M. (1991). *Origins of the modern mind*. Cambridge, England: Cambridge University Press.

Donaldson, L. (1985). *In defence of organization theory*. Cambridge, England: Cambridge University Press.

Drory, A., & Romm, T. (1990). The definition of organizational politics: A review. *Human Relations, 43*(11), 1133-1154.

Dyer, G. W., Jr., & Wilkins, A. L. (1991). Better stories, not better constructs, to generate better theory: A rejoinder to Eisenhardt. *Academy of Management Review, 16*(3), 613-619.

Eccles, R. C., & Nohria, N., with Berkeley, J. D. (1992). *Beyond the hype: Rediscovering the essence of management*. Boston: Harvard Business School Press.

Edelman, M. (1988). *Constructing the political spectacle*. Chicago: University of Chicago Press.

Einhorn, H. J. (1986). Accepting error to make less error. *Journal of Personality Assessment, 50*(3), 387-395.

Einhorn, H. J., & Hogarth, R. M. (1987). Decision making: Going forward in reverse. *Harvard Business Review, 65*(1), 66-70.

Eisenhardt, K. M. (1989). Building theories from case study research. *Academy of Management Review, 14*(4), 532-550.

Eisenhardt, K. M. (1991). Better stories and better constructs: The case for rigor and comparative logic. *Academy of Management Review, 16*(3), 620-627.

Eisenhardt, K. M., & Bourgois, L. J., II. (1988). Politics of strategic decision making in high-velocity environments: Toward a midrange theory. *Academy of Management Journal, 4*(31), 737-770.

Ellis, P. (1982). The phenomenology of defensible space. In P. Stringer (Ed.), *Confronting social Issues* (pp. 123-144). San Diego, CA: Academic Press.

Etheredge, L. S. (1985). *Can governments learn?* Elmsford, NY: Pergamon Press.

Fantini, M. D. (1986). *Regaining excellence in education.* Columbus, OH: Merrill.

Forsterling, F. (1988). *Attribution theory in clinical psychology.* New York: Wiley.

Frase, L., & Hetzel, R. (1990). *School management by wandering around.* Lancaster, PA: Technomic Publishing Co.

Frontline: The disillusionment of David Stockman. (1986. April). Transcript from PBS station WRBH, Boston.

Gabbard, G. O. (1991). Do we need theory? *Bulletin of the Menninger Clinic, 55,* 22-29.

Gardner, J. W. (1990). *On leadership.* New York: Free Press.

George, A. (1972). The case of multiple advocacy in making "foreign policy." *American Political Science Review, 67,* 751-785.

Giddens, A. (1976). *New rules of sociological method.* London: Hutchinson.

Gill, J., & Johnson, P. (1991). *Research methods for managers.* London: Chapman.

Golding, D. (1991). Some everyday rituals in management control. *Journal of Management Studies, 28*(6), 569-584.

Golembiewski, R. T., & Corrigan, S. B. (1970). The persistence of laboratory-induced changes in organizational styles. *Administrative Science Quarterly, 15,* 330-340.

Golembiewski, R. T., Hilles, R., & Daly, R. (1987). Impacting burnout and worksite features: Some effects of multiple OD interventions. Paper presented at the annual meeting of the Society for Public Administration, March, Boston.

Goodlad, J. I. (1975). *Dynamics of educational change.* New York: McGraw-Hill.

Goodlad, J. I. (1984). *A place called school.* New York: McGraw-Hill.

Grant, G. (1988). *The world we created at Hamilton High.* Cambridge, MA: Harvard University Press.

Greenberg, J., & Folger, R. (1988). *Controversial issues in social research methods.* New York: Springer-Verlag.

Hackman, J. R. (1987). The design of work teams. In J. W. Lorsch (Ed.), *Handbook of organizational behavior* (pp. 315–342). Englewood Cliffs, NJ: Prentice-Hall.

Hackman, J. R. (Ed.). (1989). *Groups that work (and those that don't): Creating conditions for effective teamwork.* San Francisco: Jossey-Bass.

Hackman, J. R., & Walton, R. (1986). Leading groups in organizations. In P. S. Goodman & Associates, *Designing effective work groups* (pp. 72–119). San Francisco: Jossey-Bass.

Halperin, M. H. (1974). *Bureaucratic politics and foreign policy.* Washington, DC: Brookings Institution.

Hassard, J. (1991). Multiple paradigms and organizational analysis: A case study. *Organization Studies, 12*(2), 275–299.

Hawley, K. E., & Nichols, M. L. (1982). A contextual approach to modeling the decision to participate in a "political" decision. *Administrative Science Quarterly, 27,* 105–119.

Heath, D. H. (1971). *Humanizing schools.* New York: Hayden Book Co.

Heider, F. (1958). *The psychology of interpersonal relationships.* New York: Wiley.

Hirschhorn, L. (1988). *The workplace within.* Cambridge, MA: MIT Press.

Hirschhorn, L. (1991). *Leaders and followers in a post-industrial Age: A psychodynamic view.* Philadelphia: Wharton Center for Applied Research.

Hirschhorn, L., & Young, D. (1991). Dealing with the anxiety of working: Social defenses as coping strategy. In M.F.R. Kets de Vries & Associates, *Organizations on the couch* (pp. 215–240). San Francisco: Jossey-Bass.

Hong, B. (1986). *Last chance for our children.* Reading, MA: Addison-Wesley.

Hopwood, A. G. (1990). Ambiguity, knowledge and territorial claims: Some observations on the doctrine of substance over form: A review essay. *British Accounting Review, 22,* 79–87.

Hoyle, E. (1988). Micropolitics of educational organizations. In A.

Westoby (Ed.), *Culture and power in educational organizations* (pp. 255–269). New York: Open University Press.

Jackson, N., & Carter, P. (1991). In defence of paradigm incommensurability. *Organization Studies, 12*(1), 109–127.

Jackson, P. W. (1968). *Life in classrooms.* Troy, MO: Holt, Rinehart & Winston.

James, L. R., Mulaik, S. A., & Brett, J. M. (1982). *Causal analyses: Assumptions, models, and data.* Newbury Park, CA: Sage.

Janis, I. L. (1972). *Victims of group think.* Boston: Houghton Mifflin.

Janis, I. L. (1989). *Crucial decisions: Leadership in policymaking and crisis management.* New York: Free Press.

Janis, I. L., & Mann, I. (1977). *Decision making: A psychological analysis of conflict, choice, and commitment.* New York: Free Press.

Jaques, E. (1951). *The changing culture of a factory.* London: Tavistock.

Jaques, E. (1976). *A general theory of bureaucracy.* London: Heinemann.

Jones, S. (1987). Choosing action research: A rationale. In I. L. Mangham (Ed.), *Organization analysis and development* (pp. 23–46). New York: Wiley.

Kahn, R. L., Wolfe, D. M., Quinn, R. P., Snoek, J. D., & Rosenthal, R. A. (1964). *Organizational stress: Studies in role conflict and ambiguity.* New York: Wiley.

Katz, D., & Kahn, R. L. (1966). *The social psychology of organizations.* New York: Wiley.

Kaufman, H. (1977). *Red tape.* Washington, DC: Brookings Institution.

Kaufman, H. (1981). *The administrative behavior of bureau chiefs.* Washington, DC: Brookings institution.

Keggunder, M. N., Jorgensen, J. J., & Hafsi, T. (1983). Administrative theory and practice in developing countries: A synthesis. *Administrative Science Quarterly, 25,* 66–84.

Kellerman, B. (Ed.). (1984). *Leadership: Multidisciplinary perspectives.* Englewood Cliffs, NJ: Prentice-Hall.

Kelley, H. H. (1967). Attribution theory in social psychology. In D.

Levine (Ed.), *Nebraska symposium on motivation, 15* (pp. 192–238). Lincoln: University of Nebraska Press.

Kelman, H. C., & Hamilton, V. L. (1989). *Crimes of obedience: Toward a social psychology of authority and responsibility.* New Haven, CN: Yale University Press.

Klayman, J., & Ha, Y. W. (1987). Confirmation, disconfirmation & information in hypothesis testing. *Psychological Review, 94,* 211–218.

Kukla, A. (1989). Nonempirical issues of psychology. *American Psychologist, 44*(5), 795–802.

Kumar, P., & Ghadially, R. (1989). Organizational politics and its effects on members of organizations. *Human Relations, 4*(42), 305–314.

Kunda, Z. (1990). The case for motivated reasoning. *Psychological Bulletin, 108*(3), 480–498.

Latour, B. (1987). *Science in action.* New York: Open University Press.

Lawler, E. E., III, Mohrman, A. M., Jr., Mohrman, S. A., Ledford, G. E., Jr., Cummings, T. G., & Associates (1985). *Doing research that is useful for theory and practice.* San Francisco: Jossey-Bass.

Lawrence, P. R., & Lorsch, J. W. (1967). *Organization and environment: Managing differentiation and integration.* Boston: Harvard Business School Press.

Lawrence, P. R., & Lorsch, J. W. (1969). *Developing organizations: Diagnosis and action.* Reading, MA: Addison-Wesley.

Lee, A. S. (1989a). Case studies as natural experiments. *Human Relations, 42*(2), 117–137.

Lee, A. S. (1989b). A scientific methodology for M.I.S. case studies. *M.I.S. Quarterly,* Mar., 33–50.

Lee, A. S. (1991). Integrating positivist and interpretive approaches to organizational research. *Organizational Science, 2*(4), 342–365.

Levine, C. H., Ruben, I. S., & Wolohagran, G. G. (1981). *The politics of entrenchment.* Newbury Park, CA: Sage.

Lewin, K. (1935). *A dynamic theory of personality.* New York: McGraw-Hill.

Lewin, K. (1948). *Resolving social conflicts* (G. W. Lewin, Ed.). New York: HarperCollins.

Lewin, K. (1951). *Field theory in social science* (D. Cartwright, Ed.). New York: HarperCollins.

Lewin, K., Lippett, R., & White, R. K. (1939). Patterns of aggressive behavior in experimentally created social climates. *Journal of Social Psychology, 10,* 271–301.

Lieberson, S. (1991). Small N's and big conclusions: An examination of the reasoning in comparative studies based on a small number of cases. *Social Forces, 70*(2), 307–320.

Lightfoot, S. L. (1983). *The good high school.* New York: Basic Books.

Likert, R. (1961). *New patterns of management.* New York: McGraw-Hill.

Lindon, J. A. (1991). Does technique require theory? *Bulletin of the Menninger Clinic, 55,* 1–21, 30–37.

Locke, E. A. (1986). *Generalizing from laboratory to field study.* Lexington, MA: Heath.

Locke, E. A. (Ed.). (1991). Theories of cognitive self-regulation. *Organizational Behavior and Human Decision Processes, 50*(2), 151–410.

Lowman, R. L. (1985). What *is* clinical method? In D. N. Berg & K. Smith (Eds.), *Exploring clinical methods for social research* (pp. 173–188). Newbury Park, CA: Sage.

Luthans, F., & Krectner, R. (1975). *Organizational behavior modification.* Glenview, IL: Scott, Foresman.

Luthans, F., & Martinko, M. (1987). Behavioral approaches to organizations. In C. L. Cooper and I. T. Robertson (Eds.), *International review of industrial and organizational psychology* (pp. 35–60). New York: Wiley.

Luthans, F., Paul, R., & Baker, D. (1981). An experimental analysis of the impact of contingent reinforcement on salespersons' performance behavior. *Journal of Applied Psychology, 66*(1), 314–323.

Lynn, L. E., & Whitman, D. deF. (1981). *The president as policy maker: Jimmy Carter and welfare reform.* Philadelphia: Temple University Press.

McClelland, D. (1985). *Human motivation.* Glenview, IL: Scott, Foresman.

McFarland, A. S. (1969). *Power and leadership in pluralistic systems*. Stanford, CA: Stanford University Press.

McGrath, J. E., & Brinberg, D. (1984). Alternative paths for research. *Applied Social Psychology Annual, 5,* 109–129.

McGrath, J. E., Martin, J., & Kukla, R. A. (1982). *Judgment calls in research*. Newbury Park, CA: Sage.

Malave, J. (1991). Organizing as event structuring: Some elements for a process oriented approach to organization theory. Unpublished manuscript, Instituto de Estudios Superiores de Administración, Caracas, Venezuela.

Mangham, I. L. (1987). *Organization analysis and development*. New York: Wiley.

Manz, C. C., & Sims, H. P. (1986). Beyond imitation: Complex behavioral and affective linkages resulting from exposure to leadership training models. *Journal of Applied Psychology, 71*(4), 571–578.

Manz, C. C., & Sims, H. P. (1989). *Super-leadership*. Englewood Cliffs, NJ: Prentice-Hall.

Mayes, B. T., & Allen, R. W. (1983). Toward a definition of organizational politics. In R. W. Allen & L. W. Porter (Eds.), *Organizational influence processes* (pp. 361–368). Glenview, IL: Scott, Foresman.

Mill, J. S. (1949). *A system of logic*. London: Longmans, Green. (Original work published 1843.)

Mohr, L. B. (1982). *Explaining organizational behavior*. San Francisco: Jossey-Bass.

Morgan, G. (1983). *Beyond method*. Newbury Park, CA: Sage.

Morgan, G., & Smircich, L. (1980). The case for qualitative research. *Academy of Management Review, 5*(4), 491–500.

Nagel, J. H. (1991). Psychological obstacles to administrative responsibility: Lessons of the M.O.V.E. disaster. *Journal of Policy Analysis and Management, 10*(1), 1–23.

NAPA. (1983). *Revitalizing federal management: Managers and their overburdened systems*. Washington, DC: Author.

National Board for Professional Teaching Standards. (1989). *Towards high and rigorous standards for the teaching profession*. Washington, DC: Author.

Neustadt, R., & Fineberg, H. V. (1978). *The swine flu affair*. Washington, DC: Department of Education.

Neustadt, R. E., & May, E. R. (1986). *Thinking in time*. New York: Free Press.

Olafson, T. A. (1967). *Principles and persons: An ethical interpretation of existentialism*. Baltimore: Johns Hopkins University Press.

Paige, G. D. (1977). *The scientific study of political leadership*. New York: Free Press.

Perrow, C. (1984). *Normal accidents: Living with high risk technologies*. New York: Basic Books.

Peters, M., & Robinson, V. (1984). The origins and status of action research. *Journal of Applied Behavioral Science, 20*(2), 113-124.

Pfeffer, J. (1992). *Managing with power: Politics and influence in organizations*. Boston: Harvard Business School Press.

Popper, K. (1959). *The logic of scientific discovery*. New York: Basic Books.

Presidential Commission. (1986). *On the space shuttle challenger accident*. Washington, DC: U.S. Government Printing Office.

Pressman, J. L., & Wildavsky, A. B. (1973). *Implementation*. Berkeley: University of California Press.

Quine, W. V. (1992). Methological reflections on current linguistic theory. In D. Harman and G. Davidson (Eds.), *Semantics of natural language* (pp. 442-454). Dordrecht, Netherlands: D. Reidel.

Rentsch, J. R. (1990). Climate and culture: Interaction and qualitative differences in organizational meanings. *Journal of Applied Psychology, 75*(6), 668-681.

Reynolds, D. (1985). *Studying school effectiveness*. London: Falmer Press.

Rosen, M. (1991). Coming to terms with the field: Understanding and doing organizational ethnography. *Journal of Management Studies, 28*(1), 1-24.

Rothschild, Lord. (1971). A report by Lord Rothschild. In *The framework for government research and development: Memorandum by the government*. Command paper 4814. London: Her Majesty's Stationery Office.

Runkel, P. J. (1990). *Casting nets and testing specimens*. New York: Praeger.

Sander, K. (1990). Organizational development as a political process. In F. Massarek (Ed.), *Advances in organizational development* (Vol. 1). Norwood, NJ: Ablex.

Sayles, L. R. (1989). *Leadership*. New York: McGraw-Hill.

Schein, E. H. (1985). *Organizational culture and leadership: A dynamic view*. San Francisco: Jossey-Bass.

Schein, E. H. (1987a). *The clinical perspective in fieldwork*. Newbury Park, CA: Sage.

Schein, E. H. (1987b). *Process consultation* (Vol. 2). Reading, MA: Addison-Wesley.

Schick, F. (1991). *Understanding action: An essay on reasons*. Cambridge, England: Cambridge University Press.

Schön, D. (1979). Generative metaphor. In A. Ortany (Ed.), *Metaphor and thought* (pp. 254-283). Cambridge, England: Cambridge University Press.

Schön, D. (1983). *The reflective practitioner: How professionals think in action*. New York: Basic Books.

Schön, D. (1987). *Educating the reflective practitioner: Toward a new design for teaching and learning in the professions*. San Francisco: Jossey-Bass.

Scott, W. R. (1981). *Organizations: Rational, natural and open systems*. Englewood Cliffs, NJ: Prentice-Hall.

Scribner, H. B., & Stevens, L. B. (1975). *Make your schools work*. New York: Simon & Schuster.

Seashore, S. E. (1985). Institutional and organizational issues in doing useful research. In E. E. Lawler III, A. M. Mohrman, Jr., S. A. Mohrman, G. E. Ledford, Jr., T. G. Cummings, & Associates (Eds.), *Doing research that is useful for theory and practice* (pp. 45-59). San Francisco: Jossey-Bass.

Shoham, Y. (1990). Nonmonotonic reasoning and causation. *Cognitive Science, 14*, 213-302.

Simon, H. A. (1969). *The science of the artificial*. Cambridge, MA: MIT Press.

Simon, H. A. (1976). The business school: A problem in organizational design. In H. A. Simon (Ed.), *Administrative behavior: A study of decision-making processes in administrative organization* (pp. 335-357). New York: Free Press.

Simon, H. A. (1990). Invariants of human behavior. *Annual Review of Psychology, 41,* 1–20.

Sizer, T. R. (1984). *Horace's compromise: The dilemma of the American high school.* Boston: Houghton Mifflin.

Spencer, L. M., & Cullen, B. J. (1978). *A taxonomy of organizational development research.* Boston: McBer.

Spielberger, C. D. (1977). State-tract anxiety and interactional psychology. In D. Magnusson & N. S. Endler (Eds.), *Personality at the crossroads: Current issues in interactional psychology.* Hillsdale, NJ: Erlbaum.

Stockman, D. H. (1986). *The triumph of politics: How the Reagan revolution failed.* New York: HarperCollins.

Stringer, P. (Ed.). (1982). *Confronting social issues* (Vol. 2). San Diego, CA: Academic Press.

Torbert, W. (1976). *Creating a community of inquiry: Conflict, collaboration and transformation.* New York: Wiley.

Torbert, W. (1983). Initiating collaborative inquiry. In G. Morgan (Ed.), *Beyond method.* Newbury Park, CA: Sage.

Van Maanen, J. (1982). Introduction. In J. Van Maanen, J. M. Dabbs, Jr., & R. R. Faulkner (Eds.), *Varieties of qualitative research* (pp. 11–30). Newbury Park, CA: Sage.

Von Hayek, F. A. (1967). *Studies in philosophy, politics, and economics.* Chicago: University of Chicago Press.

Vroom, V. H., & Jago, A. G. (1988). *The new leadership: Managing participation in organizations.* Englewwod Cliffs, NJ: Prentice-Hall.

Vroom, V. H., & Yetton, P. W. (1973). *Leadership and decision-making.* Pittsburgh: University of Pittsburgh Press.

Weick, K. E. (1969). *The social psychology of organizing.* Reading, MA: Addison-Wesley.

Weiner, B. (1986). *An attributional theory of motivation and emotion.* New York: Springer-Verlag.

Weiner, B. (1991). Metaphors in motivation and attribution. *American Psychologist, 46*(9), 921–930.

Westoby, A. (Ed.). (1988). *Culture and power in educational organizations.* New York: Open University Press.

Wheelan, S. A., Pepitone, E. A., & Abt, V. (1990). *Advances in field theory.* Newbury Park, CA: Sage.

Whyte, W. F. (1991). *Social theory for action: How individuals and organizations learn to change.* Newbury Park, CA: Sage.

Wilson, J. Z. (1989). *Bureaucracy.* New York: Basic Books.

Wood, R., & Bandura, A. (1989). Social cognitive theory of organizational management. *Academy of Management Review, 14*(3), 361–384.

Woods, P. (1979). *The divided school.* London: Routledge & Kegan Paul.

Name Index

Subject Index

Breinigsville, PA USA
13 August 2010
243597BV00001B/1/P